W9-BLR-411

N HORIZONS IN
ARATIVE POLITICS

Mexico:
From Corporatism
to Pluralism?

George W. Grayson
Class of 1938 Professor of Government
College of William & Mary

Harcourt Brace College Publishers
Fort Worth   Philadelphia   San Diego
New York   Orlando   Austin   San Antonio
Toronto   Montreal   London   Sydney   Tokyo

To the College of William & Mary's
Class of 1938 for their love of, generosity
to, and support of their alma mater.

Publisher: Christopher P. Klein
Acquisitions Editor: David Tatom
Product Manager: Steve Drummond
Project Editor: Mary K. Mayo
Art Director: Garry Harman
Production Manager: Linda McMillan
Cover Photograph: Charlie Steiner, International Stock

 This book is printed on
acid-free recycled paper.

ISBN: 0-15-505365-5

Library of Congress Catalog Card Number: 97-73399

Copyright © 1998 by Harcourt Brace & Company

Address for Editorial Correspondence: Harcourt Brace College Publishers, 301 Commerce Street, Suite 3700, Fort Worth, TX 76102.

Address for Orders: Harcourt Brace & Company, 6277 Sea Harbor Drive, Orlando, FL 32887-6777 1-800-782-4479.

Web site address: http://www.hbcollege.com

Printed in the United States of America

7 8 9 0 1 2 3 4 5 6 066 9 8 7 6 5 4 3 2 1

Table of Contents

Foreword

Mexico is at a crucial turning point in its history with profound implications both for Mexico and for the United States.

For at least five hundred years, Mexico has been dominated by an authoritarian, top-down political, social, and economic system that has prevented the growth of liberal democracy. The authoritarian tradition stems from Mexico's indigenous past (Mexico was one of the main centers of pre-Columbian Indian civilizations) and from three centuries of Spanish colonial rule. Authoritarianism was perpetuated after Mexico's independence from Spain by a succession of men-on-horseback and, more recently, by a single-party regime that has monopolized political power for nearly seventy years. In all of its colorful and often violent history, Mexico has enjoyed only eleven or twelve years of democracy.

Now Mexico is changing rapidly. Economically, its markets are more open and it has joined with the United States and Canada in the North American Free Trade Agreement (NAFTA) and with the world's most advanced countries in the Organization of Economic Cooperation and Development (OECD). Politically, Mexico now has a freer press, strong opposition political parties on both the Left and Right, and elections in which the ballots are honestly tabulated. Socially, Mexico has become more literate, urban, and middle-class. For the first time in its history, Mexico seems poised to evolve away from its authoritarian past toward greater economic liberalism, democracy, and social pluralism.

However, the road is rocky and Mexico may not make it. The economy has been going through a wringer, which has resulted in lower living standards for the majority of Mexicans. For a long time, Mexico has been an organic-corporatist or group-organized society, and it is not clear if the country can function on a U.S.-style individualistic and democratic basis. In addition, Mexico has an *institutionalized* system of patronage and authoritarianism that has been in power for over sixty years, and it is much harder to evolve away from such deeply entrenched authoritarianism. Mexico may progress toward democracy and free markets, but one should not rule out the possibilities for increased fragmentation and breakdown. If that should happen, given Mexico's 2000 mile border with the United States, the implications for both Mexico and the U.S. would be enormous.

These are the themes explored in this book by George W. Grayson. Dr. Grayson, who is the Class of 1938 Professor of Government at the College of William & Mary, is one of the country's leading experts on Mexico. He has written extensively on Mexican history, politics, social changes and economics, and he is also involved in policy-making toward Mexico. In preparing this volume, Professor Grayson has interviewed hundreds of Mexican politicians, businessmen, labor leaders, government officials, and journalists. He travels to Mexico regularly and knows the country well. There is no one better qualified to contribute a book on Mexico to the New Horizons in Comparative Politics Series.

Professor Grayson analyzes Mexico employing the concept of corporatism—the hierarchical, centralized, and group-based organization of the social and political system brought to Mexico from Spain (with its roots in indigenous practices). He contrasts Mexican corporatism and authoritarianism with the greater individualism and democracy of the United States. At the heart of Grayson's analysis is the clash between Mexico's traditionalist, patrimonial, stratified political system and the now global aspiration for democratization and more open markets. Mexico has already begun the transition from the former to the latter, but the outcome remains uncertain, and that is what makes Mexico—and Professor Grayson's book—so interesting. Will Mexico ascend into the ranks of free, democratic, and prosperous nations? Will we see a reaction on the part of those being deprived of their political power seeking to restore the traditional system? Or will Mexico destabilize and become ungovernable, thus calling forth a likely U.S. reaction?

Mexico is *one of the most important countries in the world* to the United States—not in an economic sense like Japan, but in its ability to affect the United States in multiple ways. For that reason it is imperative that we begin to understand Mexico's internal politics, and there is no better place to do that than in Professor Grayson's book.

HOWARD J. WIARDA
University of Massachusetts and
Center for Strategic and International Studies
Editor, New Horizons in Comparative Politics Series

Preface

F rank Tannenbaum, the renowned Latin Americanist, once described the experience of a young scholar from the United States who traveled to Venezuela to study that nation's constitutional history. When people in Caracas learned of his plans, they observed: "Why, he must be a poet."[1]

Like their Mexican counterparts, most Venezuelans could imagine that their constitutions might arouse literary or theoretical interest. The nineteenth-century novelist Stendhal, after all, had pored over the limpid, inspired prose of the Napoleonic Code to hone his writing style. But no Venezuelan or Mexican would have believed that these compacts reflected the true allocation of power, much less an effective and respected basis of state authority. As everyone knew—grandiose charters, earnest assertions of rights and obligations and ambitious schemes of political engineering notwithstanding—the holders of real power paid little heed to the written code. Military strongmen ran the show in Venezuela and most of Latin America at that time—and did so with frank contempt for glittering legal and political principles. For the *norteamericano* scholar's Venezuelan hosts, the chief dividend from reading their country's fundamental laws lay in discerning the evolution of the Spanish language in their proud Andean nation whose inhabitants prize men and women of letters more than politicians.

In Mexico, the military, although an important contributor to stability, has played a far less significant role in national politics than it has elsewhere in Latin America during the last sixty-five years—with the possible exception of the late 1950s and the early 1960s. Yet here, too, the organization of real power bears little resemblance to the formalities of the Mexican constitution. The document envisions a political system that—superficially, at least—mirrors that in the United States: Formal separation of powers, establishment—if not observation—of checks and balances, and dispersal of authority among executive, legislative, and judicial branches with distinct and specified duties, complete with a presidential veto. Just as with the White House occupant, Mexico's chief executive commands the armed forces, can mobilize state militias, and takes the lead in treaty-making and other foreign-policy initiatives. Moreover, the country's official name, "The United States of Mexico," implies a federal system of government. Mexico's thirty-one states also approximate their neighbors north of the Rio Grande in terms of formal organization, institutions, and rights vis-à-vis the national government. In addition, like the District of Columbia, Mexico's capital—also known as the federal district, *Distrito Federal* or D.F.—exists as a quasi-independent enclave and seat of national power.

Of course, its drafters inserted provisions in Mexico's charter alien to the philosophy of America's Founding Fathers: an emphatic anticlericalism; strong guarantees for small private farms and collectivized communal holdings known as *ejidos*; reaffirmation of the old Iberian doctrines of state control over oil and other subsoil minerals; and utopian regulatory principles affecting workplace conditions and compensation of Mexican labor. Furthermore, the authors of Mexico's constitution vested their president with a greater role in proposing laws and budgets than his U.S. counterpart, and they eliminated the office of vice-president lest a *número dos* conspire against a *número uno*.

Relying on nominal written and rhetorical descriptions of Mexico's politics today—as with the case of the visitor in Venezuela in the mid-twentieth century—will blind contemporary students to the underlying distribution of power. While differences between the Mexican and U.S. political systems have narrowed of late, especially in a *de jure* sense through the adoption of the North American Free Trade Agreement (NAFTA) and other external influences, a huge gulf continues to separate the two systems on a *de facto* basis.

At the heart of this disparity lies the phenomenon of corporatism, a social concept with ancient origins that is virtually absent in U.S. political discourse and traditions. This study contends that Mexican politics is best understood by viewing its evolution as a progressive adaptation of Iberian corporatism in response to both local and global political and economic developments. Before proceeding, however, it is worth asking: What are the intellectual origins of corporatism? Why did corporatism mesh so well with Ibero-Hispanic society? How does corporatism as a strategy for organizing social power differ from liberalism and Marxism?

Corporatism's Intellectual Origins

Although some prominent political scientists such as Samuel Beer doubt that corporatism represents "a single, logically consistent system of thought,"[2] the concept retains impressive analytic value for understanding Iberian-American societies.

Corporatism can be defined as a sociopolitical system organized on the basis of functional groups rather than individualism or one man-one vote; it tends to be top-down, mercantilist, statist, and authoritarian: a mechanism for controlling change and keeping interest groups in line. It is usually anti-liberal, anti-pluralist, and anti-free enterprise.[3]

Thus described, corporatism emerges from several intellectual streams. Plato and Aristotle embraced the idea of "natural" social classes and developed the concept that the political community, or state, is guided by a moral purpose or *telos*, which Aristotle defined as governing to advance the general welfare and common good. He insisted that the interest of the whole took precedence over the particular interests of society's different parts, which should enjoy only that freedom compatible with the organic functioning of society. Later, Ciceronian and Stoic thought stressed the presence of a social hierarchy stemming from individual functions. The notion of the organic state required that all legitimate corporate bodies be chartered by political authorities. In exchange for this official imprimatur, these groups accepted duties and acquired special privileges (*fueros*) that solidified chains of mutual dependence between the state and its body politic. The guilds that benefited from licenses and monopolies, for instance, met their obligation to the sovereign by producing high-quality goods and paying taxes. During the Middle Ages, classical philosophy and Christian theology were integrated into a coherent view of a divinely ordered universe.[4]

The systematic works of St. Thomas Aquinas (1225–1274) comprise the crowning achievement of that medieval synthesis,[5] in which "the hierarchic idea portrays a world of particulars . . . ordered on a principle" of more or less whole fundamental natures.[6] At the apex of this "great chain of being" stands the Trinity, followed by seraphim, cherubim, archangels, and angels; with bishops, priests, and Christian laymen afterward; all of whom rank above innumerable masses of infidels and pagans. This ordering encompassed all types of animate and inanimate matter and spirit, proceeding along St. Augustine's maxim "*non essent omnia, si essent aequalia*—if all things were equal, they would not exist."[7]

Throughout the history of early modern Europe, the distinction between noble and non-noble remained crucial, "since communities became structured in terms of orders with distinct legal rights and duties in a fixed, unchanging hierarchy that manifest God's will."[8] Most medieval thinkers considered this organization a reflection of what Richard M. Morse has called the "Thomistic-Aristotelian notion of functional social hierarchy,"[9] which explains both society and polity as a richly patterned tapestry of classes and castes. The various groups, as dictated by their members' stations in life, expressed interests through separate juridical tribunals appropriate to the estates, religious and military cadres, or functional corporations to which they belonged. These bodies—each highly autonomous in the regulation of its internal affairs—derived their legitimacy from an overarching system of hierarchy which found its vertex in a single figure, the sovereign monarch.[10] Ambition and attainment were limited by one's social group: "Men were expected to accept their station in life; there could thus be little questioning of the system and little mobility. Little change could or did take place."[11]

Twelfth-century Europe witnessed the rise of the first actual "corporations" in history. Scarcely comparable to modern commercial or industrial firms featured daily in the *Wall Street Journal*, these medieval institutions included craftsmen's guilds, the military, universities, religious orders, and city-states themselves. In keeping with the Thomist model, such functional and vocational entities allowed individuals to earn a living, endowed them with an identity, regulated their lives, invested them with special rights and duties, and enabled them to participate in making decisions crucial to their group's welfare. The corporatist system yielded an entire spectrum of social goods to each individual according to his position in the social structure implied by "natural law."[12] As Beer has noted,

> in the corporatist society the individual of lesser degree can be brought by the proper training and discipline to understand and to accept the good pertaining to his station . . . and to . . . its performance. He cannot grasp the idea of the common good . . . into which his particular good fits. Therefore, as Aquinas repeatedly asserts, in human society there must be a separate power which fits the particular goods of the parts into the common good of the whole. The ruled need their rulers . . . [and will] consent voluntarily to the rule of the wise and holy.[13]

In addition, the system allowed citizens to take part in politics not as atomized individuals, but instead by pooling their political influence into the corporate groups to which they belonged. Exponents of Thomism believed that collective representation better served the common good than parliaments or other bodies constituted on a territorial basis. As it sprang to life, the corporatist state—without absorbing any groups—fostered a dynamic tension between functional entities and the state, as well as among the groups themselves. One writer observes that the European experience from 1300 to 1600 essentially illuminates how emerging nation-states sought "to expand their authority at the expense of these largely autonomous corporations, and of the latter seeking to hang onto power in the face of an encroaching central government."[14]

Summarizing the development of corporatism, Beer writes that "[t]he medieval synthesis of classical and Christian thought locked Western man into political [hierarchy] . . . [T]he ruler was endowed with powers of the soul that set him off from the ruled . . . In the [corporatist] tradition, both secular and ecclesiastical government enjoyed the consent of the governed, but it was the consent of deference, not self-government."[15]

Compatibility between Corporatism and Ibero-Hispanic Society

Major movements that swept Western Europe—the Protestant Reformation, the Counter-Reformation, the Renaissance, the Enlightenment, and the Industrial Revolution—shook the very ground on which corporatism stood throughout the heart of the Continent. Between 1450 and 1850, intellectual, artistic, and political attention in most European societies shifted emphatically from the collective to the individual.

Yet, as Howard Wiarda has noted in a seminal work on corporatism's role in Latin American development, both Spain and Portugal remained cut off and isolated from these modernizing currents, adhering to fragments and remnants of a peculiarly Iberic-European tradition that at its heart was fundamentally two-class, authoritarian, traditional, elitist, patrimonial, Catholic, stratified, hierarchical, and corporatist.[16]

Corporatist institutions survived in Iberia more fully than anywhere else in Europe, despite, and often in aggressive reaction to, the wholesale intellectual, political, and social transformations that reverberated throughout the remainder of the Continent from the fifteenth to the eighteenth centuries. During this period, the major city-states of Spain and Portugal transplanted their now-distinctive social order to Latin America. The conquistadors, adventurers, and prelates whom they dispatched built a legacy far more profound and enduring than any merely political connection. Their sustained efforts gave rise to a system wherein:

> a corporate and hierarchical social order, an authoritarian-patrimonialist polity, an exploitive, "milk-cow," semi-feudal-early-capitalist, "colonial trader" economic system, a fixed and immutable religion and law *all formed part* of the structure that Spain, and in a more easy-going form Portugal, first established at home and then transplanted to the New World.[17]

These social structures, Wiarda argues, thrived and endured in the Spanish and Portuguese colonies through adaptation, accommodation, and cooperation—all in classic corporatist-patrimonial strategic style. Considering the resilience of corporate orders on the Iberian Peninsula, and the profound influence that the Iberic nations exercised over their overseas protectorates for several centuries, it is no wonder that the corporate model still provides a vital prism through which to analyze the contemporary politics of nations like Mexico.

Contrasts among Corporatism, Pluralism, and Marxism

The contours of political development in modern Mexico often appear clearer and more pronounced when viewed as the products of tension among three key ideological traditions—namely, corporatism, pluralism, and Marxism.

For its advocates, corporatism offers a humanistic alternative to both interest group liberalism identified with the United States and other Western democracies, and communism as practiced in China, Cuba, North Korea, or the former Soviet Union.

As expressed in the *Federalist Papers*, for example, James Madison and other pioneers of interest group liberalism view collective power as dangerous. Madison argues that the greatest protection for an individual's political and economic rights lies in multiplying the sources and number of "factions" in a pluralistic state. Since each citizen group must yield some portion of its claims, a balance is struck and the dangers of group domination through the state are minimized. What Thomas Hobbes termed the "war of all-against-all" state of nature is avoided not by establishing a Leviathan, but by dividing and sharing public authority.

Still, even in successful liberal-pluralist societies, citizens often decry their inability to influence policy because of the remoteness of state structures from their lives. Furthermore, even when citizens do effectively transmit their preferences to government officials, policymakers must contend with a chorus of mighty power-contenders, proficient at drowning out the *vox populi*. Finally, one might argue that corporatist regimes possess greater legitimacy, stability, and solidarity than pluralist societies, since the practice of corporatism requires leaders to maintain the appearance of a connection between government and governed, while pluralism simply assumes that link exists through labor unions, professional associations, peasant leagues, and other intermediate groups.

Ironically, in the United States and other industrialized nations, exploding complexity has resulted in the formation of effective social institutions much like those found in corporatist societies, such as bodies with memberships determined not by individuals, but by power arrangements in the organizations themselves. In theory, such modern interest groups serve as capillaries between that state and rank-and-file members. Public policy arises from negotiation, bargaining, and compromise among several group leaders, such as feminist organizations and health providers, labor and management, or environmentalists and manufacturers. Yet as Theodore Lowi demonstrated in *The End of Liberalism*, the expanding scope of government activity and diversification of liberal polities has "eroded clear standards for administrative accountability and consequently ha[s] led to a crisis of public authority over the role and purposes of government in society."[18]

Some observers criticize liberal pluralism as lacking the virtues of a more hierarchical system. They note that as opposed to the diffusion of power in pluralism, shared experience in the exercise of power in small entities provides members of corporatist bodies with their own motivation for social stability. Others view society as inherently "oligarchic and undemocratic" and so better suited to resolve conflicts through an array of broad-based highly static groups rather than by democratic competition. Further, they assert understandably that plural representation does not guarantee balanced outcomes, and so societies would actually mitigate their risks by cushioning the blow of new policies through a corporatist system of accommodating each functional grouping. Advocates of corporatism note that, in the execution of their social model, corporatist regimes—unlike their pluralist counterparts—have direct lines of influence to private economic interests, for example, chambers of commerce, other employer associations, and labor unions. Also, the concentration of power at the level of group elites tends to reduce conflicts to questions over the means of policy rather than its ends. In addition, defenders of corporatism cite the widely acknowledged shortcomings of democratic political parties in fully translating popular wishes into policy results.

Whatever virtues interest group pluralism may exhibit in theory, corporatists contend that in practice such a system represents a thin veil for rapacious capitalism. They view pluralism's alleged checks and balances as weak or nonexistent—with strong, influential, and affluent groups running roughshod over their weaker competitors. And with rare exceptions, the truly powerless segments of society find themselves completely frozen out of the bargaining that gives rise to policy. Needless to say, its critics argue that Mexico's revolutionary regime has often ignored or suppressed individuals who raised their voices against the corporatist regime and its leaders.

Corporatists decry communism as equally divisive and inhumane. After all, Marxism-Leninism originates in a dialectical view of history driven by class struggle toward the establishment of a classless society. The experience of the Soviet Union and its satellites has proven that what emerged was anything but a "proletarian" dictatorship based on the application of communist theory to nineteenth-century conditions. For millions of people throughout Eurasia during three decades of Stalinism, socialist rule spelled bloody repression rather than earthly paradise.

Marxism has never attained a durable foothold in Mexico for several reasons: the anti-communism of the late revolutionary period; the coincidence of vigorous industrialization and the adoption of an emphatic Cold War stance by Presidents Miguel Alemán Valdés and Adolfo Ruiz Cortines (1946–1958)—marked by the timely replacement of radical labor leader

Vicente Lombardo Toledano, always more nationalist than socialist, with the more tractable Fidel Velázquez Sánchez; and the basic religiosity of its citizenry. Perhaps because of its dialectical character, its materialist rejection of the forces of nationalism and religion, its political absolutism, and its focus on "class struggle," Marxism has failed to furnish a popular alternative to Mexico's entrenched system of corporatist accommodation and distribution. Mexico's Left has also suffered from rampant personalism and sectarianism, which have worked against forging a compact, coherent front against a ruling party adroit at appropriating revolutionary symbolism.

Chapter 1 reviews how Iberian colonialism introduced corporatism into Latin America, and describes the model's evolution in the hemisphere generally and in Mexico particularly. Especially important are the ways in which corporatism crystallized in the formation of a dominant governing party, precursor to the ruling Institutional Revolutionary Party (PRI). Chapter 2 analyzes how pervasive state involvement in the economy through the strategy of import-substitution industrialization (ISI) reshaped and enhanced Mexico's variant of corporatism. Chapter 3 concentrates on the presidency, an office which seized upon both a functionally based ruling party and government's pervasive penetration of the economy to become the supreme force in the nation's corporatist regime. Chapter 4 assays the corrosive impact on corporatism of Mexico's expanding integration into a rapidly evolving, global economy—a process spearheaded by President Carlos Salinas de Gortari (1988–1994) and highlighted by Mexico's joining NAFTA. Chapter 5 examines how Salinas's successor, Ernesto Zedillo Ponce de León, an Ivy League-educated technocrat and accidental chief executive with modest ties to traditional power-brokers, championed a political opening that threatened to administer the *coup de grâce* to the remaining bastions of corporatist power. Chapter 6 describes how the twin blows of economic liberalization and political reform notwithstanding, Mexico has again modified, but not discarded, a corporatist approach to organizing politics for the sake of preserving the country's cherished stability, albeit at the cost of genuine democratization and pluralism throughout an ever-more politically diverse nation.

Acknowledgments

Like every author I owe an enormous debt of gratitude to the many persons who have helped in various ways in the preparation of this book. Howard J. Wiarda not only encouraged me to embark upon this study for the New Horizons in Comparative Politics Series he edits for Harcourt Brace College Publishers, but he graciously enriched my knowledge of both Mexico and corporatism. In addition to offering astute and constructive comments on the manuscript, he even lent a hand in tracking down arcane references—

a chore that transcends the job description of a man who is both a keen editor and an incredibly prolific scholar. Two colleagues at the College of William & Mary—Michael T. Clark, Assistant Director of the Reeves Center for International Studies, and James C. Livingston, Mason Professor of Religion—made welcomed additions to my understanding of corporatism and applying the concept to Mexico. Dr. Clark's expertise in political philosophy, political development, Latin American affairs, and the English language never ceases to amaze me. His assistance was matched only by that of Oscar Aguilar Asencio, a distinguished political science professor at Mexico City's IberoAmerican University, who carefully reviewed the manuscript, offering dozens of suggestions that shaped and sharpened my analysis. Similarly, Ramzi Nemo, my former research assistant at William & Mary and a current graduate student at the American University, contributed greatly to this project through his adroitness and imagination in research and his wordsmithery par excellence. Further, Dr. Carmen Brissette Grayson, an incomparable companion for 35 years and a remarkably gifted historian, took time from crafting the seminal work on Maj. Gen. Montgomery C. Meigs, Lincoln's Quartermaster-General, to instruct me on the writings and ideas of St. Thomas Aquinas and the context in which they originated.

Karen Hammer and Alicia Jones cheerfully and expertly typed the manuscript; Jamie Brown, a graduate student in William & Mary's Thomas Jefferson Program in Public Policy, made countless trips to the Swem Library for me; Anne Shepherd performed yeoman's work assisting with research and with the meticulous polishing of my roughly hewn prose; and Michael Abley along with the infamous "two Ellens"—Powers and Moncure—carefully proofread the text.

I wish to express appreciation to Nancy Hoepli-Phalon, Editor-in-Chief at the Foreign Policy Association, for allowing me to draw liberally from a monograph entitled *The North American Free Trade Association*, which I wrote and she edited in 1993. Equally obliging was Dr. M. Delal Baer, Director of the Mexico Project at the Center for Strategic & International Studies, who has forgotten more about Mexico than I will ever learn. She permitted me to include material from both *The Church in Mexican Politics* and *A Guide to the 1997 Mexico City Mayoral Election*, which CSIS brought out, respectively, in 1992 and 1997.

Both William & Mary's Class of 1938, which endowed the chair that I am honored to occupy, and the College's Faculty Research Committee, which provided me with a research leave, played instrumental roles in my completing this study. Of course, I would have floundered more than usual if some 100 Mexican and U.S. politicians, civil servants, labor leaders, diplomats, scholars, and journalists had not taken time from busy schedules to open my eyes to the Byzantine workings of Mexico's corporatist system.

Above all, thanks are due to Mary Kathryn Mayo, project editor at Harcourt Brace, for patiently and professionally accomplishing the Herculean task of readying for publication the manuscript of a writer whose vocabulary lacks the words, "no more changes."

With such abundant support, the defects in this book are obviously my own.

Notes

1. Frank Tannenbaum, *Ten Keys to Latin America* (New York: Alfred A. Knopf, 1965), p. 148.
2. Samuel Beer, *To Make a Nation: The Rediscovery of American Federalism* (Cambridge: Harvard University Press, 1993), p. 31.
3. For the definition of an "ideal-type" of corporatism, see Philippe Schmitter, "Still the Century of Corporatism?" in Frederick B. Pike and Thomas Stritch (eds.), *The New Corporatism: Socio-Political Structures in the Iberian World* (Notre Dame: University of Notre Dame Press, 1974), pp. 93–94.
4. Peter F. Klarén, "Lost Promise: Explaining Latin American Underdevelopment," in Roderic Ai Camp, *Democracy in Latin America: Patterns and Cycles* (Wilmington, Del.: Scholarly Resources, 1996), p. 116.
5. J. M. Roberts, *History of the World* (New York: Oxford University Press, 1993), p. 428; see, in particular, St. Thomas Aquinas, *On Kingship: To the King of Cyprus* (Toronto: The Pontifical Institute of Mediaeval Studies, 1949).
6. Beer, *To Make a Nation*, p. 34.
7. Arthur Lovejoy, *The Great Chain of Being* (Cambridge: Harvard University Press, 1964) p. 67.
8. Roberts, *History of the World*, pp. 447-48.
9. Richard M. Morse, "Recent Research on Latin American Urbanization: A Selective Survey with Commentary," *Latin American Research Review* 1 (Fall 1965): 41.
10. Howard J. Wiarda, "Toward a Framework for the Study of Political Change in the Iberic-Latin Tradition: The Corporative Model," *World Politics* 25 (January 1973): 210–11.
11. Wiarda, "Toward a Framework for the Study of Political Change," pp. 217–18.
12. Antony Black, "St. Thomas Aquinas: The State and Morality," in Brian Redhead (ed.), *Political Thought from Plato to NATO* (London: Ariel Books, 1988), pp. 66–67.

13. Beer, *To Make a Nation*, p. 53.

14. Wiarda, "Dismantling Corporatism: The Problem of Latin America," a review of Jorge E. Bustamante, *La república corporativa* (Buenos Aires: EMECE, 1989) in *World Affairs* 156 (Spring 1994): 199–203.

15. Beer, *To Make a Nation*, p. 64.

16. Wiarda, "Toward a Framework for the Study of Political Change," p. 209.

17. Wiarda, "Toward a Framework for the Study of Political Change," p. 218.

18. Lowi, *End of Liberalism: the Second Republic of the United States* (2nd ed.; New York: Norton & Co., 1969), p. 127.

1

Corporatism in Mexico

Introduction

From the time of Hernán Cortés when general corporatist principles were first introduced, the people of Mexico have participated in the adaptive re-creation of a social and political order that has absorbed within itself "virtually all the systems of society that have ever governed men's affairs . . . Thomism, divine-right monarchy, feudalism, autocracy, liberalism, and all the rest."[1] Mexico's protean corporatist structure has continually evolved, occasionally with startling rapidity and ingenuity in response to changing economic and social conditions. With each new adaptation, however, the basic pattern of ownership and wealth persisted; past values and behavioral norms endured; the system of *fueros* or special courts, patronage, exemptions, and privileges continued; and the underlying configuration of power and society remained hierarchical, elitist, authoritarian, and corporative. New constituencies, ideologies, and technologies achieved assimilation, but always on terms defined by, and consistent with the interests of, the older ruling groups and norms.

By establishing a huge, multi-sectoral party virtually indistinguishable from the government and its distributive agencies, Lázaro Cárdenas del Río—populist president from 1934 to 1940—demonstrated his genius at political engineering. He designed a system that would guarantee the stability and continuity of the revolutionary experiment by creating a broad base of support for the venture. Above all, he had to fortify the Mexican state, which—since ratification of the 1917 Constitution—had suffered the debilitating blows of three military uprisings, a religious war, and Obregón's assassination. Even more than Plutarco Elías Calles before him (1924–1928), Cárdenas used the hardy dynamics of corporatist politics as a means to cobble together a structure within which diverse and antagonistic social interests could be integrated to produce badly needed political peace.

Corporatism, adopted as the dominant political structure by successive generations in Mexican politics, has endowed its practitioners with extraordinary flexibility.[2] Governments in corporatist societies typically direct all legitimate associations, not only granting or withholding recognition but also dispensing funds and favors. In a society where autonomous association is rare, the power to sanction social groupings becomes a central means of government. Consequently, state administration absorbs politics, and the population gains representation functionally, through membership in recognized functional segments. When it performs well, the government acts as a gyroscope—balancing competing corporate interests by integrating them into the state apparatus. Unlike liberal pluralism, however, the state also seeks to control the corporate groups that swirl around it.

In Mexico, corporatist practices have proved to be strikingly resilient in the face of powerful modern ideological challenges such as liberalism and a notably nationalist variant of communism. Reform-minded leaders like Benito Juárez, Francisco I. Madero, the Flores Magón brothers, Alvaro Obregón, Venustiano Carranza, and Pascual Orozco have appealed again and again to the pluralist strain of Mexican politics over the past 125 years. Their genuine attempts to limit succession for senior elected officials, open political participation to all citizens, eliminate *fueros*, and diminish centralized economic power align them with the classic-liberal tradition of John Locke, Jeremy Bentham, and John Stuart Mill. Among other measures, the Liberal Plan of 1906 called for basic civil rights, restrictions on the death penalty, the establishment of detailed labor laws, and the end of the hacienda economy as characterized by the *tiendas de raya* or company stores. The more hortatory and radical Plan Orozquista of 1912 sounded many of the same notes.[3]

In the Mexican context, the attempt to invest private citizens with the initiative for choosing individual identity and affiliations comprises pluralism's strongest motive force. Yet despite occasional gains, pluralism has demonstrated only limited staying power through most of Mexican history—at least until the latter part of the twentieth century. Severely chastened by the bloodshed that accompanied the country's 1910–1920 revolution, Mexico's political elites have only gingerly approached controversial social issues, preferring until recently, at least, to adapt with the familiar embrace of an enduring corporatist and statist tradition.

From Conquest Toward Independence

When they arrived in 1518, Mexico's Iberian conquerors began to infuse a new corporatist outlook into what they called "New Spain," which appeared more like the Spanish regions of Andalucía, Aragón, or other monarchical dependencies than an overseas colony.[4] As such, a corporatist view of society permeated New Spain just as this perspective pervaded the mother country. As in Iberia, no institution more effectively translated this viewpoint than the Roman Catholic Church. Originally commissioned to convert natives to the "true faith" and minister to their souls, the messianic church increasingly involved itself in the construction of imposing places of worship—from quasi-medieval style structures with simple naves in the sixteenth century to domed, baroque extravaganzas in the seventeenth and eighteenth.[5] Nonspiritual matters conflicted with the paternalistic care of Indians. Membership in the clergy provided a route to high secular office: At least ten archbishops of Mexico received appointment as the king's viceroy. The close relationship between the ecclesiastical and governing spheres appears most conspicuously in the church's coordination of its parish records with imperial tax assessments.

During Spanish colonization, church officials made desultory efforts to protect the indigenous population, or at least to save their souls. One historical record details competition between monastic orders: The Dominicans accused the Franciscans of preventing the Indians from working in their houses and pointed out that the followers of Saint Francis had a far greater number of edifices. The Franciscans in turn charged the brothers of Saint Dominic with envy.[6] In urban areas, corruption became the norm, as priests gambled and sought to enrich and glorify themselves instead of pursuing their vocations. The self-serving acts of European clergy, including the selling of indulgences, rapidly spread to the New World. Nevertheless, there were significant traits that distinguished common priests in the hinterland from their more prosperous superiors in the cities. Baron Alexander Von Humboldt wrote that "what is really distressing is to find in a diocese whose bishop enjoys an annual income of 650,000 francs, priests of Indian villages who have not five or six hundred francs a year."[7]

While the organization and function of the colonial church typify the basic pattern of corporatist practices, it is important to note that the crown also introduced specific institutional measures to contain the worst misdeeds. *Audiencias* and *cabildos*—established by Madrid to discharge administrative, legislative, and judicial responsibilities, as well as to serve as a counterpoise to the viceroy—also reinforced corporatist principles. The *audiencias reales*—or "royal courts"—represented the authority of the monarch himself in New Spain: In addition to the viceroy or captain-general who presided *ex officio*, the *audiencia* included a regent, three judges, a notary, a constable, and two attorneys—one for civil and the other for criminal cases. While the viceroy did not have to accept the *audiencia*'s recommendations, he strove to avoid conflict.[8] After all, the *audiencia* could hear appeals even against the actions of the viceroy, as well as communicate directly with the king, exemplifying this corporatist entity's flexibility, permeability, and capability for absorbing newer currents—without undermining the traditional structures in the process.

Furthermore, in staffing *audiencias*, the crown took steps to ensure members' loyalty, as most were born in Spain, and none could marry while serving in the colonies.

The crown administered New Spain with advice from a "Council of the Indies," a committee of courtiers who had previously served in colonial administration, and ostensibly had acquired expertise in profitably managing Spanish holdings. The Council issued decrees and appointed the viceroy and other local officials. Unfortunately, administrators on the ground often found themselves charged to execute conflicting orders. In other cases, public servants would simply ignore or distort direct commands; a seemingly astronomical distance separated New Spain from Madrid. In keeping with the corporatist emphasis on accommodation and distribution of benefits, the crown would rarely interfere in the details of administration so long as gold and other commodities poured into Spain on time and in the amounts expected.

The task of local government fell to *cabildos*, composed of *regidores* or aldermen appointed by the monarch. The *regidores*, in turn, elected two *alcaldes* who also served on the panel, and functioned much like modern mayors. One of the main avenues to power, selection of *alcaldes* always occurred under a real threat of corruption. In addition to sizable salaries from the Royal Treasury, officials could also dip into the public trough by funneling resources to themselves under the pretext of supporting local initiatives. Also, few opportunities for oversight meant that officials could exploit their populations through arbitrary taxation and administrative abuse.

A system of special executive-judicial *fueros* conferred on churchmen, military officers, residents of certain municipalities, and members of other preferred groups distinct rights, prerogatives, and exemptions from judgment unavailable to average citizens.

The *fueros* were privileges of corporate bodies and of the professions; of the clergy, called public or common; and of the monks, canons, inquisitions, colleges and universities; the entitlements of royal tax collectors; the general prerogatives of the armed forces, which also extended to the militia, marines, engineers, and members of the artillery. An individual enjoying these advantages was elevated above civil authority and—whether as plaintiff or defendant—answered only to the leader of the organization to which he belonged, both in civil and criminal cases.

In addition, corporatist influences also manifested themselves through the division of the New World's residents into four well-recognized classes. *Peninsulares* or European-born individuals occupied the highest social stratum. Though its members numbered fewer than 15,000 at the height of colonial rule—less than three-tenths of 1 percent of the population—this class dominated political and economic life in New Spain. Only five of more than 120 viceroys and only a dozen of several hundred captains-general claimed American birth, illustrating the *peninsulares'* tight hold on political opportunity. American or *criollo* identity offered no appreciable benefits and many disadvantages as compared to the status of *peninsulares*. One viceroy even suggested that *criollos* should receive only menial posts in government so as to keep them "submissive and humble."

Mestizos arose from mixed marriages between Spaniards and Indians. Not surprisingly, many Indian women sought to bear children by *peninsulares* or *criollos* in the hope of enhancing their offspring's lot in life. The mestizos filled an unenviable social niche between advantaged full-blooded Europeans and the purebred Indians who suffered only hardship and toil at the hands of their Iberian masters. The church paid mestizos a backhanded compliment by subjecting them to the Inquisition, as opposed to Indians, whom the Roman Catholic hierarchy considered childlike and incapable of engaging in heresy. In the final stage of the colonial era, the mestizos found themselves trapped again between Europeans and Indians, since both groups viewed the mestizos as the other's ally in social conflict.

Native Indians eked out a living at the base of a distended social pyramid. Thanks in large measure to the crusading of Dominican friar Bartolomé de Las Casas, Spain abolished slavery in the 1550s, and Queen Isabella decreed that no one could enslave the Indians under pain of death. However, the native population, tied economically to land owned by others, enjoyed little real freedom, and high officials often flouted the regulations protecting them. While mestizos could achieve limited social mobility through the army, small-parish priesthood, or low-level management posts in agriculture or manufacturing, Indians had absolutely no hope of social advancement, regardless of their ability or initiative. The introduction of black slaves proved expensive, and, during periods when diseases decimated the ranks of potential workers, employers were forced to offer advances to induce Indians to work. In response, landholders indentured their farm hands, then limited their buying and selling of goods to the company stores they owned; as the

Indians' commitment drew to a close, plantation owners would return them to virtual servitude by presenting them with a list of charges for food, clothing, and lodging amassed during their service.

History would not preserve Mexican colonial society in amber. Over time, successive waves of revolution, rationalism, and industrialization would transform the world and, with it, Mexico's economic and ideological contours. Yet the basic Iberian pattern of Mexico's corporatist political order not only survived but remained paramount.

Independence and Beyond

During the 1800s, political and social change in Europe and in the Western Hemisphere itself confronted Mexican society with palpable and substantial alternatives to its centuries-old social order. Historical developments—most significantly, the country's attainment of independence from Spain in 1821— left Mexicans with many vexing social issues to resolve. Their attempts to do so would be powerfully informed and influenced not only by Mexicans' own emerging national identity, but also by powerful currents from abroad.

In the words of Wiarda:

> New, agonizing questions were asked: Who are we? Spanish? New World? What? What shall be our relations with North America, Europe, Spain, or Portugal? How did we become what we are, and what is our destiny as a continent and as a people? In the absence of restraints imposed by the Spanish Crown on the questioning of established truths and as a result of contact with the outside world, the dominant tradition was subjected to the increasing challenge of new ideas and conceptions.[9]

Napoleon's occupation of Iberia in 1808 gave impetus to appealing doctrines of empiricism and the social thought of the Enlightenment, but these ideas touched only an elite circle of politicians and intellectuals. The Wars of Independence enabled American "republics" to separate from *la madre patria*, yet the fundamental character of society changed little. Creole aristocrats, generals, and political strongmen quickly stepped into the boots of the Spanish and Portuguese viceroys.

On paper, the new states adopted representative and democratic forms of government; in fact, these nascent regimes happily retained the centralized, elitist, authoritarian, hierarchical, corporate heritage bequeathed by Iberia. The direction of political thought in Latin America exhibited an impressive continuity both before *and* after 1810. Importantly, historians record that the expulsion of Spanish forces from Mexico (1820–1822) by Agustín de Iturbide, an ex-seminarian-turned-soldier whose father was Basque and mother Mexican, happened as a direct result of King Ferdinand's embrace of "mildly anticlerical" and civil-libertarian provisions in Spain's Constitution of 1812: "Ironically, a conservative [and thoroughly corporatist] colony would thus gain independence from a temporarily liberal mother country."[10]

Significantly, history recalls that Iturbide's *Ejército de las Tres Garantías* (Army of the Three Guarantees) owed its eponym to promises of post-war constitutional monarchy, maintenance of the Catholic Church as a preeminent social institution, and equal treatment of *peninsulares* and *criollos*. Within a year of his anti-liberal uprising, a popular demonstration in Mexico City proclaimed Iturbide Agustín I, emperor of "Mexican America," a post he held for only ten months. Despite the earnest pluralizing and progressive efforts of Father Miguel Hidalgo y Costilla, Juárez, the Lerdo de Tejada brothers, Emiliano Zapata, and others over the next century, politics in Mexico was dominated for decades by competing military chiefs, or *caudillos*, who would bargain with opponents for an ever-greater share of that nation's wealth, and who found military power a tempting instrument to advance their own self-interest. This period of turbulence among the elite would "vindicate the apathy of the rural Mexican, for his life would change little, if at all. The fate of the Mexican Indian continued to rest totally in the hands of others. . . . His privations went unnoticed. He could take little solace in the fact that the politically articulate groups in Mexico City that completely overlooked his interests demonstrated precious little ability to govern even themselves."[11]

In short, once Creole aristocrats, *caudillos*, and the armed forces flooded into the power vacuum left by the withdrawal of Spanish troops, the traditional structure resurged. New institutional arrangements appeared, but the essential elements of the Iberic-Latin tradition remained undisturbed by independence.

La Reforma

Freedom from Spanish hegemony plunged the nation into a condition of Hobbesian anarchy. Only Mexico's first president, the goodwilled, unpretentious, naive, Guadalupe Victoria, a devotee of republicanism, managed to struggle through his four-year-plus term (1824–1829). During the half-century after independence, some forty-eight regimes rose and fell in kaleidoscopic fashion as thirty different men occupied the National Palace from which viceroys formerly ruled. This procession of leaders included two emperors—one indigenous, Agustín I (1822–1823); the other French-imposed, Maximilian I (1863–1867)—both of whom suffered death by execution.

Sixteen men presided over twenty-two regimes during one fifteen-year period alone. Further instability appeared in the 318 changes in key cabinet posts—War, Treasury, Foreign Relations, and Government—that transpired between 1829 and 1855. The enigmatic Antonio López de Santa Anna stood as the most contemptible of these officeholders. A cryptic, mercurial, domineering military chieftain who created armies by dint of his personal magnetism, he captured the presidency nine times between 1833 and 1855, and his name became synonymous with treachery, intrigue, and betrayal. For historian Hugh Thomas, Santa Anna's lost leg symbolized "the vast territories which his mistakes enabled the United States to capture in a sensational war in 1846–1848."

Yet the same conditions that nurtured the authoritarian Santa Anna and his ilk also produced Benito Juárez. A Zapotec Indian, born in impoverished, mountainous Oaxaca, Benito Juárez caught the eye of a devoutly religious bookbinder, who paid for the young man's education at the local diocesan seminary and law school. While pursuing legal studies, Juárez served on the town council of Oaxaca, the state capital, and in the state legislature. A defender of the rights of Indian villages, the young attorney rapidly ascended the slippery ladder of Oaxacan politics, winning election as governor in 1848. During his four-year term, he garnered praise as an honest, ardent advocate of education, public workers, and efficient government. When Santa Anna regained the presidency in 1853 on a platform of extreme centralism and reactionary conservatism, Juárez fled to New Orleans, where he and other Liberal republicans lived in penurious self-imposed exile.

Two years later, when a Liberal president triumphed in the "Revolution of Ayutla," Juárez returned from abroad to head the Ministry of Justice. He and his Liberal colleagues attacked the now-discredited institutions of Spanish origin so inextricably bound to authoritarianism, corporatism, and Roman Catholicism. The reformers insisted on breaking up church lands and expropriating monasteries to engender a new class of small property holders, who—they averred—would promote stability and order, thus obviating the appeal of Santa Anna-type suzerains. In addition, cutting the umbilical cord with Roman Catholicism would free the masses from bondage to "the past."

The Liberals promulgated the 1857 Constitution, which drew freely on the American Constitution of 1787, the French revolutionary constitutions, the Spanish Constitution of 1812, and the constitutions emanating from the European revolutions of 1848. This preeminently political document stressed individual rights and laissez-faire economics over corporation, formally limited the functions of government, separated church and state, called for secular schools, strengthened the legislative branch at the expense of the executive, terminated the exemptions from civil jurisdictions enjoyed by soldiers and clerics, and attempted to dismantle most of the corporatist aspects of Mexican life arising from the colonial era.[12] These changes sparked a bloody, three-year "War of Reform" that ended with a Liberal victory in 1861. At this point, Napoleon III answered the pleas of local conservatives and imposed Archduke Maximilian of Austria, a Hapsburg, as emperor of Mexico. The ouster of the blue-tuniced French forces—catalyzed by General Porfirio Díaz's resounding triumph in Puebla in April 1867—gave rise to the execution of the ingenuous, mildly anticlerical Maximilian. The Indians of Querétaro, the site of the Hapsburg's demise, long combed the hillside where he died in search of "magical" stones to safeguard their huts. Meanwhile, Liberal chief executives Juárez and Sebastián Lerdo de Tejada, a professor from Veracruz, implemented *La Reforma*—an ambitious program of anti-church laws that (1) established complete freedom of worship, (2) declared marriage a civil contract, (3) forbade religious institutions to rent or acquire property, (4) abolished religious oaths in civil acts, (5) banned the wearing of religious garb in public, (6) outlawed monastic vows, (7) prohibited religious instruction and worship in public buildings, (8) limited the tolling of church bells to summon the faithful to services, and (9) replaced the swearing of oaths on Bibles with simple declarations of intent. In addition, Lerdo suppressed the Sisters of Charity; banished from the country Jesuits and Sisters of San Vicente de Paulo; and closed down the Catholic newspaper *Voz de México*.

As part of their economic program, the Liberals selectively invited foreigners to build railroads, establish industries, open mines, cultivate farms, and settle vacant lands. To accommodate the newcomers, many of whom were not Catholic, the government tolerated other religions. With official encouragement, North American Protestant missionaries followed their fellow countrymen and other immigrants to Mexico. This period witnessed unprecedented religious tolerance and appeared to prefigure the demise of corporatism.

Mexico's continued economic stagnation in the face of astonishing U.S. and European growth attenuated Liberalism's appeal. When a heart attack took the life of the revered Juárez in mid-1872, his successor proved incapable of turning the "restored republic" into a golden age. Lerdo, the excelibate who ascended to the presidency, apparently decided to sow the wild oats he had spurned as a young man under watchful Jesuit eyes. Only his lust for food exceeded his penchant for dalliances. Such excesses prompted cartoons in *Ahuizote*, a satirical publication run by pro-Díaz generals, lampooning the corpulent, round-faced Lerdo as "a glutton, an erotomaniac, a nicotinmaniac, as a *great general*."[13]

Rivals seized on Lerdo's personal shortcomings and eccentricities to mobilize support against his shaky regime. Lerdo's enemies gravitated to Díaz. Díaz's friend Manuel Lozano catalyzed a recrudescence of nativism as 8,000 half-naked, religiously inspired, fanatical Nayarit Indians proclaimed a new Aztec empire and swarmed against settlers on the Jalisco plains. At the same time, enforcement of the Reform laws incited a bloody, armed revolt in Michoacán, which quickly spread to Jalisco where 2,500 staunch Catholics called *Cristeros* took up arms. Meanwhile, Washington, which resented the Liberal's failure to heed telegraphed appeals to spare Maximilian's life, looked askance at Lerdo's hostility to American investors.

The *Porfiriato*

After failing to win reelection against Sebastián Lerdo de Tejada in 1872, Díaz bided his time before again mounting a political campaign. Defeated at the polls on a second occasion in 1875, the mustachioed general, who reportedly powdered himself with talcum to disguise his Indian heritage, traded ballots for bullets to gain his objective. He returned from exile in Cuba aboard the *City of Havana* bound for Veracruz. Traveling incognito as "Dr. de la Boza," a Cuban, he wore a wig, beard, tinted glasses, a ridiculous suit, and pretended to have an unquenchable thirst for alcohol.[14] Once on the mainland, the hero of the war against the French exchanged his disguise for a uniform and began an inexorable march for the presidential palace, aided by fellow generals, the business community, the Catholic Church, and—above all—deteriorating economic and social conditions. Díaz's "Revolution of Tuxtepec" drove Lerdo into exile and opened the way for the general to seize Mexico City in November 1876. He assumed the presidency under the banner of "no reelection"—a mordantly ironic slogan betrayed by Díaz's three-and-one-half decades of ruthless primacy.

Even though his intransigence ultimately detonated the bloody 1910 revolution, Díaz understood his nation's craving for order, and laid the groundwork for the strong presidents who succeeded him in the twentieth century. Díaz knew as only a former general could the danger that military chiefs posed to any Mexican leader. To preserve peace, he appropriated the motto of Paolo Sarpi: "All excuses for revolt should be avoided: *bread or the club*, this should be the rule; for the greatest act of justice which a prince should perform is [to] sustain himself."[15]

Rather than brandish the club at foes, Díaz preferred to seduce them with bread—in the form of choice assignments, civilian posts, and access to lucrative business concessions. In contrast to Juárez's attempted demobilization of the army, Díaz reorganized it: He divided the country into eleven military zones, none of which overlapped with state boundaries to discourage conspiracies between generals and governors; he transferred commanders from their local bailiwicks; he weakened other generals by promoting them to governorships and dispatching their troops to distant parts of the nation; and he created the *Rurales*—a mounted constabulary, open to ex-bandits, with an *esprit de corps* like that of the Spanish Civil Guard—to suppress troublemakers. The *Rurales* struck a frightening pose in their broad felt hats, bright red ties, richly embroidered gray jackets, gray pantaloons down the sides of which marched silver buttons, and carved saddles adorned with hammered silver. These extremely well paid, lavishly costumed toughs proved faithful to their oft-repeated maxim: "Shoot first and find out afterwards—if at all." They served as gendarmes, judges, and executioners, ready—for example— to bury to their necks and gallop over villagers who protested the theft of their lands by affluent ranchers.

Díaz adhered to the slogan, "few politics and much administration." He combined the *caudillo*-like ruthlessness of Santa Anna with foresight and efficiency. His approach to governing Mexico supplanted instability and violence with tyranny and a more disciplined use of force. He ruled the country by relying on local leaders who, like him, had evolved from fervent anticlericals in their youth to church-going autocrats in later life.[16]

In keeping with the arrival of modern technological influences, the elites of the Díaz regime identified closely with the positivist philosophy of August Comte. Focusing on communal order and material progress—expedited by the rise of an educated and propertied class—positivism became for Díaz and the *científicos* or "scientists" in his government a weapon of conservative reaction. Juárez and other Liberal paladins of *la Reforma* had proclaimed democracy, equality, and secularism as their watchwords. For his part, Díaz—although nominally a Liberal—subordinated individual liberty and equal justice to social quiescence even as the church regained concessions and properties lost at mid-century. Exemplifying the successful adaptation of corporatism during the *Porfiriato*, "[t]he [modern] value of material progress was harmonized with the old conservative ideals of clerical privilege, distribution of opportunity among the few, and political dictatorship. Progress in an egalitarian sense tended to be written off."[17]

Based on an assumption that minimizing politics would facilitate "orderly economic prosperity," Díaz's regime emphasized the use of intimidation, bribery, torture, and assassination in order to impress on Mexicans that the government would accept no deviation from presidential dictates. Most Mexicans saw little point in participating in elections, viewing them more as formal pantomimes than genuine opportunities for influencing politics and policies.

Characterizing the effect of Porfirismo on Mexican society, political scientist Robert E. Scott has written, "the theories of positivism and social Darwinism found a fertile field in the minds of Díaz and his científicos . . . the aristocracy considered national government their private preserve . . . and the constitution . . . a set of rules for a . . . private game played among themselves." Not surprisingly, while industry and infrastructure grew, its benefits were not widely shared among all Mexicans.[18] In a polity in which Euro-focused bureaucratic mandarins supplied the "brain" and the ruthless *Rurales* provided the "brawn," the leaders lauded external culture over nationalism. Mexico became known as the "mother of foreigners and the step-mother of Mexicans." Industrialization introduced a new social group in cities, but elsewhere only intensified the existing distinctions between campesinos, the Creole elite, the Roman Catholic Church, and the army. Even as Díaz elevated material progress over political development, Mexico remained a decidedly corporatist society.

While Mexico provided a cornucopia of riches for Díaz and those individuals, ranchers, and businesses that basked in his favor, the majority of the population suffered economic, social, and political privations. Just after the turn of the century, the Flores Magón brothers and other union leaders spearheaded strikes to protest the suppression and exploitation of workers. Zapata in the South and Francisco "Pancho" Villa in the North mobilized an insurgency proclaiming the need to distribute feudal estates to the peasantry. And political idealist Francisco I. Madero organized a network of liberal "clubs" to bolster his candidacy against Díaz in the 1910 presidential contest.

Díaz's crude stealing of the election sparked a Madero-led uprising that attracted the important foes of the *Porfiriato*. As his once-invincible regime crumbled, the dictator fled to France—a move that vaulted Madero into the presidency. A right-wing coup cut short Madero's term in 1913, plunging the country into civil war. Ultimately, a newly emergent Constitutionalist movement in the North—headed by "First Chief" Venustiano Carranza, who had served as a minor official under Díaz and a state governor and military commander under Madero—gathered an army composed of defecting federal troops and Madero loyalists. This force vanquished elements of the old order before turning its guns on the agrarians of Villa and Zapata. In the course of events, liberal reformers lost control to radicals, who dominated the writing of the nation's new fundamental law.

The 1917 Constitution—Groundwork for Revolutionary Nationalism

Describing the eventual settlement of Mexico's civil strife of 1910–1920, Miguel Angel Centeno has asserted:

> [t]he legacy of [Carranza's and Obregón's] victory is contradictory and paradoxical. On the one hand, the 1917 Constitution may be seen as marking the birth of the first socialist state. On the other, the regime created by Obregón and his successors may also be seen as continuing the model of Don Porfirio, emphasizing the continuity of central authority and the role of private property in economic development.[19]

On first reading, the 1917 Constitution appears as a Liberal charter antithetical to corporatist doctrine and tradition. Indeed, the drafters of the compact lifted about two-thirds of its contents whole-cloth from the Lerdo-Juárez fundamental law of 1857. In addition, "Jacobins" or radical officers from the North whose work enjoyed the blessing of Alvaro Obregón—the outstanding hero of the revolutionary conflict and war minister when the delegates to the Constitutional Convention assembled in Querétaro—overshadowed the "Renovators" or gradualists linked to Carranza—First Chief of the Constitutionalist Army and interim president.

Although forced to hammer out some compromises, the Jacobins left their indelible mark on the compact's provisions. Among other steps, they:

- provided that the state offer free, universal, secular education, with private education subjected to constitutional precepts on the subject (Article 3);
- stipulated that the possession of lands and waters was vested originally in the nation, which had the right to transmit ownership to private citizens; proclaimed that the state could restrict private property as it deemed suitable, including expropriation with indemnification (Article 27);
- authorized the division of huge estates into small holdings (Article 27);
- specified that the nation owned the subsoil rights to petroleum and other mineral resources (Article 27);
- required the government to protect workers' rights; limited the maximum hours in the work-day; recognized the right of workers to form unions and to strike; established the principle of equal salaries for equal work accomplished by men and women (Article 123);
- empowered legislatures to limit the number of priests (who had to be Mexicans by birth) in their states, denied juridical personality to churches, and forbade the formation of political organizations whose names were related to religious creeds (Article 130); and
- broached a plethora of approaches—private, public, cooperative, communal—to economic development.[20]

On completing their labor, several dozen young officers who participated in the Constitutional Convention ran through the streets singing "La Marseillaise." They had prepared the most socially advanced charter in history, which—they believed—would provide the underpinnings for social progress in their strife-torn nation. However, their magnum opus suffered from several deficiencies. To begin with, it was rife with contradictions. The provision vouchsafing the sanctity of contract, for example, clashed with sweeping state discretion on the proper use of surface and subsoil holdings. In addition, the ambitiousness of the document exceeded the resources available in Mexico's prostrate economy. The benefits conferred on peasants and workers in Articles 27 and 123 were unfunded. Finally, even though his delegates had lost out on many crucial votes, Carranza had the option of either working vigorously to advance the document's social agenda or merely allowing it to gleam as a wish list on official parchment. His disdain for many of the new constitution's premises—particularly agrarian reform—led the First Chief simply to ignore their presence and even to impede parallel socioeconomic innovations sponsored by progressive governors. This defiance of the convention delegates' intentions precipitated a showdown between Carranza and his top generals, the three ardent Sonorans: Obregón, Plutarco Elías Calles, and Adolfo de la Huerta.

The participants in the convention had emphatically endorsed liberal concepts. Nonetheless, the new fundamental law provided fertile terrain in which sectoral institutions could flourish. First, in contrast to the minimalist vision of government inscribed in the mid-nineteenth century Liberal constitution, the majority in Querétaro enthusiastically backed an activist, interventionist state—one destined to prove congenial to functionally organized institutions. Second, the progressive articles relative to peasants and workers would remain largely moribund until these constituencies could be organized in ways that both legitimated their standing and limited their autonomy. Again, corporatism furnished the instrument for achieving these two goals. Third, because of the chaos that engulfed the decade, the Querétaro draftsmen fortified the presidency vis-à-vis the parliament preferred by architects of the 1857 Constitution, but deemed sixty years later to have exacerbated the ungovernability that swept Díaz to power. They endowed the chief executive with the authority and legitimacy to create and dominate an official political party, which evolved into the keystone of twentieth-century Mexican corporatism.

Indeed, examining the 1917 Constitution's provisions further buttresses the assertion that despite the congeries of forces brought to bear on Mexico in the preceding years, corporatism, centralism, and statism remained the pillars of Mexico's sociopolitical structure. Such mainstays enabled the state to emerge as the guiding force of the economy, promoting the well-being of persons and workers or seizing the assets of foreign oil companies.

When Obregón vanquished Carranza in 1920, he and his successor Calles (1924–1928) confronted a Herculean task: They needed to secure their constitutional mandates during a period of profound social transformation. Cycles of turmoil, reform, frustration, and aggravation of conflict during previous years had impressed a vital lesson on the leaders of the early constitutional period: Increasingly, ordinary Mexicans could no longer be counted on to stand idle if their interests remained unattended. Obregón and Calles blessed the burgeoning of trade unions, peasant leagues, and political parties as mechanisms to aggregate and express the concerns of their members or, at least, of their leaders. They also perceived such organizations—especially labor centrals—as part and parcel of a revolutionary state that needed a counterpoise to foreign entrepreneurs.

Among other issues, the first generation of post-civil-war political chiefs required devices for coordinating and carrying out enormous changes, especially with respect to interest groups: How many power centers should exist, and how would the government resolve conflicts among them? The new government needed to appease old-line interests while at the same time accommodating peasants and laborers who had made heroic sacrifices in the revolutionary conflict.

Obregón and Calles began a risky process of balancing organized interests that continues to the present. They turned to the constitution for legitimacy, bending its articles around corporatist principles in order to mollify successive and competing power contenders. The 1917 compact, for example, enshrined the concept of collective farms or *ejidos* so admired by revolutionary agrarians; at the same time, traditional conservatives, a sector long identified with military might, viewed communal land-holdings for peasants as anathema. The constitution had provided a preliminary blueprint for the rational management of a modern corporatist state. In the years to follow, Mexican leaders would forge the best-articulated, single-party corporate matrix in Latin American history, a model that has endured more than seventy years.

The *"Cristero* Rebellion"—Reaction against Secular Anti-Clericalism[21]

Soon after adoption of the 1917 Constitution, another series of crises erupted over government policy with respect to the church's social role, an intensely sensitive theme in Mexico's popular mind. Carranza and Obregón had essentially disregarded the anticlericalism that bristled on the pages of the 1917 Constitution, although zealots such as the governor of Tabasco had persecuted the church, an episode vividly recounted in Graham Greene's *The Power and the Glory*.

The social tumult between 1926 and 1929 marked the Mexican clergy's straightforward reaction to President Calles's attempts to implement the anticlerical provisions. In February 1926, the Archbishop of Mexico, José Mora y del Río, told a journalist that Roman Catholics could not in good conscience obey the new fundamental law. Such recalcitrance infuriated the intemperate Calles. He quickly moved to restrain the church from holding processions and operating schools, to deport foreign-born religious brothers and sisters who sought to "fanaticize" the people, to close monasteries and convents, and to require all priests to register with civil authorities. In retaliation, Mora y del Río ordered the clergy to cease discharging their official functions, including celebrating mass, baptizing the newborn, and providing last rites for the dying. Incited by local church authorities, peasants in the Western states of Colima, Jalisco and Michoacán reacted violently against Calles's regime and, in particular, against "Godless" secular schools established by his government. They provided the uprising with its name, shouting "¡Viva Cristo

Rey!" as they launched their attacks. Stalwarts in the *Cristero* Rebellion had hoped that Washington would assist them in toppling Calles. Not only did such support fail to materialize, but the United States appointed a Protestant as envoy to Mexico City, much to church officials' dismay.

After the violence had consumed more than a quarter-million Mexicans' lives, U.S. Ambassador Dwight Morrow, caretaker Emilio Portes Gil, who followed Calles as president, and Archbishop Leopoldo Ruiz y Flores, Mora y del Río's successor, crafted a settlement. The chief executive pledged to allow the Catholic hierarchy to designate priests for registration in compliance with the law. In addition, the government agreed to refrain from interference with religious instruction conducted inside places of worship, and to permit the clergy—like other Mexican residents—to seek modification of the constitution through legitimate channels. In a pastoral letter, the new archbishop urged priests to avoid political entanglements, and enjoined laymen to obey national laws.

In the end, the *Cristero* Rebellion stands as an episode in which zealots from a profoundly Catholic zone lashed out against a Jacobin political hierarchy deemed antagonistic to their traditions, values, and institutions. Major social disruptions followed this bloody confrontation, and were resolved only with the adoption of a new, flexible modus vivendi. In the travails of civil war and the complexities inherent in founding a new legal framework, agonistic violence had again reared its menacing head in Mexico.

Calles and the Crisis of 1928

In 1924, Calles, a steadfast supporter of Obregón during the civil wars, succeeded his comrade-in-arms as president. During his term, Calles took advantage of a recovering economy to accelerate the populist policies initiated by his predecessor. Calles's administration increased the amount of land redistributed to *ejidos* under the 1917 Constitution, from 3 to 8 million acres. Calles also fortified the links between the state and organized labor, especially the Mexican Regional Confederation of Workers (CROM). While Obregón had worked closely with the CROM's Luis Napoleón Morones, Calles appointed the acutely ambitious trade-unionist to the post of secretary of industry, commerce and labor, and stocked the executive and legislative branches with other CROM militants. Morones won official favor because of his tactical malleability compared with the ideological rigidity of anarchosyndicalists, syndicalists, and other radicals. In his view, labor needed "fewer ideals and more organization."

In the same period, Calles had spearheaded a constitutional revision to provide for a six-year presidency, allowing multiple periods in office so long as a chief executive did not serve them consecutively. Not surprisingly, Calles backed the ambitious Obregón's desire for another term, believing that his ally would return the favor in 1934. Rumors abounded that an Obregón-Calles alternation in office might materialize as a latter-day version of the *Porfiriato*. Obregón was the revolutionary war hero par excellence, his amputated arm serving as a constant symbol of his military courage; for his part, Calles proved a master organizer, who had gone out of his way to propitiate organized labor and, to a lesser degree, peasant interests. Yet the scheme foundered when Generals Francisco Serrano and Arnulfo Gómez, who had also proclaimed their own candidacies in the spring of 1928, flew into open revolt. Within weeks, authorities had captured and killed both upstarts. The grisly trail of political violence did not end with Serrano and Gómez, however: In August 1928, at the height of the *Cristero* Rebellion, a deranged young artist named José de León Toral fired five shots into the head of Obregón, who had won the presidency but had yet to be inaugurated for a second period.

What action could Calles take? Not even the immensely popular Obregón had sought back-to-back terms. In theory, Calles handed the reins of government over to a hand-picked interim president—Portes Gil, a lawyer and former governor of Tamaulipas. In fact, following his official presidential tenure (1924–1928), Calles exercised near-absolute authority as the power behind the throne. Commentators identified Obregón's Sonoran disciple as *jefe máximo* or "supreme chief" and his harsh domineering tenure as the *Maximato*. Though ruling indirectly, Calles ran the affairs of state essentially by fiat, using armed force and mass arrests to impose his will. During this period, Portes Gil (1928–1930), Pascual Ortiz Rubio (1930–1932), and General Abelardo Rodríguez (1932–1934) successively wore the presidential sash, but they acted cautiously, knowing that to run afoul of the redoubtable Calles would ensure their ouster.

The Formation of a Revolutionary Party

Once he had installed Portes Gil temporarily in the presidency, Calles began to prepare the foundation for a national political party. Initially, the supreme chief did not intend the new organization as a corporatist institution. Rather, he sought desperately to forge a loose cartel of regional, personalist political parties and functional interest groups to preserve order. In the aftermath of Obregón's assassination, thousands of revolutionary generals and other power seekers were poised to pursue violently both self-aggrandizement and the settlement of old scores. The notables whom Calles summoned to Querétaro in 1929 included military strongmen (epitomized by Abelardo Rodríguez of Sonora), civilian chieftains (such as Portes Gil), the "*agraristas*," and some labor leaders, taking care to exclude Morones and the communists. Calling itself the Revolutionary Nationalist Party (PNR), the new combine was dominated by military chiefs, who treated their localities as fiefdoms in which they allied themselves with grass-roots peasant and worker groups. From the beginning, these men of action downplayed ideology in favor of channeling popular support into an effective power apparatus that would facilitate maximum freedom of action in their own geographic zones. In the words of Portes Gil, "[t]he Government has the program of the Revolution; the party has the program of the Revolution and of the Government. . . . The party will be a sincere collaborator of the administration." Portes Gil himself helped strengthen the new party by requiring every federal employee to join and contribute a week's pay in the form of dues, thus forging links to the bureaucracy that would become a hallmark of the official party.

In classic corporatist fashion, the major figures at Querétaro "brought with them into the new party their entire network of followers, people whose personal loyalty was assured through one or another element of the sacred triad of personal relationships consisting of family, friendship, and [godparenthood]."[22] Evelyn Stevens has drawn attention to the PNR's lack of ideological fixation, noting that "party followers could always find a statement by some leader that seemed to reflect their own political biases. . . . [I]deological imprecision was combined with preemption of the revolutionary mystique." This example of corporatist adaptation in Mexican politics hinged on the initiation of a domestic "party-state" by Calles. Through innovative governance and forceful leadership, Calles had provided a brilliant entrée for his successor, and Mexico's first modern president, General Cárdenas.

Lázaro Cárdenas Transforms a Confederal Party into a Corporatist Organization

Several major changes in the revolutionary party's internal political procedures took place at the PNR conventions in 1932 and 1933. The delegates successfully embraced a constitutional amendment prohibiting the reelection of federal presidents and banning senators and deputies from serving consecutive terms—on the grounds that frequent turnover in office would militate against the reconcentration of power in the hands of provincial political bosses.[23] Calles and his coterie also abolished the party's regional power bases at the same time they weakened local and state governments. Then, party leaders terminated consultation with provincial activists for presidential nominations in favor of selection by PNR conclaves. This action narrowed the effective coalition required to choose the party's standard-bearer and opened the door to *el dedazo*, or "finger pointing," the enduring practice whereby incumbent presidents select their successors. In combination, these moves undermined the PNR's incipient federalism, eroded the strength of power-hungry local chieftains, and centralized decision making in Mexico City.[24] At the same time, such changes ensured that future revolutionary party presidential nominees would develop a comprehensive knowledge of the corporatist system—its machinery, mores, and key members. This tendency predominated until the 1970s. Political scientist L. Vincent Padgett has commented that "[p]ersonalism and caesarism are limited although some personal identification carries over for some Mexicans. The key difference is that the recipient of such loyalty tends himself to be a product of the system rather than its main originator and supporter."

Calles, intent on recruiting a puppet attractive to left-wingers vexed at the growing conservatism of the *Maximato*, selected Lázaro Cárdenas to carry the PNR's banner in the 1934 presidential contest. The youthful general from Michoacán had a mind of his own, however, and he set about establishing a power base independent of the supreme chief. Even though he faced only token opposition, Cárdenas barnstormed the country as if the outcome of the contest depended on every vote. He took his campaign from cavernous halls in big cities, to tree-infested squares in small towns, to windswept crossroads in the northern desert, and to dirt-poor villages in the rain forested, mountainous south. His peripatetic crusade enabled him to imprint his face and name on the psyches of millions of Mexicans, to learn the problems of the diverse nation, and to recruit fresh talent for his administration. Once in power, Cárdenas manifested both his disdain for royal trappings and his sensitivity to ordinary citizens by moving his official residence from Chapultepec Castle, Maximilian's luxurious quarters, to the less ornate, tree-shrouded Los Pinos, a former hacienda. The legitimacy and personal popularity resulting from his energetic campaign and subsequent pro-labor and pro-peasant policies enabled Cárdenas to dispatch Calles into exile when the latter lambasted the social agenda of his "puppet" in mid-1935. Even today, older Mexicans speak fondly of "Tata Lázaro" whom they compare favorably to another "tata," Vasco de Quiroga, the bishop of Michoacán who fought relentlessly for the spiritual and physical welfare of Indians in the sixteenth century.

At the time of Cárdenas's presidency, populist corporatism began to find wide expression in Latin America. Green-shirted militants in the Brazilian Integralist Action movement had championed a politics of nativism, nationalism, and mysticism, called for "an 'integral' state under a single authoritarian head of government," emphasized discipline, order, and hierarchical organization, and proclaimed as their slogan: "For family, for country and for God."[25] In contrast to Brazil's right-wing Integralists, Chilean politicians formed a National Front, modeled on similar anti-fascist coalitions in France and Spain. This government united Radicals, Socialists, Communists, Democrats, and the newly organized Confederation of Chilean Workers, focusing its policies on state involvement in economic growth, as exemplified by a government-created development bank, the *Corporación de Fomento*.

Meanwhile, in 1946 Juan and Evita Perón reached Argentina's Casa Rosada presidential palace on the shoulders of government-regimented trade unionists, affectionately called *descamisados* or "shirtless ones" by their patrons. In addition, corporatist experiments in Europe in the 1930s influenced Cárdenas's decision to create a sector-based party in Mexico.

The PNR's metamorphosis into the Party of the Mexican Revolution (PRM), overseen by Cárdenas, would at one stroke mimic these developments and also transcend them in scope and longevity. Within a single presidential term, Cárdenas and his revolutionary contemporaries pulled together under the PRM's tricolored tent most of the elements that had contended for power for centuries, while expanding state control over the national economy.

Enhancing the Regime through "Revolutionary Nationalism"

In 1938, to ensure group-focused participation for segments of Mexican society whose support was deemed crucial for the exercise of power, Cárdenas built into the party structure access for four major groups. These comprised the Peasant, Labor, Popular, and Military sectors—with the latter encompassing officers in an army inflated by the revolution. Each collectivity exerted influence through a mass-membership organization with smaller constituent parts. These included the National Peasant Confederation (CNC) for peasants, the Mexican Workers' Confederation (CTM) for workers, and in 1943 the National Confederation of Popular Organizations (CNOP) for teachers, bureaucrats, clerks, professionals, shopkeepers, and other middle-class citizens. In 1940, the party discontinued the military sector mainly because politicians wanted to prevent the armed forces' serving as the mediator of disputes and the legitimator of each new government. For their part, officers shied from the glare of public political participation. Those military men anxious to remain active in partisan affairs found a home in the PRI's popular sector, although a handful of revolutionary generals established the Authentic Party of the Mexican Revolution (PARM), which served as an appendage of the ruling party. Significantly, Cárdenas played a key role in the establishment of the CTM in 1936, as he sought a labor base separate from the CROM where Calles's influence had been so strong. In 1936 and 1937, the party-state promoted wide national membership for business entities in the National Confederation of Chambers of Commerce (CONCANACO) and the National Confederation of Industrial Chambers (CONCAMIN), which together embrace the most important private enterprises in the country.

Cárdenas regarded Mexico's workers and peasants—long reviled by elites as faceless masses—as the most important components of society. Once Cárdenas's administration had completely reconfigured the party into individual functional groups joined only through the official party's central control apparatus, the National Executive Committee, an unmistakably corporatist organization appeared. Through the PRM, trade-unionists, campesinos, and other groups could wield greater political weight through collective action. "Each sector's line of force reached from the centre through regions, states, and small localities, to provide candidates, ideas, power, and votes for the single, presidentially dominated party."[26]

Cárdenas's radical reconfiguration of the Mexican power structure displayed corporatist tenets, but in this case a left-wing version. He assigned workers and peasants to separate sectors, and divided government employees—concentrated in the Federation of State Workers' Unions (FSTSE), destined to become the popular sector's centerpiece—from their blue-collar CTM brethren. While the president required FSTSE leaders to adhere to the no-reelection principle, he placed no such restriction on the secretaries-general of labor-sector unions. He gave impulse to the organization of workers, higher wages, and improved working conditions. In addition, he bestowed on peasants land titles to more than 20 million hectares, nearly twice the total granted by his six predecessors. This land reform benefited not only individual landowners, but also *ejidos*, worked collectively by their occupants. Above all, Cárdenas endowed the presidency itself with a unique status in Mexican society. Robert Scott has shown that his ability to manipulate the sectoral entities enabled the populist leader to construct an organization politically faithful and subordinate to the chief executive.

Rules of the Game

Out of the Calles and Cárdenas experiments, certain "rules of the game" arose that endured for more than a half-century. First, reelection to the presidency and Congress was prohibited, guaranteeing that no single individual could use the massive concentration of power in the executive branch to dominate Mexican politics for more than six years.

Second, the state bureaucracy established a vise-like grip over both the party and the military. The armed forces—particularly after the abolition of the ruling party's military sector—obeyed the orders issued by civilian leaders rather than deliberate over what course to follow. Of course, this scheme embodied a fundamental tension, which continues to bedevil the revolutionary party today: Rank-and-file group members too often found themselves impotent because avaricious power brokers pursued personal rather than collective interests with the connivance of their partners in positions of public trust.

Third, the regime's leaders continually evoked the legacy of the revolution to enhance their own legitimacy and discredit opposition forces on the left and right.

Table 1.1   Land Distribution in Mexico, 1915–94

Source: Edmundo Flores, "El Reparto de Tierra Obsoleto, *Excélsior*, June 19, 1986, p. 14-A.

President	Period	Hectares	% Total	Ejido Members Benefited	% Total
Carranza	1915-20	381,949	.39	77,203	2.23
de la Huerta	1920-21	1,730,684	1.77	154,128	4.46
Obregón	1921-25	3,173,343	3.25	292,194	8.46
Calles	1925-29	851,282	.87	126,537	3.66
Portes Gil	1930-30	1,495,182	1.53	117,500	3.40
Ortiz Rubio	1930-33	2,056,268	2.11	158,262	4.58
Abelardo Rodríquez	1933-34	2,094,637	2.15	200,220	5.80
Cárdenas	1934-40	20,107,044	20.61	763,009	22.09
Avila Camacho	1940-46	5,306,922	5.44	112,107	3.25
Alemán	1946-52	4,210,478	4.32	91,054	2.64
Ruiz Cortines	1952-58	3,563,847	3.65	195,699	5.67
López Mateos	1958-64	7,935,476	8.13	255,283	7.39
Díaz Ordaz	1964-70	24,491,000	25.10	396,700	11.48
Echeverría	1970-76	12,866,416	13.19	223,462	6.47
López Portillo	1976-82	6,368,616	6.53	258,786	7.49
de la Madrid	1982-85*	937,437	.96	32,270	.93
Salinas	1988-94	0	.00	0	.00
TOTAL		**97,570,581**	**100.00**	**3,454,414**	**100.00**

*Only years available for de la Madrid.

Fourth, although indulging in antibusiness rhetoric, the party-state amalgam forged an implicit alliance with private capital: The former provided economic opportunities to entrepreneurs, who in turn lavished financial largesse on the revolutionary party, the president, and other leading actors in the regime.

Fifth, the incumbent chief executive, who consulted with key members of the revolutionary family, designated the PRI's presidential nominee from among the members of his cabinet.

Sixth, aspirants for president who failed to receive the *dedazo* promptly and publicly threw their support behind the PRI nominee—in return for which they received consolation prizes, usually in the form of a remunerative governmental post.

Seventh, the party's sectors operated on a "one for all, all for one" basis in backing each other's candidates for elective positions at all levels.

Eighth, the governing party's nominee became the focus of official attention during his presidential campaign and power flowed to him even before his inauguration.

Ninth, whether or not credible opposition existed, the PRI's presidential nominee relentlessly criss-crossed the country—à la Cárdenas in 1934—visiting all states, major cities, important towns, and scores of union halls and communal farms.

Tenth, except for debilitating illness, cabinet members, governors, and other high officials retained their posts unless removed by the president, while unwritten understandings upheld the social peace: (a) members of the revolutionary family spurned violence in settling intramural disputes; (b) incumbent presidents refrained from disparaging their predecessors or their families; (c) outgoing chief executives accomplished devaluations and other difficult economic policies so that successors could assume office under the most favorable conditions possible; and (d) former presidents maintained a low profile, while comporting themselves in a dignified manner.

Finally, the mass media abstained from openly criticizing the regime, especially the decisions and actions of the president.[27]

Conclusion

The Mexican revolution and the *Cristero* Rebellion unleashed powerful social and political forces that overwhelmed the capacities of existing institutional structures to channel and contain them. The second and third decades of the twentieth century saw a return to earlier patterns of violence and outside intervention. The first faltering steps toward rebuilding a viable political order were taken by the revolutionary *caudillo* presidents Obregón and Calles, who formed an ad hoc working alliance with potential rivals while manipulating three interim presidents. The *jefe máximo* transformed the confederal party into a hierarchical organization whose growing number of apparatchiks proved ever more independent of state *caudillos* and increasingly subservient to the chief executive. After the revolution and *Cristero* Rebellion, Mexicans hungered for political stability and economic opportunities. The untimely murder of Obregón forced Calles to organize a gestalt of forces under the rubric of the PNR. It remained for the administration of Lázaro Cárdenas, however, to discover the formula for inclusive growth and stability that would guide Mexico for the next half century. Pursuing a corporatist version of the strategy of "divide and rule," Cárdenas institutionalized the political participation of diverse social groups with their own separate organizations. As a quid pro quo for his largesse, these groups integrated themselves into a corporatist party that would both amplify their political voices and contain anti-system behavior. An intricate, often ad hoc, set of rules buttressed Mexico's corporatist state. Integrated, but only at the top, through the revolutionary party, these organizations formed the backbone of a one-party regime that, until very recently, had established a record of stability and of orderly—but undemocratic—transfer of power unrivaled in Latin America. Having achieved social peace, the chief challenge facing the Mexican government was to deliver the goods. To foster rapid growth with broad distribution, Mexico's leaders turned to a new doctrine of economic nationalism: import substitution industrialization (ISI)—which would fortify the iron triangle of president, party, and bureaucracy. The success of this approach would both shape, and be shaped by, Mexico's enduring corporatist traditions.

Notes

1. Wiarda, "Toward a Framework for the Study of Political Change," p. 214.
2. Evelyn P. Stevens, "Mexico's PRI: The Institutionalization of Corporatism?" in James Malloy (ed.), *Authoritarianism and Corporatism in Latin America* (Pittsburgh: University of Pittsburgh Press, 1977), p. 231.
3. Michael C. Meyer and William L. Sherman, *The Course of Mexican History* (New York: Oxford University Press, 1983), pp. 487, 516–517.
4. Hugh Thomas, *The Mexican Labyrinth* (New York: Twentieth Century Fund, 1990), p. 13.
5. Thomas, *Mexican Labyrinth*, p. 14.
6. Ernest Gruening, *Mexico and Its Heritage* (New York: D. Appleton-Century Co., 1934), p. 178.
7. Cited in Gruening, *Mexico and Its Heritage*, p. 183.
8. Elizabeth Wilkes Dore, "Audiencia," in Helen Delpar (ed.) *Encyclopedia of Latin America* (New York: McGraw-Hill, 1974), pp. 48–49.
9. Wiarda, "Toward a Framework for the Study of Political Change," p. 214.
10. Meyer and Sherman, *The Course of Mexican History*, p. 294.
11. Meyer and Sherman, *The Course of Mexican History*, p. 297.
12. Howard F. Cline, *Mexico: Revolution to Evolution 1940–1960* (Westport, CT: Greenwood Press, 1981), p. 136.
13. Carleton Beals, *Porfirio Díaz: Dictator of Mexico* (Westport, CT: Greenwood Press, 1971), p. 192.
14. Beals, *Porfirio Díaz*, p. 204.
15. Quoted in Beals, *Porfirio Díaz*, p. 222.
16. Thomas, *Mexican Labyrinth*, p. 16.
17. L. Vincent Padgett, *The Mexican Political System* (2nd. ed.; Boston: Houghton Mifflin Co., 1976), p. 21.

18. Robert E. Scott, *Mexican Government in Transition* (Urbana: University of Illinois Press, 1964), p. 57.

19. Miguel Angel Centeno, *Democracy within Reason: Technocratic Revolution in Mexico* (University Park, PA: Pennsylvania State University Press, 1994), p. 6–7.

20. Frank Brandenburg, *The Making of Modern Mexico* (Englewood Cliffs, N.J.: Prentice-Hall Inc., 1967), pp. 10–11.

21. This section draws on George Grayson, *The Church in Contemporary Mexico* (Washington, D.C.: Center for Strategic and International Studies, 1992), pp.14–16.

22. Evelyn P. Stevens, "Mexico's PRI: The Institutionalization of Corporatism," p. 230.

23. Story, *The Mexican Ruling Party*, p. 21.

24. Stevens, "Mexico's PRI: The Institutionalization of Corporatism?" p. 231.

25. N. Bradford Burns, *A History of Brazil* (2nd. ed.; New York: Columbia University Press, 1993), p. 354; and Peter Flynn, *Brazil: A Political Analysis* (London: Anchor Press, 1978), pp. 71–75.

26. Cline, *Mexico: Revolution to Evolution*, p. 152.

27. Centeno, *Democracy within Reason*, pp. 7–8; and "Democracia o anarquía: escenarios para el futuro político de méxico," *La carpeta púrpura*, IX (April 30, 1996): 5.

2
—

ISI, Mexico's Economic Miracle, and Corporatism

Introduction

A policy of import substitution industrialization (ISI) drove Mexico's economic development in the middle twentieth century. Widely accepted throughout the hemisphere in the 1930s, ISI proved crucial in shaping each of the PRI's corporatist constituencies. To foster the growth of domestic industrial capacities, ISI emphasized the erection of trade barriers to reduce the volume of foreign-manufactured imports. Mexican leaders sought to keep out products from abroad while fostering their nation's industrialization.

Import Substitution Industrialization (ISI)

Along with Argentina, Brazil, and Chile, Mexico also employed import substitution to cope with the catastrophic effects of the Great Depression. The marked decline of the U.S. and European economies shrunk external demand for the one or two commodities on which most Latin American nations relied to earn foreign exchange. To prevent capital flight, developed nations raised import levies on the sugar, wool, copper, silver, tin, oil, and beef that they had traditionally purchased. After decreases in both the unit price and quantity of Latin American exports, their total value between 1930 and 1934 declined 48 percent relative to the 1925–1929 period.[1] Regional leaders viewed ISI as a means of reducing dependence on their traditional suppliers of food products, clothing, and consumer durables like automobiles and household appliances. They also hoped to generate employment for a restive and expanding urban work force, and to broaden their array of potential exports.

Mexico concentrated on domestic priorities during the 1930s, especially on implementing elements of the 1917 Constitution, and later, President Cárdenas sought to preserve social peace and invigorate the state by organizing and recruiting peasants, workers, and other neglected segments of the population into the revolutionary party. To achieve these objectives, he energetically expanded land reform, nationalized the railroad and petroleum industries, and recognized scores of labor unions and campesino associations.

Although the Mexican economy contracted sharply between 1926 and 1932, the country recovered much earlier than most other Latin American nations. In fact, new investment enabled manufacturing to supplant agriculture as the leading economic activity by the mid-1930s. Several factors explain this turnabout. First, two-thirds of the population lived in small villages, many at or beyond the margin of the market economy, mitigating the impact of the international crash. Second, Mexico enjoyed luck in the "export commodity lottery." Compared to mono-crop exporters like Colombia with coffee and Chile with copper, Mexico shipped abroad grains, tropical fruits, coffee, unfinished industrial materials, precious metals, and oil. Global demand for two of Mexico's key products—silver and petroleum—proved both strong and inelastic. Finally, Cárdenas abandoned the goals of a stable peso and a balanced budget in favor of an expansionary fiscal and monetary policy.

Cárdenas raised spending on social programs and infrastructure from 36 percent of the federal budget to 60 percent. Outlays on rural schools, potable water systems, irrigation facilities, roads, railroads, electrification, and the newly formed state oil monopoly—officially known as *Petróleos Mexicanos* (Pemex)—buoyed aggregate demand. Orders flooded into construction firms and factories turning out steel, cement, and other producer goods. In another era, Mexico's businessmen might have sunk their profits into fancy ranches, haciendas, or stables for their racehorses. Uncertainty over the future of land reform, however, meant that "only a very ignorant or a very courageous investor would have made large-scale investments in rural land."[2]

World War II severely curtailed Mexico's access to items manufactured abroad and gave impetus to an expansion in industrial capability. Many entrepreneurs who had immigrated to Mexico from Eastern Europe and the Mideast championed import substitution. Some of the newcomers had begun selling socks, underwear, and other clothing door-to-door or in small shops until they amassed sufficient capital to purchase or construct small mills. This so-called "New Group," which formed the National Chamber of Manufacturers (CANACINTRA) in the 1950s, joined middle-class businessmen in seeking sufficient protection to ensure the profitability of their enterprises. As a result, successive presidents, beginning with the courtly Manuel Avila Camacho (1940–1946), constructed a wall of tariffs to shield virtually every infant industry established in Mexico from foreign competition. At the same time, Avila Camacho concentrated the resources of the Nacional Financiera development bank—established in 1934—on issuing loans or purchasing stock to promote basic industries. The federal government, private entrepreneurs, and U.S. institutions including the Export-Import Bank supplied funds for these large-scale investments.

Miguel Alemán (1946–1952), the country's first elected civilian president since the revolution, succeeded Avila Camacho. The new chief executive depended even more heavily on tariffs to stimulate private sector investment. He kept duties low on raw materials purchased abroad, while imposing tax rates that often exceeded 100 percent on imported manufactures. By the late 1950s, Mexico had replaced tariffs with import licenses as the principal tool of protectionism. Revenues from these permits stimulated Mexican industrialization and, since licensing limited Mexican purchases of foreign goods, the policy also conserved valuable foreign exchange for only the most essential purposes. Currency devaluations of 1949 and 1954 provided an additional safeguard to emerging industries by markedly undervaluing the peso, thereby discouraging imports. Licensing in the economic sphere found a parallel in the licensing of interest groups, which kept them under the government's corporatist thumb.

Incentives for industrialists complemented the protectionist barricade of tariffs, import permits, and an undervalued currency. Among other advantages, Mexican businesses benefited from tax concessions, low-interest loans, inexpensive energy, a malleable and manipulated union movement, and the construction of an elaborate infrastructure system. The weakening of the church during the revolution and Cárdenas's redistribution of large landowners' holdings effectively removed two possible foes of ISI.

As the Mexican market grew and memories of Cárdenas's popular nationalism faded, foreign investors began to open assembly and processing plants. Alemán's stand with the Allied Powers during World War II and his anticommunism at the outset of the Cold War reassured American executives. U.S. investment, followed by loans, flowed across the border at an accelerating pace, expanding fivefold between 1950 and 1970—from $566 million to $2.822 billion. General Motors, Dow Chemical, Pepsi-Cola, Coca-Cola, Colgate, Goodyear, John Deere, Ford Motor Company, Procter and Gamble, and Sears, Roebuck flocked to Mexico in the postwar period.[3] Gaudy neon signs flashed invitations to "Fume Raleigh" ("Smoke Raleighs") and "Tome Coca-Cola—La Pause Que Refresca"("Drink Coca-Cola—the Pause that Refreshes")—as Madison Avenue made its impact felt along Insurgentes and other broad shop-lined boulevards. In fact, during the half-century between 1920–1970, trade with the United States accounted for approximately two-thirds of all commercial intercourse in the region. The early 1960s witnessed the establishment of the twin-plant *maquiladora* program—with capital-intensive work performed in the United States; labor-focused tasks carried out in Mexico; and preferential tariffs applied to goods shipped back to the United States. This system greatly spurred Mexican exports. Government-directed policies sparked an "economic miracle," demonstrated by a growth rate that averaged more than 6 percent between 1955 and 1971, before opportunities for domestic production waned.

ISI and Corporatism

The myriad permits, tariffs, rules, and regulations required to implement protectionism spawned a vast state apparatus with a vested political interest in preserving and expanding government controls. The ranks of public servants grew in proportion to the state's intervention in the economy. Thanks to nationalizations—foreshadowed by Nacional Financiera's purchase of a minority interest in the Altos Hornos de México steel company in 1942—the number of public firms mushroomed, and the state eventually generated approximately one-third of national economic activity. By the early 1980s, the federal government employed more than 3 million people.

Import substitution inflated the ranks of the bureaucracy and facilitated its dominance over the Party of the Mexican Revolution, progenitor of today's PRI. An expanding and intrusive federal regime provided employment for the party faithful and their allies. As a condition of employment, these men and women had to join FSTSE, formed in 1938 as a charter organ of the official party. When CNOP sprang to life five years later as an umbrella body for the rapidly growing popular sector, FSTSE became its largest component. Approximately half of the federation's members comprised teachers and other school staff members who belonged to the National Union of Educational Workers (SNTE), Latin America's biggest union.

President Alemán and his successors lavished resources on the popular sector in general and on FSTSE in particular. Such largesse reinforced the top-down relationship between the country's leadership and corporatist entities. The chief executive and his confidants viewed loyalty from public workers as important to maintaining stability as the bureaucracy expanded dramatically. In addition, this sector boasted the official party's best educated, most articulate, and most politically adept members. Finally, no equivalent to the Agrarian Code or the Federal Labor Law manacled the middle-class representatives of the CNOP to the state. As Dale Story has noted, "whereas the agrarian sector is totally dependent upon the state for land, and the labor sector depends on the state for many jobs and for its rights to organize and to be recognized legally, the popular sector is not asymmetrically beholden to the state for any necessary resources."[4]

The advantages accruing to the popular sector, particularly to FSTSE members, included access to low-cost housing, short-term loans, generous pensions, and broad health care coverage. A major federal agency, the Institute for Social Security and Social Services for State Employees (ISSSTE) administered these far-reaching programs.

Popular sector loyalists filled the lion's share of high-level government posts. In the late 1950s, for example, twice as many CNOP members held elective positions compared to activists in the party's labor and peasant organs. The popular sector's portion grew rapidly in subsequent years, especially among cabinet members and governors.

Still, this largely white-collar, bureaucrat-dominated grouping lacked cohesion and autonomy. Its leadership won appointment from on high, and grass-roots members had few effective channels through which to influence the selection of chiefs. CNOP suffered from internal rivalries that plague all public administrations. Furthermore, the absence of a professional civil service meant that a government official had no job security when a new president, with his own adherents to reward, took office. Such employment vulnerability bred both corruption within the bureaucratic apparatus and a tendency to allocate resources on politically motivated rather than objective grounds. To conduct business legally in Mexico entailed running a formidable gauntlet of obscure regulations, multiple official agencies, and extremely sticky palms. Insiders regularly refer to the last year of the *sexenio*, the six-year presidential term, as the Año de Hidalgo—after the austere priest whose stern, pinched face once graced the peso coin—when public officials steal egregiously to provide for an uncertain future. Insecurity also found senior bureaucrats devoting a disproportionate amount of their time to *camarillas*, ubiquitous political teams that concentrated on the mutual political advancement of their members rather than policy objectives. The circulation of elites provides opportunities for profit as well as power. In a corporatist system, "the personalistic nature of . . . politics promotes [corruption], and once [it] pervades the system, it feeds on itself."[5]

ISI also profoundly affected Mexico's labor movement. In contrast to Argentina, Brazil, Chile, and other Latin American countries, the creation of Mexico's corporatist arrangement preceded enactment of import substitution, stretching all the way back to the colonial era. Thus, Mexican leaders boasted a mechanism by which to control and manipulate the growing blue-collar workforce resulting from increased industrialization, thus militating against the ascent of Mexican versions of populist politicians like Argentina's Perón and Brazil's Getulio Vargas. Still, ISI helped Mexican presidents draw organized labor more firmly into the government party web.

In light of the anti-labor sentiment pervading the local business community, Vicente Lombardo Toledano—secretary-general of the Confederation of Mexican Workers from 1936 to 1941—wholeheartedly endorsed replacement of imports with domestic goods produced under the direction of an activist state. To him, the ISI strategy signified national control of more firms in which labor organizations could recruit followers, a growing labor force, higher wages, and an expanded bureaucracy, whose unionized party members enjoyed comparatively attractive salaries. When in early 1945, the U.S. delegation to the Chapultepec Conference in Mexico City urged nations of the Hemisphere to slash tariffs and welcome foreign investors, the socialist Lombardo Toledano joined Mexican capitalists in denouncing Washington's attempt to thwart Latin America's industrial development.[6] While anxious for the CTM's support of import substitution, Avila Camacho feared that Lombardo Toledano's radicalism could harm the nation's investment climate. After all, the labor firebrand had once described himself as "a rich man . . . rich in the hatred of the bourgeoisie." In addition, the chief executive wanted union leaders whom the government could readily manipulate. As a result, Avila Camacho replaced the left-leaning Lombardo Toledano with the more pliable Fidel Velázquez. "Don Fidel," as friends and foes alike would call the former head of the dairy workers' union, believed in "revolutionary nationalism"—an eclectic set of principles that venerates the president, the revolution, the constitution, and the governing party. At the same time, this ideology advocates central planning in a mixed economy and furnishing generous social benefits for workers. That Velázquez, unlike Morones and Lombardo Toledano, harbored no ambition for the presidency also appealed to Avila Camacho.

Despite the new CTM leadership, labor–government tension marked the first few years of Velázquez's tenure. Inflation, caused by a persistent balance-of-payments deficit, eroded workers' buying power and elicited protests from the CTM, which endorsed controls on prices and profits. Between 1947 and 1951, some labor leaders—determined to maintain at any cost the strength and autonomy of their unions in the face of Alemán's cooptive, pro-business administration—spearheaded strikes in the railroad, petroleum, and mining sectors.

With few exceptions, authorities had repressed these "pro-communist" activists by the early 1950s. In so doing, the government reinforced its hegemony over Velázquez and his allies. Labor officials' subservience to the state ensured the dominance of pragmatic bosses within the CTM, and the Confederation's political preeminence within organized labor for three decades. While stridently demanding higher salaries and increased benefits for the labor movement, Don Fidel generally discouraged strikes, supported presidential initiatives, backed PRI candidates, and behaved like an advocate of "responsible syndicalism." By making revolutionary nationalism the credo of the union movement, he inoculated rank-and-file members against Marxism and other disruptive ideologies, while furnishing the Labor and Government ministries with information about dissident groups throughout the country. Also, Velázquez helped burnish the ruling party's "pro-worker" image, even as its policies skewed the income distribution in favor of the affluent. In addition, he often threw his weight behind the regime's anti-inflation initiatives.

In return for the loyalty of "official" labor organizations, the government allowed their members' salaries to rise. In most cases, increases resulted from "collective contracts" that the CTM and other official unions negotiated with an industry under the watchful eye of the Labor Ministry. In the event of an impasse, aggressive union representation would threaten to call a strike. Often, before the work stoppage began, the leaders would meet with the president or labor secretary, who would magnanimously compromise with the aggrieved workers. Their officials learned the value of cooperating with the regime—in the interest of their members and for the sake of their own careers, which—after all—could be prolonged through multiple reelections. Once again underscoring the corporatist hierarchy's function, salary increases sprang from the benevolence of *señor presidente*, and the Mexican state—not from the strength of an increasingly coopted labor movement.

Labor chiefs who rebuffed the government's carrots often suffered the merciless impact of its stick. The most notable case involved the Railroad Workers, who launched a strike in 1959. When negotiations broke down, the government arrested and jailed their key activists, Valentín Campa and Demetrio Vallejo, on vague charges of subversion. Authorities finally brought these men to trial in 1964, resulting in a conviction for violating the Law of Social Dissolution, which equated political dissent with sedition. Thanks to international pressure, they served only a fraction of their sixteen-year sentences, and the Mexican Congress repealed the statute during the Echeverría administration (1970–1976). In the 1970s, Vallejo, along with Professor Heberto Castillo of the National Autonomous University of Mexico (UNAM), organized the Mexican Workers' Party (PMT), composed of many supporters of the railroad strike. The government helped purge dissident leaders who spearheaded reform movements among electrical workers— "Tendencia Democrática" of the Electrical Workers' Union (SUTERM)— and Nuclear Workers (SUTIN).

Such intervention expanded government influence over corporatist entities, whose newly installed leaders enjoyed increasing power at the expense of union locals and the rank-and-file. In the words of Kevin J. Middlebrook, "this system of [domineering] control ultimately rested on state officials' authority to approve union statutes and certify union elections."[7] For their part, compliant union leaders readily watched as workers' benefits multiplied, profit-sharing became a reality, and PRI-affiliated labor organizations gained recognition as the legal bargaining agent for a given plant or industry. This policy assisted the CTM and, to a lesser extent, the pro-regime CROM and the Revolutionary Confederation of Workers and Peasants (CROC), created in 1952 by the Alemán administration to unify disparate labor groups and to serve as a counterpoise to the CTM. In the CROM—which reigned over national labor politics during the decade after its founding in 1918—artisans and blue-collar workers achieved joint representation for the first time.

Within the framework of the corporatist PRM, the government supported union candidates for elective office and rubber-stamped Don Fidel's designees as representatives on Federal Conciliation and Arbitration Boards (JFCA), established by the Labor Ministry to resolve workplace conflicts. CTM designees also served on the governing bodies of the Mexican Social Security Institute (IMSS), National Fund for Workers' Housing (INFONAVIT), and the National Fund for Workers' Needs (FONACOT), which furnished workers with low-cost household appliances. CTM loyalty partially explains the establishment of a Workers' Bank (Banco Obrero) in 1977. Confederation affiliates supplied most of the bank's working capital; their members received a preponderance of loans; and Velázquez acted as "general advisor" to an institution that proclaimed itself: "A Bank for All." The bank's first manager, Alfredo del Mazo González, took advantage of close ties with Don Fidel to win union, PRI, and presidential backing for the governorship of Mexico state in 1981. Sixteen years later, the CTM enthusiastically supported Del Mazo's bid for mayor of Mexico City.

The actions of Joaquín "La Quina" Hernández Galicia epitomized the complex relationship that powerful labor chiefs developed with state agencies, their peers, and their followers. In the early 1960s, Hernández Galicia emerged as the head of the Oil Workers' Union (STPRM), an organization notable for its affluence and strategic economic role and proclivity for violence against challengers to La Quina's hegemony. The union's wealth derived from its symbiotic relationship with Pemex, the state oil firm. Through its collective agreement with the monopoly, the STPRM obtained 2 percent of the value of all the company's contracts for "social works" undertaken at the absolute discretion of La Quina and his henchmen. The agreement also gave the STPRM control over the maritime shipment of oil from one Mexican port to another. In addition, the union involved itself in such lucrative ventures as well drilling, the disposal of "slop oil," and the performance of maintenance at petroleum installations. Moreover, Pemex indirectly subsidized union-operated stores where prices often exceeded those charged for similar items in commercial establishments. Finally, the government provided a vast array of schools, clinics, hospitals, housing complexes, and recreational facilities for the *petroleros*. Hernández Galicia even managed to construct a network of savings institutions, commercial properties, and ranches, making his union the wealthiest in the country. In La Quina's home locale in Ciudad Madero (Sección 1), the PRI headquarters long occupied a STPRM-owned building.

Patently illegal activities gave rise to a veritable "river of gold," in the words of one observer, that flowed into the leaders' pockets. The most conspicuous of these crimes involved ubiquitous job-selling: 2,000 pesos for a transitory position—up to 28 days, 40,000 pesos for an ordinary worker's slot, and 150,000 for a tenured mechanical engineering post.[8] In mid-1978, unscrupulous STPRM leaders even demanded sexual favors from women seeking temporary secretarial jobs. Furthermore, the union stole Pemex property, obtained compensation from the government for work never performed, and forced retirees to "donate" labor on STPRM-owned ranches. Men such as Heriberto Kehoe Vincent, Oscar Torres Pancardo, and "Chico" Balderas who crossed swords with the redoubtable *petrolero* boss died under strange circumstances. Old-timers regale visitors to union halls with tales of wanna-be bigshots who committed "suicide" by firing several bullets into their heads. While not averse to using blackmail and brute force against foes, Hernández Galicia preferred to present himself as the "paterfamilias" of the petroleum workers.

The author observed this role while waiting to interview him in Ciudad Madero in 1978.[9] While I watched from outside the gate of his modest suburban home, scenes reminiscent of *The Godfather* unfolded. Men gathered to plead for work or a handout; women sought to have unfaithful or alcoholic husbands disciplined; children delivered shiny, cellophane-wrapped gifts; and sycophantic politicians strove to ingratiate themselves with the man who could launch or ground their careers.

His retainers spread the word that Hernández Galicia was at one of the union's many ranches outside town and would not receive visitors that evening; nevertheless, at least sixty people came by to inquire about his schedule, chat with associates, or drop off messages. La Quina did arrive that evening, around 7:30, in a three-vehicle caravan, apparently for protection. As his truck appeared, the twenty-five or so people still on hand scurried to see and be seen. They obsequiously opened the gate to his yard, held doors, and cleared a path for him among the faithful, who formed a semicircle at a respectful distance from their hero. One by one those fortunate enough to be summoned approached La Quina, who intently listened to each plea as if the petitioner were the only other person on earth. The tête-à-tête—analogous to a penitent importuning a priest—ended with La Quina's giving an order to a fawning subordinate or jotting a note to the appropriate person who could satisfy the petitioner's request. In classic patronage politics the boss provided favors, jobs, and benefits in return for submission, loyalty, and service.

Although critics condemned the oil sector as a "petroleum jungle," several presidents gave La Quina the right of *picaporte*, or immediate access, to Los Pinos presidential palace. Hernández Galicia's power sprang in large measure from the billions of pesos that he controlled. He also exhibited incredible skill as an organizer, which not only enhanced his dominance of appreciative, well-compensated union members, but earned the respect of politicians, who feared he could paralyze a crucial sector of the economy at will. Moreover, if attacked by the government, the STPRM leader could publicize the names of Pemex officials and political cronies who had feathered their own nests while turning a blind eye to—or aiding and abetting—unlawful union activities.

The ability of La Quina, Don Fidel, the CTM, and constituent unions to "deliver the goods" through their ever-stronger ties to the government-party alliance enhanced their ability to consolidate and expand their grass-roots support, even as national leaders augmented their power at the expense of local leaders and the rank-and-file. Authoritarianism, centralization, hierarchy, and paternalism all characterized the labor movement. For example, when an average worker ran into a bureaucratic stonewall while seeking a driver's license, social security card, access to a hospital, a loan, or some other document or service, he looked to the head of his local for relief. If necessary, the low-level leader turned to his superior in the union movement—with the inquiry progressing upward through the corporatist structure as necessary. Even though labor chieftains propitiated their members with raises, fringe benefits, and favors, they owed their positions to kingpins in Mexico City or in state capitals. Higher-ups had appointed local bosses and could cut short their careers. Big players in the system also favored union loyalists with opportunities to run for public office, to obtain bureaucratic sinecures, or to become immensely wealthy, often through illicit practices. As a result, power and initiative flowed downward from the top in an increasingly corrupt, ISI-reinforced corporatist system.

Compared to organized labor, the National Peasants Confederation obtained far fewer advantages from import substitution. Well-to-do farmers prospered because of escalating demand for their specialty fruits and vegetables grown on vast irrigated ranches concentrated in the north. In contrast, ejido-dwellers constituted the CNC's biggest component, yet wielded the least influence. However, they did register gains. Specifically, truck farmers in the north benefited from the erection of dams for irrigation, flood control, and power generation. Mexico cooperated with the United States to construct the Falcon Dam in the lower Rio Grande Valley; to the south, the lot of farmers in the states of Puebla, Veracruz, and Oaxaca improved after the harnessing of the Papaloapan River. Road building and other infrastructure projects also helped the agricultural sector. In contrast, land reform—vigorous in the Cárdenas administration—slowed to a crawl, and hundreds of thousands of young people left communal farms in search of work in the industrial zones that sprouted up around Mexico City, Guadalajara, and Monterrey.

Clearly, companies that flourished thanks to protectionism backed the regime, whose policies had enabled them to earn unprecedented profits. As part of the corporatist structure he consolidated in the 1930s, Cárdenas required businesses to join national producer organizations or chambers of commerce. As mentioned earlier, these groups included CONCANACO, CONCAMIN, and later, CANACINTRA. Still, Cárdenas stopped short of adding a business sector to the revolutionary party. After all, he regarded labor as a substantially more powerful and reliable ally than business. Moreover, rolling out the red carpet for large companies—one of the nemeses of the Cárdenas era—would have run afoul of the party's ideology of revolutionary nationalism that venerated workers. Nonetheless, the captains of industry who prospered under ISI developed interlocking relations with PRI governments.

According to Mexico expert John J. Bailey, these links crystallized in several ways. For instance, Avila Camacho invited private-sector representatives to join the boards of directors of newly created parastatal industries. Representatives of various chambers also served on advisory committees formed by the Ministry of Industry and Commerce. In this capacity, businessmen instituted and strengthened contacts with bureaucrats and politicians belonging to the ruling party's popular sector. In addition, chambers appointed members to the above-mentioned tripartite arbitration boards supervised by the Labor Ministry. Here they rubbed elbows with politicians and union leaders. Finally, General Braulio Maldonado Sánchez—a governor of Baja California Norte under Adolfo Ruiz Cortines—cultivated along with other wealthy, pro-business politicians their own contacts with the private sector. Noteworthy successors to Maldonado included Antonio Ortiz Mena, finance secretary under Ruiz Cortines, Adolfo López Mateos, and Gustavo Díaz Ordaz before becoming president of the Inter-American Development Bank in 1971; Alfonso Martínez Domínguez, who served as PRI president under Díaz Ordaz, as Mexico City's mayor under Luis Echeverría Alvarez, and governor of Nuevo León under José López Portillo and de la Madrid; the legendary Carlos Hank González, a man with a fortune exceeded only by his political curriculum vitae, including federal deputy, director-general of the National Food Distribution Company (CONASUPO), two cabinet posts—Tourism and Agriculture—as well as the governorship of Mexico state and mayoralty of Toluca and Mexico City; and Miguel Alemán Velasco, the son and heir to the fortune of ex-president Alemán, the husband of a former Miss Universe, and a successful candidate for a Veracruz Senate seat in 1992.

Corruption flourished as bureaucrats and politicians conferred contracts on businessmen, slashed the regulatory "red tape" that complicated their lucrative deals, and obtained official approvals required for economic transactions. The quid pro quo for such favors involved greasing the palms of obliging officials, lavishly contributing to the PRI, or cutting the helpful party activist into the money-making venture. "Corruption beset [Alemán's] administration, and many new millionaires emerged between 1946 and 1952. The displays of sprawling mansions, yachts, and airplanes, paid for with bribes brought to mind the venality of the days of Santa Anna."[10]

Problems with ISI

For several reasons, import substitution proved a mixed blessing for Latin American economies. First, hopes of curbing reliance on industrialized nations faded, as developing states found themselves dependent on imports of machinery and other sophisticated capital goods required by the nascent firms that they had nurtured. ISI did not eliminate Mexico's dependency, only changing its symptoms. Second, imported manufactures commanded ever-higher prices, compared to stagnant or declining prices in world markets for many of Latin America's major exports. Expressed simply, adverse terms of trade meant that Mexicans had to export more and more bags of coffee, wheat, or sugar to purchase each successive tractor, generator, or airplane. Third, having copied first-world production techniques, many infant industries featured capital-intensivity, thus creating relatively few jobs. Fourth, continued protection for the new businesses—even after they had matured—shielded them from competition. Such hothouse conditions enabled these companies to produce goods dear in price but cheap in quality. As a result, income transferred from consumer to producer, benefiting industrialists and their network of managers and professionals at the expense of workers, small farmers, and the lower-middle-class. Finally, in terms of Mexico's corporatism, extensive ISI induced intrusion into the economy provided the regime with incomparable resources with which to suborn and subordinate workers, peasants, and public servants. The government took advantage of the potential for such intricate transactions, suffusing protectionism throughout the economy to devise a reward system for loyalists within the PRI's three sectors—with, of course, bureaucrats being especially well placed to exchange favors for *mordidas* or bribes. The elites thus managed to elude corporatism's controls whereas lower classes often found them repressive.

By the late 1960s, many of the spry, eager, infant industries of Mexico's previous generation had grown swag-bellied, lethargic, whiny, and inefficient. Sheltered from competition at home, hundreds of these firms could not hold their own in foreign markets. The first "captains of industry" had shown entrepreneurial talents that earned the esteem of the authorities. Such respect faded over time as the private sector became more reliant on protectionist measures. Indeed, as Luis Rubio has asserted, "hence, the second- and third-generation *empresarios* were more subordinate to, and dependent on, the government, and more risk-averse."[11]

Just as the draconian Smoot-Hawley Tariff chilled international commerce and alerted U.S. lawmakers to the pitfalls of protectionism in the early 1930s, Mexico's experience with coddling infant industries demonstrated the eventual shortcomings of sustained import substitution in the late 1960s. In many branches of the economy, the market was saturated, and short production runs and other inefficiencies resulted in prices as much as 300 percent above the cost of imports in their countries of origin.[12] Clashes sparked largely by political disputes between the government of President Díaz Ordaz (1964–1970) and segments of the middle class foreshadowed the tensions inherent in the slow-down and then the exhaustion of ISI-inspired growth.

During the protracted economic miracle, Mexico's governing system had furnished abundant opportunities for members of the growing and increasingly heterogeneous middle class to make money. On one hand, these new bourgeois did look askance at the coercion, corruption, and censorship marring a regime that largely excluded them from the ever-more Byzantine political game, denying them structured channels through which to express grievances and influence policy. Nevertheless, the system had generated both employment for themselves and the prospect of upward mobility for their children.

Flagging growth did, however, exacerbate the essentially political tension that burst forth in 1968 as students, doctors, teachers, and other elements of the middle class seeking higher salaries and political liberties encountered first indifference and then repression. As Newell and Rubio have found, "the majority of middle-class members, intellectuals, students, and business people were altogether relegated to a nonparticipant role, one that simply did not fit with either their social or economic status or their aspirations. They shared this relegated status with labor and peasants, who had also lost in the economic arena."[13]

Strains on the Corporatist System

Student dissatisfaction with both political conditions and economic inequality, erupted in the mid-1960s. In early 1966, a student movement at UNAM gave rise to the resignation of its rector. Later in the year, the government dispatched military units to restore order at the University of Morelia—an action repeated the following year at the University of Sonora. The cynical, authoritarian Díaz Ordaz tended to see student activism as part of a plot. Indeed, he often quoted the French novel *Clochemerle* to hammer home his view that violence, however trivial it may appear at the outset, can cascade out of control.[14]

In 1968, the president perceived himself as the target of young, leftist conspirators whose counterparts in France and the United States, respectively, had confronted the regimes of Charles DeGaulle and Lyndon B. Johnson, ultimately driving both haughty statesmen from office. University demonstrations began with a pro-Castro event on July 26—with some forty-seven protests bursting forth during the next two weeks. In mid-August, the student strike committee shifted from a series of sporadic marches to a huge rally that drew 150,000 demonstrators to Mexico City's Zócalo central plaza on August 13. There protesters implicated Díaz Ordaz in police and army violence, waving placards reading: "Criminal," "Hated Beast," and "Assassin." Just as American youths had sought to pressure their government by demonstrating at Chicago's Democratic Party Convention earlier that year, Mexican students knew that the proximity of their action to the start of the Mexico City Olympics in October would add to their protest's potency. In their view, the Mexican government could ill afford any evidence contradicting the image of a developing, innovative, and unified nation used by Díaz Ordaz to attract the games to a Third World country for the first time. Government–student conflict came to a head on October 2, 1968, when army and police units fired on several thousand unarmed students, housewives, and office workers decrying the lack of freedom in their country, killing several hundred protesters and innocent bystanders

Díaz Ordaz portrayed the attack as a reasonable response to the danger posed to national security by the alleged "subversives." After all, the youthful activists announced their intentions to make common cause with peasants, demanded the release from prison of railroad-strike firebrands Campa and Vallejo, and staged their agitation at the same time that teachers, hospital employees, and railroad workers had stridently demanded higher wages and other concessions. Such justifications aside, the president emerged from the Tlatelolco massacre a broken man. He increasingly delegated responsibilities to Luis Echeverría Alvarez, his secretary of government who had supervised the bloodbath.

In retrospect, Tlatelolco represented a watershed in modern Mexican history. The event loomed so large not because Díaz Ordaz had employed violence—though most previous presidents had resorted to force only selectively—but instead because of the massacre's targets. The victims came not from the peasantry, workers, or shantytown dwellers, but from the middle class. Within a few hours, Mexico's image shifted from that of an emerging democracy to a heavy-handed authoritarian regime. As one political insider summarized the situation,

> Díaz Ordaz has endangered the system by being unable to manipulate it in a traditional way—through skill in manoeuvering, guile, blandishments, promises, some concessions and where necessary bribes, with force kept in the background as the ultimate threat to be used, if at all, only with the utmost discretion.[15]

Upon becoming president in late 1970, Echeverría sought to relieve the social tensions that had overwhelmed his predecessors and diminished the party-state's legitimacy. Although continuing ISI despite its obvious limitations, the new chief executive—rebuffed by the business community when he tried to reform the tax system early in his administration—shifted from the "stabilizing" development that characterized the post-World War II boom to "shared" development. The latter strategy combined continued benefits to the private sector with greater outlays for health care, education, nutrition, housing, and social security. Increased government intervention in the economy would prove central to the success of Echeverría's bold approach. New agencies popped up, their expenditures partly offsetting the growing reluctance to invest of long-pampered entrepreneurs, while the self-proclaimed "populist president" made increasingly demagogic appeals to trade unionists, campesinos, and the urban poor.

In the face of anemic domestic savings, Echeverría relied heavily on the printing of pesos at home and borrowing greenbacks from abroad to finance his expenditures on infrastructure and social programs. Government spending, which totaled 13.1 percent of GNP in 1970, more than tripled to 39.6 percent in 1976. Meanwhile, the number of state companies grew tenfold under Echeverría to 845, eventually soaring further to 1,155 in the early 1980s. During this period, the ranks of bureaucrats ballooned from 616,000 (1970) to 3.3 million (1983). When orthodox economists at the Finance Ministry and Central Bank tried to curb what they considered imprudent policies, the president shifted more responsibility to his inner circle. In much the same way that John F. Kennedy circumvented the State Department by investing the design of foreign policy in the National Security Council staff within the White House, Echeverría turned "the presidency into a shadow economic cabinet that persistently and often successfully fought with older institutions."[16]

To jump-start the shared-development initiative, Echeverría recruited younger loyalists, many displaying technical rather than political credentials, posting them to new and expanded federal agencies responsible for planning and implementing social programs. In the process, he bypassed a generation of politicians who had expected rewards for their loyalty to the revolutionary family. For example, future president Carlos Salinas de Gortari and many other U.S.-trained colleagues began their public service at this time. These young technocrats carefully concealed any qualms they might have had about the politically correct statist policies of the 1970s.

In the absence of higher taxes, prices rose steadily during Echeverría's sexennium, even as the business community—which had intensified its political organizing—encountered sagging profits. Their hostility to the president's populism mounted as he began to excoriate "greedy industrialists," "emissaries of the past," and other "bad Mexicans." Echeverría suffered from especially strained relations with the "Monterrey Group" of industrialists in northern Nuevo León state, some of whom descended from Basques, Sephardic Jews, and the poor who settled the barren scrubland a century after the Spanish conquest. Tough, self-reliant, and nationalistic, many of these entrepreneurs enjoy bonds of kinship or business activity to the immensely wealthy Garza Sada clan.

In September 1973, the simmering feud boiled over when guerrillas belonging to the 23rd of September Communist League killed Eugenio Garza Sada, patriarch of the group and father of Monterrey's industrialization, during an abortive kidnapping. Arriving at the airport to pay his respects to the family, Echeverría learned that the victim's widow adamantly refused to receive him. Later, the bishop delivering the funeral mass deliberately talked at great length while the national leader twiddled his thumbs in his limousine outside the cathedral—Mexican presidents do not enter churches. At the gravesite, a spokesman for the local private sector stated bluntly in Echeverría's presence that the government had to bear responsibility for terrorist activities, and that officials had tried "to foment hate and division within social classes." Rarely has a chief executive anywhere faced a more studied public insult. Echeverría's mercurial behavior, erratic pronouncements, and inept handling of economic problems alienated both the right and left: the former because of resentment toward the government's blustering, economic micromanagement, and the chief executive's diatribes against entrepreneurs; the latter because of the disparity between Echeverría's populist image and lower classes' quality of life, even though the 1970-76 *sexenio* was the last in which the minimum wage rose faster than inflation.

To his credit, Echeverría attempted to relax the rigid political controls inherited from Díaz Ordaz in order to broaden access to the political system, especially for individuals and groups outside the PRI who increasingly vented their anger at the sclerotic regime by taking to the streets or to the mountains. His "political opening" included (1) expanding opposition representation in Congress, (2) bestowing amnesty on political prisoners, (3) lowering the voting age to eighteen, (4) reducing the minimum ages for deputies to twenty-one from thirty and for senators to thirty from thirty-five, (5) creating institutions of higher education such as the Metropolitan Autonomous University as alternatives to UNAM, (6) authorizing annual revisions of collective labor contracts, and (7) granting greater press freedom.

Echeverría lost any credibility he had attained as a reformer by orchestrating a 1976 attack on *Excélsior,* a Mexico City daily whose independence had won it a world-wide reputation. In the president's eyes, the newspaper sinned not so much because it criticized official actions. After all, conservative editors had taken his administration to task for "leftist" pursuits—criticism that bolstered the regime's revolutionary image. Rather *Excélsior* had the audacity to castigate the administration's foreign policy, its failure to alleviate poverty, its involvement in corruption, its disdain for political freedom, and its failure to involve workers in economic decision making. Social, political, and economic pressures ousted the paper's editor, Julio Scherer García, and his team, marking the triumph of "gray," the "color of conformity and passivity," according to intellectual Octavio Paz.

In the final analysis, this president subsidized conflicts as opposed to resolving them. To avoid harsh political and economic choices, the government increased spending indiscriminately and profligately, swelling Mexico's foreign debt from $3 billion in 1970 to $19.6 billion in 1976. In an attempt to divert attention from his economic missteps with domestic businessmen, Echeverría clamped more controls on foreign investment. At the same time, he launched various initiatives to diminish the Third World's vulnerability to industrialized countries and Mexico's dependence on the United States. Despite the president's policy objectives, Mexico's reliance increased because of his need to agree to an austerity plan linked to loans from the International Monetary Fund (IMF) intended to stabilize the shaky economy Echeverría bequeathed to his successor.

The Short-Lived Oil Boom

The wrongheadedness of statist economics became patently evident during the administration of Mexico's next president, José López Portillo, who campaigned on the innocuous, mollifying slogan, "We are all the solution." Immediately upon donning the red, white, and green presidential sash, the karate-practicing ex-finance secretary leveraged his country's newly discovered petroleum deposits into economic growth, enhancing Mexico's stature as a leader both in Latin America and throughout the developing world. Expanding exports of "black gold" increased the gross domestic product by approximately 8 percent each year between 1978 and 1982. This windfall generated vast profits for the private sector and helped create 1 million new jobs annually.

Mexico's success became the envy of a world foundering in recession. Such glamour, however, diverted attention from the beginnings of "petrolization," the neologism used to describe the process of an economy's becoming superheated by oil revenues; an overvalued currency; mounting dependence on external credits to import escalating amounts of food, capital, and luxury goods; a moribund agricultural sector; and, above all, outsized budget deficits spawned by prodigious spending in a rapidly expanding bureaucracy. López Portillo insisted that his country was "not so much underdeveloped as underadministered." The shortage of skilled workers amid widespread unemployment—as well as bottlenecks in port services, storage, and transport—only compounded Mexico's problems. The government had built highways with capacity for only one-fifth of actual traffic by the 1980s, while railroads had changed little since the days when Pancho Villa and his roughly hewn troops rode them during the revolution. Rather than raising taxes, Mexican leaders chose to cover budget shortfalls by printing stacks of crisp new peso notes to pay its bills.

Excessive spending drove prices ever higher. The rate of inflation dropped from 20.7 percent in 1977 to 16.2 percent in 1978 only to climb back to 28 percent in 1980. A dearer peso relative to the dollar discouraged tourism, inhibited the export of relatively labor-intensive manufactures, and intensified Mexico's reliance on oil and its derivatives to earn dollars. Petroleum, which accounted for 21.9 percent of the nation's export earnings in 1977, produced three-fourths of these revenues six years later.

Like a heroin addict who sells his blood in the morning to get a "fix" from an eager, well-heeled supplier at night, Mexico reacted to petrolization pressures by exchanging oil for loans. All told, the country's private and public obligations exceeded $100 billion by the early 1980s. In the spring of 1981, however, foreign bankers stopped flooding into Mexico City when an international oil glut appeared, and a buyer's market for oil emerged. Determined not to "rat on OPEC," with which Mexico had coordinated policy, the government adhered to overvalued oil prices—even as clients abandoned Pemex for either random purchases on the "spot market" or from exporters offering discounts.

A series of disquieting changes broke during an eight-week period beginning June 3, 1981. First, Mexico cut its oil prices $4 a barrel. Then Jorge Díaz Serrano—a López Portillo confidant, Pemex's director-general, architect of the sharp price reduction, and aggressive aspirant for the presidency—abruptly resigned under fire. Patrimony Secretary José Andrés Oteyza—an inveterate nationalist and proponent of shared development—assumed control of oil policy. Finally, Pemex provided 109.15 million barrels for the U.S. Strategic Petroleum Reserve. When the smoke cleared, López Portillo faced the reality that Mexico earned just $14.6 billion from oil, gas, and petrochemical sales for the year, barely two-thirds of the amount projected.

Mexico's only hope lay in a $10 billion rescue scheme, fashioned by the Reagan administration in response to a desperate August 1982 appeal to Washington from Finance Secretary Jesús Silva Herzog Flores and Central Bank President Miguel Mancera Aguayo. The plan prevented the country's defaulting on its foreign debt, though López Portillo's acquiescence in an IMF stabilization scheme was crucial to the success of the bailout. López Portillo became increasingly withdrawn, sleeping late, failing to shave, and padding around the presidential mansion during the day in his dressing gown. To those familiar with his condition, he appeared as a "hermit," a man who wished to shield himself from Díaz Serrano's apparent perfidy over oil prices and the abject failure of his presidency. "The President is sounding defensive and apologetic and—that's the worst thing that can happen in Mexico," said a prominent politician, reiterating the preeminence of each Mexican chief executive as a symbol of corporatist power and stability.[17] Wrote one British scholar, "he had neither the intellectual preparation nor the psychological resources to cope with the economic downturn after 1981."[18] As the end of his term approached, López Portillo had all but handed over the reins of economic decision making to Miguel de la Madrid Hurtado, the PRI's presidential candidate in the 1982 election. The outgoing chief executive named close associates of de la Madrid to head the Finance Ministry and Central Bank.

Still, López Portillo would leave one final mark during his presidency. While negotiations with the IMF hung fire, he flaunted his "revolutionary" credentials by expropriating the private banking system—an impromptu act that caught all but the Mexican leader's closest advisers by surprise. Ironically, the man who had once warned his countrymen to end "panic-stricken and frantic activity" justified the September 1, 1982, nationalization on the grounds that bankers had "betrayed" Mexico by facilitating speculation against the peso, which had lost 75 percent of its value during 1982. "I can affirm," he said, "that in recent years a group of Mexicans led, counseled, and supported by private banks, have taken more money out of the country than all the empires that have exploited us since the beginning of our history." In reality gross fiscal mismanagement by the party-state, not a plot by financial gnomes, had sparked the capital flight. Nevertheless, the nationalization inflicted a long-felt trauma on the country's private sector, which had recorded huge profits during the four-year oil boom. After all, the banks controlled scores of major corporations through stock, debt obligations, and board memberships.

This "profoundly revolutionary measure" by an outgoing leader seemed reminiscent of Echeverría's populism. López Portillo had designed the seizure to arrest the collapse of his popularity, identify a scapegoat for his earlier failure to remedy the country's social ills, secure a place for himself alongside Lázaro Cárdenas in the country's pantheon of heroes, and placate the left. At the PRI's behest, some 300,000 workers, peasants, and civil servants flocked to Mexico City's central plaza to praise the intrepid action of "the patriotic president." In the opinion of one analyst, "López Portillo was looking increasingly like a bullfighter awarded both ears and the tail" because of his undaunted move.[19] Demagoguery soared to its zenith when the president began collecting "voluntary" contributions from laborers, campesinos, and government employees to compensate the owners of Mexico's banks—a program in which the military refused to participate.

Conclusion

Corporatism proved crucial to Mexico's stability. The economic modernization launched by Alemán and Ruiz Cortines precipitated a series of violent strikes by fire-breathing union leaders. The regime responded by selecting for the only time in history a labor secretary, López Mateos, to assume the presidency in 1958. The intelligent, energetic, youthful chief executive—later compared to John F. Kennedy—declared himself to be "left within the Constitution." Yet he came down like a ton of bricks on communists and others deemed outside the fundamental law. For example, he removed the communist head of the teachers' union, jailed the secretary-general of the Railroad Workers, and even imprisoned world-renowned muralist David Alfaro Siqueiros for organizing a student uprising in 1960. At the same time, he curried favor with CTM members by initiating profit-sharing; won accolades from the PRI's peasant sector by resuscitating the land-reform program; and appealed to nationalists by purchasing a foreign electric company—action heralded on mammoth electric signs that proclaimed: *"La electricidad es nuestra"* ("The electricity is ours"). Young people also resonated to his buying the motion-picture industry from its U. S. owners and keeping ticket prices so low that the masses could enjoy films. A skilled, attractive administrator could energize the corporatist machine and use it to suppress dissidents.

Historians will identify López Mateo's personal choice, Díaz Ordaz, as the last "revolutionary" president who could act with impunity. The exhaustion of ISI, followed by the failure of shared development, and the collapse of the oil boom exacted a heavy toll on Mexico's corporatist regime. Resources that once fortified a smooth-running system of patronage, official funding, and economic expansion had dried-up, depriving the party-state of its lubrication. Stagnation amid rising prices undermined the legitimacy of the "revolutionary leader's" economic stewardship in the eyes of a burgeoning, ever-more assertive middle class. Regrettably for Díaz Ordaz's successors, the students, professionals, and housewives who clamored in the streets, wrote scathing editorials, and organized clandestine groups wanted more than the material rewards that lay at the heart of pre-1968 demands on the government. They also sought fundamental political reforms, the achievement of which would shatter the foundations of a corporatist regime contrived to adjust and balance the economic interests of a limited number of stakeholders in the system. Meanwhile, Díaz Ordaz, Echeverría, and López Portillo broke several key rules of the corporatist game. Díaz Ordaz, for example, employed violence against the middle class, previously the target of cooptation. Echeverría failed to reward party stalwarts who paid their dues to the revolutionary system, but found themselves passed over for posts to which they believed themselves entitled. And Echeverría's populism and López Portillo's bank nationalization alienated the business community, which—although not a formal sector of the PRI—had long since made a profitable peace with the corporatist regime: The *hombres de negocios* invested heavily in the economy in exchange for preferred treatment by the party-government system. The high-handedness of Echeverría and López

Portillo—most notably the latter's takeover of the banks—convinced important business leaders of the imperative of democracy to obviate future acts of individual caprice. Manuel J. Clouthier, president of the powerful Business Coordinating Council (CCE) at the time of the nationalization, took the lead as the 1988 presidential candidate of the National Action Party (PAN). Other hard-charging entrepreneurs—self-described "Northern barbarians"—followed "Maquío" Clouthier into *panista* politics. With their coffers nearly empty, PRI politicians—particularly those from the labor and peasant sectors—had to move from corporatist accommodation to repression and authoritarianism, relying increasingly on intimidating their members and capturing elections through fraud. As each sector's leaders lost their legitimacy among rank-and-file workers, they became even more beholden to a government that could now dole out resources only selectively. Even though he had flirted with Don Fidel's foes, President Echeverría rewarded the geriatric union chief for his loyalty by creating out of fiscal thin air both the Banco Obrero and the INFONAVIT housing agency. At the same time, he required white-collar Pemex employees to join La Quina's STPRM.

Such rewards from the country's political Mount Olympus epitomized the practice of modern Mexican corporatism: Important members of the executive branch at Los Pinos enhanced their stature among the chiefs of trade unions, peasant organizations, and the bureaucracy; and each sectoral elite did the same within his own constituency with no oversight from or accountability to other power centers, much less the increasing number of Mexicans excluded from the corporatist system. Moreover, through an overextended fiscal policy, Echeverría disrupted the key organizational structure of traditional corporatism, undermined the bureaucracy's institutional autonomy, and arrogated near-exclusive power to an already dominant presidency. Miguel Angel Centeno has contended that apocalyptic warnings about the future awaiting a top-heavy Mexico emblazoned the covers of studies published in the 1980s: *Mexico in Crisis*,[20] *Mexico: Chaos on Our Doorstep*,[21] and *Despues del milagro*:[22] If in the past the president was first among equals in the "Revolutionary Family," after Echeverría *señor presidente* strove to become the only one who mattered.[23]

Notes

1. Thomas E. Skidmore and Peter H. Smith, *Modern Latin America* (3rd ed.; New York: Oxford University Press, 1992), p. 53.
2. Raymond Vernon, *The Dilemma of Mexico's Development: the Roles of the Private and Public Sectors* (Cambridge: Harvard University Press, 1963), p. 96.

3. Meyer and Sherman, *The Course of Mexican History*, p. 646.

4. Dale Story, *The Mexican Ruling Party: Stability and Authority* (New York: Praeger, 1986), p. 96.

5. Daniel Levy and Gabriel Székely, *Mexico: Paradoxes of Stability and Change* (Boulder, CO: Westview, 1983), p. 109.

6. Kevin J. Middlebrook, *The Paradox of Revolution: Labor, the State, and Authoritarianism in Mexico* (Baltimore: Johns Hopkins, 1995), p. 213.

7. Middlebrook, *The Paradox of Revolution*, p. 149.

8. Interview with Hebraicaz Vázquez Gutiérrez, President, the National Petroleum Movement, Mexico City, May 31, 1978.

9. This section draws on George W. Grayson, *The Politics of Mexican Oil* (Pittsburgh: University of Pittsburgh Press, 1980), pp. 88–102.

10. Meyer and Sherman, *The Course of Mexican History*, p. 644.

11. Luis Rubio F., "The Changing Role of the Private Sector," in Susan Kaufman Purcell (ed.), *Mexico in Transition: Implications for U.S. Policy* (New York: Council on Foreign Relations, 1988), p. 33.

12. Douglas K. Ballentine, "Mexico: The Door Opens Wider," *International Commerce*, June 6, 1996, p. 15

13. Roberto G. Newell and Luis Rubio F., *Mexico's Dilemma: The Political Origins of Economic Crisis* (Boulder, CO: Westview Press, 1984), p. 110.

14. Philip, *The Presidency in Mexican Politics*, p. 25.

15. *Latin America*, September 11, 1970.

16. Miguel Angel Centeno, *Democracy within Reason*, p. 83.

17. *New York Times*, May 22, 1982, p. 2.

18. Philip, *The Presidency in Mexican Politics*, p. 132.

19. *Latin America Weekly Report*, November 19, 1982, p. A-20.

20. Judith A. Heller (2nd. ed.; New York: Holmes & Meier, 1983).

21. Sol Sanders (Lanham, Md.: Madison Books, 1986).

22. Héctor Camín Aguilar (Mexico City: Cal y Arena, 1988).

23. Centeno, *Democracy within Reason*, p. 81.

3

The Presidency and Corporatism

Introduction

Considering the top-down exercise of power in a corporatist system, emphasizing limited pluralism and elite initiative over democratic and inclusive consultation, any study of Mexican politics must focus on the biggest corporatist chief, Mexico's president. The creation of a dominant party with functional sectors helped Mexicans drive their military to the wings of the political stage, thereby ensuring civilian primacy. After 1940, Mexico's *jefe* no longer had to keep one eye on the barracks while he attempted to govern. In addition, import substitution industrialization expanded the ranks and resources of the bureaucracy, which inexorably eclipsed the PRI itself in importance. Within the public administration, however, the budgeting, planning, and finance sectors magnified their influence, thanks to the emergence of Mexican presidents for whom economic issues held as much salience, if not more so, than political matters. Though occupying a position long at the apex of a corporatist regime, the failure of successive leaders to adapt Mexico's polity to changes at home and abroad ultimately sapped their own power and that of the PRI.

Legacy of Presidential Power

Observers have characterized Mexico's chief executive as a "combination of U.S. president, British prime minister, and pope" or even, according to Tannenbaum, an extension of the Aztec emperor. In the words of journalist Alan Riding:

> Like the Divine Right of Kings and the infallibility of the Pope, [the myth of presidential omnipotence in Mexico] maintains the mystery of the office. The President is, after all, the heir to a pre-Hispanic tradition of theocratic authoritarianism that was enormously reinforced by the political centralism and religious dogmatism of the Spanish Colony.[1]

Riding could have included several other factors that nourished the custom of strong executive leadership in Mexico. Centralized authority characterized Iberia's rulers for 2,000 years: In 31 A.D., after Augustus routed Mark Antony at the Battle of Actium, the Romans completed their conquest of the Peninsula. They suffered defeat at the hands of the Visigoths and other Germanic tribes during the fifth century and the Muslims occupied at least part of Spain for 700 years, until driven from Granada by warriors loyal to Ferdinand and Isabella in 1492. For their role in the Reconquest, many of the conquistadors received land grants in New Spain, where they encountered—and subdued—the Aztec and other Indian cultures that practiced authoritarian, hierarchical rule long before Cortés arrived in Veracruz in 1519 to take power in Charles I's name. As discussed in Chapter 1, a series of viceroys governed in the name of the crown until Fathers Hidalgo and Morelos spearheaded the movement that culminated in independence in 1821. Even though his intransigence precipitated the bloody 1910 revolution, Porfirio Díaz understood his nation's craving for order, and laid the groundwork for the strong presidents who succeeded him in the twentieth century. A onetime general officer himself, Díaz knew the importance of eliminating the anarchy and chaos that had afflicted his countrymen during most of the early post-independence period. He combined the artifice and cunning of Santa Anna with the competence and acumen befitting a chief executive.[2] An eminent historian explains his approach to governing Mexico as one "replacing instability and disorganized violence with tyranny and organized violence."[3]

Díaz—one of Santa Anna's most important successors—concentrated on taming the rambunctious, rebellion-prone, and unreliable officer corps. He cashiered one-quarter of the army's 100 generals and ousted some 400 lower-ranking officers. He provided rivals deemed too dangerous to confront with boundless access to graft and plunder, assuming that "a dog with a bone in its mouth cannot bite." He propitiated the rest with attractive salaries, generous expense accounts, and opportunities for self-enrichment. In addition, the Machiavellian leader began rotating commands in the nation's newly created eleven military regions. Not only did he periodically reassign generals from one zone to another, but he also rotated staff officers, lest they cultivate a strong base among enlisted personnel and the local population.

Ultimately, Díaz felt confident enough to retire rivals or elevate them to governorships. In the words of Lieuwen, "[b]y 1892, after a dozen years of effort, the army was finally under Díaz's firm control."[4] To combat bandits and brigands, the wily president created the *Rurales*, an elite force like the Texas Rangers or the Royal Canadian Mounted Police, except that Díaz's constabulary ruthlessly eliminated opponents to the despotic system. Amid this enforced tranquility, Díaz acted as national patron, dispensing favors to loyalists and repressing those who dared question his rule. In addition, his *científico* advisers had attracted foreign investment and loans, spurring unprecedented economic growth, including 15,000 miles of new railroad, urban electrification, construction of factory complexes and ports, and the commercial development of resources in industrial metals and petroleum. Even though he had Mixtec blood and hailed from the impoverished southern state of Oaxaca, Díaz channeled the benefits of his rule to an affluent elite, while the masses continued to scratch out a living in abject poverty.

Enhancing his power, in what observers called a "monarchical" presidency, Díaz maintained a politically supine judiciary and a suborned Congress, existing only to rubber-stamp executive initiatives.

His trappings of power and fawning advisors blinded Díaz to the rise of forces virulently hostile to his regime. As discussed in Chapter 1, sharing only the common denominator of loathing Díaz, liberal intellectuals like Madero, agrarian reformers like Zapata and Villa, and northern Jacobins like Carranza and Obregón committed themselves to expelling the dictator and creating a new political order.

The revolution gave rise to hundreds of generals, many self-appointed, as well as other freewheeling "officers" who commanded portions of the 80,000 men who took up arms between 1910 and 1920. A potpourri of ruffians, desperados, stragglers, and opportunists constituted the rank-and-file of the notably overstaffed, poorly disciplined army. "It lacked regulation uniforms, arms, training, and tactics. Its numbers rose and fell with fluctuations in the ambitions and power of its leaders."[5] Three generals-turned-president—Obregón, Calles, and Cárdenas—acted decisively to return the military genie released during the revolution to the bottle in which Díaz had first encased him. They boldly added the revolutionary generals to the federal payroll; purged disloyal officers, replacing them with well-prepared professionals; sent promising young men abroad to learn modern war fighting; engaged the army in road building, dam construction and other public works; decreed rigorous promotion standards unattainable for most revolutionary *militares*; shifted commands; and—through the official party—forged a civilian counterforce to an ever smaller and better trained armed force.

The decline of rebellious officers reflected the success of these reforms. In 1923, approximately half the officer corps cast their lot with insurgents against Obregón; in 1927 less than a quarter participated in the abortive coup against Calles; and in 1940, few—if any—regular army officers joined General Juan Andreu Almazán in taking up arms against Cárdenas after Almazán—the most senior general and a prosperous landowner—lost the 1940 presidential election to Avila Camacho by a margin of 17 to 1. Shortly thereafter the revolutionary party eliminated its military sector, and no officer has held a high party post since the mid-1960s.

Executive power expanded as that of the military waned. Indeed, the president's roles included chief of state, head of government, commander-in-chief of the armed forces, de facto boss of the revolutionary party, number-one patron, chief diplomat, and—with the advent of Echeverría—manager of the economy. In the words of a careful student of the executive, the "Mexican system is a set of arrangements consistently being redefined . . . around its only fixed element . . . which is the presidency."[6]

The official party functions mainly as an electoral machine at the beck and call of the revolutionary party candidate for president even before he wins election. Once identified, the heir-apparent, or *destapado* (unveiled one), places his loyalists in strategic party posts so they can run the campaign in accord with his wishes. The outgoing chief executive, however, keeps a trusted member of his team at the party's helm to monitor and supervise the conduct of the campaign. Once in office, the new *número uno* shifts his confidants from the party to key slots in his administration, while replacing his predecessor's choice for party leader with one of his own. As party head, Mexico's president has customarily appointed and dismissed party officials, laid down the party's official line, and dispensed boodle. In addition, he has given governors, legislators, and judges their marching orders; forged—or shattered—alliances with other political forces; and hand-picked official party candidates for every post from city councilman to president. While alien to a Jeffersonian democracy, the incumbent's selecting his political heir through the *dedazo* preserved discipline in the sometimes fractious ruling party during most of his six-year presidential term. Yet, the "no-reelection" provision in 1917's fundamental law limited the president's hegemony to a fixed term, after which he had to rely on a successor to continue any programs that he had initiated. This reform ultimately separated the individual from the office.

In managing political affairs, the president's right-hand man within the cabinet is the secretary of government (*Gobernación*). In contrast to the chief executive, whose presidential campaign constituted his first foray into elective politics since 1970, typically the government secretary exhibits the shrewdness and *olfato político* (political sensitivity) of a veteran politician, who knows the state and local power brokers from the Rio Grande to the Guatemalan border. While post-revolutionary presidents often served their predecessors as defense secretary, between 1940 and 1970—a period of recurring domestic political consolidation—government secretaries Alemán, Ruiz Cortines, Díaz Ordaz, and Echeverría ascended to Los Pinos. The government secretary has often served as the link between the administration and the official party, the president of which was usually another cunning political animal.

Formal and Informal Presidential Powers[7]

Traditionally, presidents satisfied several formal and informal qualifications. The formal qualifications for the presidency included:

- possessing native Mexican citizenship;
- attaining the age of 35 by the time of election;
- having both parents born in Mexico (no longer required after 1999);
- residing in Mexico for the year preceding election;
- registering no affiliation with an ecclesiastical order or any religious vocation;
- if a member of the armed forces, leaving active duty six months before election;
- during six months before election, not serving as a cabinet secretary, undersecretary, or secretary general of an executive department; attorney general; governor; or mayor of Mexico City;
- evincing ten years of party membership, held a party office, and elected to office (beginning in 2000); and
- never before occupying the presidency, whether in an elected, interim, or provisional basis.

Informal qualifications, which also loomed large, embraced:

- being male;
- boasting PRI membership;
- belonging to an important political team or *"camarilla"*;
- enjoying the confidence of the incumbent, who plays a major role in selecting the PRI nominee;
- coming from the Federal District or a large, prosperous state;
- pursuing a career in the capital to make the contacts crucial for attaining the nation's highest office;
- participating actively in the outgoing chief executive's own campaign, often as campaign manager;

- holding a cabinet post before election;
- presenting the image of a good family man;
- enjoying a reputation as being *muy hombre* (a he-man)—but not a philanderer;
- exhibiting reasonably good health and energy;
- being neither a Protestant nor a militant atheist—he can be a practicing Roman Catholic, but not a *fanático*;
- evincing a middle-class background;
- since 1946, having no active connection to the armed forces; and
- upon completing his term, refraining from commenting publicly on his successor's policies in return for the incumbent's turning a blind eye to his, his family's, and his entourage's enrichment in or out of office.

Observers used to trumpet the "pendulum theory": The PRI—for the sake of political balance and cohesion—would alternate its nominees among different tendencies within the party, with participation in the 1910–1917 revolution serving as a unifying factor. As a result, Cárdenas, a leftist, preceded a centrist, Avila Camacho, who in turn bestowed the presidential sash on a conservative, Alemán. During subsequent *sexenios*, the pendulum would shift back to the center with Ruiz Cortines before returning to the left with López Mateos. He, in turn, selected the rightist Díaz Ordaz, who gave way to the leftist-populist Echeverría.[8]

The overwhelming importance of economic issues and the escalating impact of global affairs on Mexico's policy agenda has obviated any such process, if indeed it ever existed. For the last generation, the PRI has emphasized youth, a university background, graduate study abroad, fluency in English, a good media presence, proficiency in economics, and rapport with the financial and banking communities in North America, Europe, and Asia.

The traits possessed by presidential candidates of the center-right, pro-business, National Action Party (PAN) have also evolved. Until recently, one could count on the *panista* standard-bearer to be a longtime party activist respected by his peers, but given no chance of victory. His candidacy strove to (1) legitimate the party's claim to national status, (2) assist PAN nominees for the Chamber of Deputies, (3) enable the party to disseminate its message more widely, (4) recruit more followers, and (5) discourage personalism inasmuch as the PAN organization urged the faithful to cast ballots for the party, not the candidate heading the ticket.[9] Now that their party enjoys national stature and a large following, prospective nominees may turn out to be relative newcomers to the PAN rather than men and women with many years of activism in the party's ranks. The newest current arose in the northern business community, attracted to elective politics in reaction to Echeverría's land expropriations in Sonora in 1976 and López Portillo's bank nationalization six years later. As noted in Chapter 2, many of these "Northern barbarians" drew inspiration from the late Manuel Clouthier, the burly, outspoken businessman from Nuevo León who captured 3.3 million votes as the PAN's aspirant in the 1988 presidential campaign. Future PAN nominees will be serious contenders for the presidency, all the more so since they will probably have garnered experience and name recognition as a mayor of a major city or as a governor. In mid-1997, PAN leaders headed states, cities, and towns whose collective population exceeded one-third of the country's 95 million inhabitants. Although the dispute over personalism rages, ambitious *panistas* no longer cloak their ideas and personas under the party's blue-and-white banner. Briefly stated, they have become genuine competitors rather than propagandists with coattails for those lower on the party's ticket. The use of democratic local assemblies to select some 1,126 delegates to a national nominating convention in 1994 enhanced the transparency of the PAN's selection process and the legitimacy of its candidate.

The Democratic Revolutionary Party (PRD) has had only one presidential nominee—Cuauhtémoc Cárdenas in 1994—making it impossible to generalize about characteristics sought by the party's leadership. Having served as a governor, senator, and cabinet undersecretary, Cárdenas was a consummate PRI insider until age 53. In 1994, he won the PRD's nomination through an orchestrated *dedazo*, reflective of the party's fondness for authoritarian, manipulative practices which many of their movers and shakers learned while part of the revolutionary family. In early 1993, several hundred people "acting as individuals" met in a Mexico City restaurant to draft Cárdenas as their nominee. He agreed to run because he perceived "a strong current within the democratic movement of our country that expresses its confidence in me." He also emphasized that his was not a "personalistic candidacy" and that he would step aside if a more appropriate competitor were found.

Crisis of Legitimacy

The Tlatelolco massacre, presaging the exhaustion of ISI, struck a resounding blow to the legitimacy of both the presidency and the corporatist regime over which he presided. By the early 1970s, Echeverría administered another setback to the government-PRI system when his populist, shared development policies alienated the domestic business community, contributed to a gaping trade deficit, and ultimately led to the devaluation of the peso and an IMF-imposed stabilization plan.

Echeverría's successor, López Portillo, sought to revive public support for the country's widely discredited regime. To mend fences with the private sector, he muted the government's leftist rhetoric, made clear his disdain for his predecessor's eleventh-hour land expropriations, consulted entrepreneurs on policy matters, faithfully attended their social events, and invited business leaders to take part in his administration, most notably appointing Santiago Roel García of Monterrey to become head of the Foreign Relations Ministry (SRE), long a bastion of anti-U.S., anti-business, and pro-Third World positions. "In comparison with the last president, we feel like we're in heaven. His ministers not only listen to us . . . they pay attention," beamed Alberto Santos, president of Monterrey's major industrial organization.

Captains of industry also rejoiced in the appointment of Díaz Ordaz as ambassador to Spain where he boasted excellent contacts with the private sector. Mexican entrepreneurs hoped that the hard-line ex-president could coax up to a billion dollars of Iberian investment into their country, attract an influx of free-spending Spanish tourists, and facilitate Madrid's using Mexico as a launching pad for its economic initiatives in Latin America. Much to the dismay of business communities in both nations, Díaz Ordaz resigned twelve days after reaching Iberia. He attributed his abrupt departure to worsening eye problems. The more plausible explanation lay with his comments to reporters about Echeverría's attacks on the Franco regime after it executed five Basque revolutionaries. "You musn't judge Mexicans by what Echeverría did," averred the erstwhile chief executive. Such a pronouncement—no matter how true—violated the system's unwritten rules about the behavior of former presidents, and abbreviated Díaz Ordaz's diplomatic career.

Even while striving to mend fences with business, López Portillo strove to demonstrate his sympathy for the corporatist labor sector, and backed efforts to define the PRI as a "workers' party"—a symbolic gesture in view of labor's shrinking slice of the economic pie. In a more substantive act, the president virtually handed over the housing agency INFONAVIT to the CTM, which promptly changed the agency's policy by according preference to unionized over nonunionized workers in the allocation of low cost housing. This move conferred on CTM leader Don Fidel and his lieutenants powerful tools with which to reward friends and punish enemies—construction contracts and keys to new living units. Meanwhile, the Labor Ministry stood by as the Confederation took over representation of INFONAVIT employees. "Moreover, individual CTM leaders derived multiple benefits from the [worker housing] program: They purchased land and sold it to INFONAVIT at inflated prices; they often owned or received kickbacks from the construction companies responsible for building housing; and they selectively distributed completed housing units to loyal supporters in order to strengthen their political position."[10]

In an initiative that not even the populist Echeverría would take, López Portillo satisfied a long-standing demand by Velázquez by creating the Banco Obrero, dominated by young technocrats acceptable to the CTM hierarchy. In addition, the president backed the unification of all electricity workers, thus uniting one of the nation's only independent unions (SUTERM) with the CTM. He also agreed to allow Joaquín Gamboa Pascoe, Don Fidel's immensely wealthy son-in-law and head of CTM workers in the Federal District, to chair the Permanent Commission, which supervises legislative matters during the eight months when Congress stands in recess. Similarly, López Portillo gave short shrift to the independent unions that Echeverría had encouraged early in his administration. For his part, the CTM's Velázquez continued to perform as the system's number-one corporatist, limiting the labor movement's salary demands, discouraging strikes, and toeing the PRI party line.

In October 1977, López Portillo attempted to play the role of reformer by introducing the Federal Law of Political Organizations and Political Processes (LOPPE). This initiative: (1) lowered the registration requirements for minor political parties to either winning 1.5 percent of the votes cast in the last election or signing up a minimum number of members in electoral districts and states where they sought to present candidates; (2) allocated one-quarter of the 400 seats in the Chamber of Deputies to proportional representation from at-large contests; and (3) provided access to media, mailing privileges, and subsidies to opposition parties. The president also backed amnesty for those held or sentenced for "sedition, incitement to rebellion or conspiracy." As he stated in his 1978 State of the Nation address, "dissidence is not synonymous with violence, and opposition should not be associated with crime."

Although López Portillo hailed the LOPPE as a "giant step toward democratization," he and his brilliant government secretary, Jesús Reyes Heroles, actually sought to give critics of the PRI-government alliance more forums, opportunities, and information so that they could become effective watchdogs of a regime whose leaders adroitly used *sub rosa* decision making for self-advancement, intrigue, and enrichment. The single-party formula that had served pre-industrial Mexico so well had become insensitive to the needs and aspirations of the masses. The system increasingly appeared "totally outdated, and incapable of reforming itself from within."[11]

Secondarily, Reyes Heroles sought to open the door for the registration of left-wing parties to offset the growth of the Mexican right. Conservative insurgency had emerged particularly in the north, where an increasing number of businessmen disenchanted with the PRI resonated to National Action, although growing tensions between the brash northerners and traditional conservatives attenuated the PAN's cohesion. In addition to dividing the opposition, López Portillo wanted to make it easier for radicals inclined toward guerrilla activities to enter the political system. After all, authorities believed that the 23rd of September Communist League bore responsibility for the murder of Hugo Margaín Charles, the son of Mexico's ambassador to Washington. This strategy bore fruit in the 1979 congressional elections in which seven parties debuted, six of which vied for votes along the fragmented left of the political spectrum. One of these, the Communists, had not been allowed to present candidates for forty years. The PAN, Communists, and Mexican Workers' Party lambasted LOPPE as "antidemocratic and totalitarian." Yet its passage enhanced participation in the political process, and "legitimacy levels climbed."[12]

To improve further the government's reputation, López Portillo pledged to wage a no-holds-barred war against corruption. His administration first targeted the Finance Ministry, accusing twenty-five auditors and inspectors of corruption. Authorities charged with wrongdoing Echeverría's communications secretary, Eugenio Méndez Docurro, and director of the Mexican Coffee Institute, Fausto Cantú Peña. The former president's agrarian-reform secretary, Félix Barra García, enjoyed the distinction of becoming the first ex-cabinet member arrested for corruption. After five days of intensive questioning, Barra—a former CNC head and rumored presidential aspirant—confessed to extorting $450,000 from a "small" landowner in northern Coahuila state. While hardly a paragon of virtue, Barra appeared as the sacrificial lamb slaughtered to appease mighty landowners and their private sector friends, who still smarted from Echeverría's frenetic seizure of efficient and productive holdings in Sonora and Sinaloa, states contiguous to Coahuila. A month before Barra's incarceration, the central figure in this expropriation, the wily Augusto Gómez Villanueva, suddenly resigned the presidency of the Chamber of Deputies to become ambassador to Rome. *Proceso* magazine suggested that López Portillo jailed Barra to reassure owners of well-run productive estates, even if larger than the law permitted, that the "Constitution protects . . . [well-to-do ranchers] wearing collars and ties but not those [dirt-poor peasants] wearing rope sandals."[13]

López Portillo also occupied Los Pinos at a time when Pemex sharply increased output from recently discovered hydrocarbon reservoirs on the Isthmus of Tehuantepec and in Campeche Sound. Within a month of taking office, the president announced that Pemex's proven reserves had doubled to 11.1 billion barrels and would impel the nation's development. Mexico City's cartoonists found in such predictions an irresistible theme for their work. Some depicted *el petróleo* as a guardian angel, fluttering down to save the nation; others showed it as a latter-day Virgin of Guadalupe, also playing a redemptive role; finally, it was sketched as black gold, flowing profusely from a cornucopia-shaped vessel resembling Mexico itself.

These artists captured the hopes and ambitions of politicians, who saw in petroleum the answer to their country's pressing economic and social problems. On the eve of President Jimmy Carter's visit to Mexico City in February 1979, López Portillo proclaimed that Mexicans "are bent on solving our own problems with our own resources based on our unity and always seeking political and economic independence." Even more effusive was Pemex director-general Jorge Díaz Serrano, who told the Chamber of Deputies: "For the first time in its history, Mexico enjoys sufficient wealth to make possible not only the resolution of economic problems facing the country, but also the creation of a new permanently prosperous country, a rich country where the right to work will be a reality."

During the short-lived boom, growth averaged 8.4 percent annually, jobs multiplied, salaries increased, and opportunities for the private sector mushroomed even as public expenditures swelled from 34 percent of GDP in 1979 to nearly 42 percent in 1981. As indicated in Chapter 2, the hydrocarbon-filled economic balloon burst even more quickly than it had inflated. The petroleum glut that appeared in the spring of 1981 left bridges half-erected, roads only partially constructed, and the Panglossian dreams of López Portillo and Díaz Serrano shattered. The average Mexican, however, noticed not just the incomplete, extremely expensive infrastructure and the plethora of unfulfilled promises, but evidence of the most egregious venality ever witnessed in a country infamous for ill-begotten gains.

There is a popular saying in Mexico that "oil, a gift of the gods, is the temptation of the devil." The freewheeling atmosphere of the late 1970s and early 1980s metastasized the corruption that had long infected the petroleum industry, but was exacerbated by the enormous projects and huge earnings arising from the surge in production. The wrongdoing occurred principally in the Oil Workers' Union (STPRM) to which Pemex Director-General Díaz Serrano granted the right to undertake 50 percent of the monopoly's construction projects without bidding. Furthermore, the union involved itself in job-selling, property theft, collecting the salaries of nonexistent employees, coercive thuggery against dissident members, and exaction of large commissions from Pemex for work never accomplished, poorly done, or subcontracted to third parties. This peculation reached into Pemex's highest echelons, perhaps into the presidential palace itself. Popular outrage focused on ex-president López Portillo's moving into a posh, five-home compound on 7.5-acre "Dog Hill" outside the capital. The name of the venue prompted upper-middle-class patrons of restaurants frequented by López Portillo and his entourage to make barking sounds to express their dismay when the erstwhile chief executive entered. "It doesn't matter if they steal a bit," a taxi driver used to forking over *mordidas* to police for real or trumped-up traffic infractions told a *New York Times* reporter, "but they shouldn't steal so much."

Stealing "so much" exactly summarized the accusation leveled against former Mexico City police chief Arturo Durazo Moreno. On January 20, 1984, authorities ordered the arrest of the sunglasses-wearing, portly ex-cop, widely known as "El Negro" or "The Black One." Authorities charged Durazo—to whom López Portillo had awarded the rank of three-star general to irritate the army's brass—with smuggling, stockpiling outlawed weapons, and tax fraud. These charges followed a police raid on two palatial houses that he had built: One near the capital—reportedly worth $2.5 million—contained large quantities of firearms and other illegal goods, as well as a discotheque, casino, heliport, and gymnasium. The other, allegedly constructed on land granted by the government to peasants in Zihuatanejo on the Pacific coast, held marble and gold bathrooms, fountains, statues, and enormous guest rooms in which beds had baroque rose-colored velvet and gold-leaf head-boards, in an architectural style crudely blending Greek revival with California ranch-house modern. Mexicans joked that the Greek Minister of Culture, actress Melina Mercouri, would on her next visit to Mexico seek the return to Athens of the "pantheon," as journalists derided Durazo's pseudo-Greek mansion. The public's seething anger at these publicized abuses helped persuade López Portillo to spend the early part of his successor's *sexenio* in Europe.

Like López Portillo before him, President Miguel de la Madrid Hurtado sought to burnish the badly tarnished image of the chief executive and the regime he headed. In his campaign for the presidency in 1982, the Harvard-educated technocrat promised to cleanse official wrongdoing through a pro-gram of "moral renovation," beginning with the state oil monopoly. In mid-1983, his attorney general charged then-senator Díaz Serrano—former Pemex director-general, impresario of Mexico's short-lived oil boom, and a would-be presidential candidate—of participating in a $34 million fraud in-volving the purchase of two seagoing vessels. According to authorities, in April 1980 Pemex entered into a contract with the Liberian firm, Navigas International, to buy two natural gas tankers built by a Belgian shipyard. As an intermediary in the transaction, Navigas received $158 million from Pemex, but paid the Belgian company only $124 million, giving rise to $34 million in "undue profit."

Besides his intimate involvement in the deal, Díaz Serrano reportedly lied to the government agency responsible for approving the acquisition, falsely claiming that the ships met the monopoly's specifications. Congress stripped the senator of his legislative immunity, the court sentenced him to ten years in prison for fraud, and ordered him to pay $54 million in damages. De la Madrid threw the book at Díaz Serrano to symbolize his commitment to moral renovation, not to excise the cancer of corruption that lay at the heart of the corporatist system. After all, the ex-Pemex chief was a businessman-turned-politician and only a nominal *priísta* or PRI member, whose power scarcely went beyond that of his personal relationship with the now discred-ited López Portillo.

In contrast, Secretary of Planning and Budget Carlos Salinas joined with Mario Ramón Beteta—a former finance secretary and the incorruptible new head of Pemex—to attack a pillar of the corporatist party, La Quina. For ex-ample, they deprived the Oil Workers' Union of their right to drill 40 per-cent of all onshore wells. Henceforth, a system of sealed bids would determine the award of contracts for the well-drilling and maintenance functions that the union had previously performed as a matter of right. These innovations earned for Salinas and Beteta the unremitting hatred of the STPRM's Hernández Galicia.

Hernández Galicia did nothing to disguise his contempt for the courtly Beteta, whom he dismissed as a "banker who didn't know beans about oil." In hopes of finding common ground, Beteta invited La Quina to breakfast several times at his home. Sometimes Hernández Galicia showed up with a toady, Salvador "Chava" Barragán, the STPRM's crass, loutish secretary-general. On other occasions, La Quina brought along not his wife, Doña Carmelita, but his mistress Elena Ríos, a.k.a. "La Estrellita," and throughout the meal the foul-mouthed La Quina cooed and flirted with the former cabaret singer.

Clearly, the labor chief, who reminded one guest of a "love-crazed teen-ager," wanted to impress his inamorata with his importance. No fool, La Quina also realized that Ríos's presence would offend the Betetas and their guests. Still the gesture allowed the street-smart boss to indirectly, but unmistakably, thumb his nose in the face of the aristocratic Beteta, his equally refined wife, and other agents of the system who might dare challenge his STPRM fiefdom. Even though some members of the cabinet voiced support for the strike against Hernández Galicia, others demurred, believing that La Quina would have no compunctions about sparking work stoppages, sabotage, and other acts harmful to the distressed energy sector in retribution. Indeed, Pemex executives believed the union responsible for the numerous death threats directed at Beteta, who several times found eavesdropping devices hidden in his office. Jesús Silva Herzog remembers that de la Madrid took no action after the Finance Ministry, at the request of Los Pinos, supplied a thick file on tax evasion committed by the Oil Workers' Union and its leaders.[14]

Although the bidding requirements remained in effect, de la Madrid's administration failed to purge Pemex of its most venal elements. On the contrary, it extended the olive branch to STPRM leaders, recalling the pivotal role of striking Iranian oil workers in toppling the Shah from his Peacock Throne in Iran.

"The only way to cow the union is to have a coup d'état. You actually have to use the army or don't try at all," said Rogelio Ramírez de la O, director-general of business consultants Ecanal. "Maintaining social peace is a creed in Pemex," according to José Luis García-Luna Hernández, director of the Mexican Petroleum Institute, adding that "[y]ou can't push the union to the point of having an explosion." Such a catastrophe seemed possible because, in the view of union dissidents, La Quina's forces had trained teams of saboteurs already in place at key facilities.[15] Indeed, many Pemex insiders attributed the November 19, 1984, explosion of a gas bottling plant, LPG storage facility, and gas pipeline to union skulduggery. More than 452 people died in the San Juanico disaster in Mexico state.

In lieu of scouring the union's Augean stable, Beteta initiated a rapprochement with La Quina in May 1984. The director-general, whom the STPRM chieftains treated with crude disdain, praised the "pristine patriotism" demonstrated by union leaders who "understood the necessity to support without reservation . . . the policy of Miguel de la Madrid." After a Munich-like appeasement statement by the chief executive himself, Hernández Galicia and his comrades lauded "[their] good friend" even as they escalated their verbal assaults on Beteta, fearful that the honest, renowned economist, and the president's confidant might become the nation's next chief executive. Ultimately, La Quina and his allies succeeded as Beteta, passed over for the post of energy secretary, left Pemex to become governor of Mexico state. The governorship of the nation's most important state constituted a wondrous consolation prize, but it obviated a seat in the cabinet, from which came future presidents.

De la Madrid also reneged on promises to ensure honest elections and to open up the PRI at the grass-roots level. On December 5, 1982, four days after the presidential inauguration, Dr. Salvador Nava, a staunch critic of PRI *caciques*, or bosses, in the state, captured the mayorship of San Luis Potosí. Eight months later, the PAN scored landslides in municipal elections in its northern strongholds. Mayoral posts fell like tenpins as the *panistas* rolled to victory in the state capitals of Chihuahua, Durango, Sonora, and San Luis Potosí, raising to seven the number of PAN mayors in capitals of the 31 states. In Chihuahua alone, PAN candidates emerged on top in towns embracing three-fourths of the state's population.

These successes raised hackles among the PRI's corporatist barons. As discussed earlier, these so-called "dinosaurs" never perceived the ballot as a mechanism for citizens to select their representatives. Rather, elected positions formed part of a patronage system to reward party members for loyalty, cooperation, conformity, and years of service. CTM leaders had opposed de la Madrid's selection as the PRI presidential standard-bearer because of his reformist rhetoric. Now they openly decried his recognition of PAN victories, their anger all the more intense because Labor Secretary Arsenio Farell Cubillas had sought to broaden the revolutionary party's base by building up the CROC, the CROM, and other labor confederations at the expense of Don Fidel and his CTM votaries. PRI President Adolfo Lugo Verduzco excoriated party members who didn't vote, saying "in this defining hour, one is with the party or against it." Ex-PRI top dog General Alfonso Corona del Rosal claimed that the economic and financial crisis had led timid *priístas* to turn their backs on the party—"something that would never have happened [in the good old days] and shouldn't have happened this time." In early 1983, Velázquez emphasized that the PRI needed a change in its policies "not its men." Later, he and Gamboa Pascoe, the scurrilous leader of Mexico City's CTM, openly chided de la Madrid.

PRI diehards sought out scapegoats for their setbacks. Catholic clergy-men in general and particularly Bishop Manuel Talamás Camandari of Ciudad Juárez and Archbishop Adalberto Almeida Merino of Chihuahua became favored targets. Such men of the cloth had, the hard-liners averred, manipulated women and other naive voters through sermons and propaganda. Bishop Talamás denied that the church had coordinated the distribution of PAN material with a diocesan-produced brochure: "Votar con responsabilidad, una orientación cristiana" ("Vote Responsibly, a Christian Orientation"). While mentioning no names, this pamphlet cited parties that articulate two ideologies antithetical to Christianity: "liberal capitalism" and "collectivist marxism."

Just as he had aborted his moral renewal initiative in the petroleum sector, de la Madrid did a volte-face on electoral reform. In 1984, he quietly shelved a proposal to allow local party members to select mayoral nominees from lists prepared by the state party leadership. The following year, he unleashed his party's "alchemists"—specialists in transmuting electoral losses into victories—to ensure a PRI landslide in the midterm legislative elections held in July 1985. To work their magic, these modern-day wizards manipulated electoral rolls, voted the dead, and stuffed ballot boxes. They also disqualified unreliable voters, encouraged multiple voting by flying squads of "aviators," diverted pots of public funds into campaign coffers, finagled the results, and managed local news reports. As a result, the PRI garnered 289 of 300 congressional seats chosen by direct election, nearly all of the 845 mayoral contests, and the seven governorships that were on the line.

A year later, equally flagrant vote-stealing marred elections in the states of Sonora and Chihuahua. In the latter, the PRI showed no subtlety in rigging the results to trounce the popular, attractive PAN gubernatorial candidate, Francisco Barrio Terrazas, and to regain the seven municipalities that the PAN had previously won.

PRI excesses ignited a veritable firestorm of protest. Churches closed their doors; PRI women, many the wives of government officials, begged for mass to be said; socialist leaders termed the church's action "legitimate"; *panistas* jubilantly welcomed a caravan of protesting peasants; and the commander of the Federal Highway Police, dispatched to open a road clogged by activists, wound up making the Churchillian "V" sign to show solidarity with the demonstrators.

PAN leaders expressed their ire through speeches, communiqués, marches, and sit-ins. Chihuahua City Mayor Luis H. Alvarez, a 67-year-old retired cattleman and textile entrepreneur who had run for president and governor, garnered national attention with a forty-day hunger strike. How did the frail, bespectacled businessman account for his valiant action?

My decision could be explained as the member of a political party; but this isn't the case: I am doing this because I think that my first responsibility as mayor is to safeguard the full enjoyment of human rights by the inhabitants of the city. I am concerned and outraged by the abuses suffered by *panistas;* but I am equally offended by the curbs on the rights and liberties of other Chihuahuans.[16]

The exceptional magnitude of the corruption led northern churchmen to take extraordinary steps. Father Camilo Daniel Pérez, a veteran in the base community movement, joined with local political leaders to create the Democratic Electoral Movement (MED), which launched a civil disobedience campaign. To protest a "monstrous electoral fraud," the MED mobilized peasants, convened rallies, occupied public buildings, blockaded major highways, and staged a sit-down action on the international bridge linking Ciudad Juárez to El Paso, Texas. At the same time, Bishop Talamás lambasted the government for perverting the people's will, and accused those responsible for the fraud of having sinned against God and their fellow citizens. These diatribes paled in comparison to Archbishop Almeida's homily on July 13, 1986, just a week after the electoral tampering. Recounting the parable of the Good Samaritan, he explained that the decent people of Chihuahua had fallen prey to political robbers. To protest this larceny, he announced that priests would not hold masses in the archdiocese on July 20. Only the Vatican's intervention, urged by Government Secretary Manuel Bartlett Díaz, prevented the closing of churches to protest the fraud and to make "a strong sign on our part to those whose eyes still remain blindfolded or who are blinded by their own guilt."[17]

De la Madrid sought to boost his regime's stock in late 1986. He championed the LOPPE, which introduced proportional representation into the Chamber of Deputies and state legislatures, with the opposition guaranteed one-third of the seats. In addition, he replaced hard-line PRI President Lugo Verduzco with the more diplomatic Jorge de la Vega Domínguez to project a better image for the party as it entered the 1988 presidential campaign. Nevertheless, the president's own standing dropped like a brick in a well. In 1983, 45 percent of respondents to a public-opinion survey indicated that the government was doing a "good" job; four years later, de la Madrid's approval rating had fallen to 29 percent. Further, on July 26, 1986, many of the 100,000 spectators at a World Cup soccer match in Mexico City greeted the president's entry into Aztec Stadium with Mexico's sibilant version of the Bronx cheer.

The *El Grande* earthquakes that struck Mexico City and four other states in September 1985 took an enormous toll in lives and property, not to mention the legitimacy of the chief executive and the system over which he presided. Any ward politician worth his patronage allotment would have clamped on a hard hat, rolled up his sleeves, and waded into the smoking rubble after the shocks killed at least 10,000 people and left tens of thousands homeless. Yet, as Mexicans from every walk of life organized to rescue family members, neighbors, and fellow workers, de la Madrid impressed one foreign diplomat more as an "accountant scrutinizing a balance-sheet" than as concerned patriarch of a tormented national family.

The president neither appeared at a press conference called after the first quake—registered at 8.1 on the Richter scale—nor, following the second shock, did he show up on the balcony of the Presidential Palace to offer sympathy and succor to grieving families assembled in the Zócalo below. Soon he became the butt of bitter jokes: "Why did de la Madrid make only twelve visits to earthquake-devastated sites?" The answer, according to cynical disaster victims in the middle-class neighborhood of Tlatelolco: "Because he owns only a dozen leather jackets"—a reference to his sartorial elegance displayed during televised appearances in afflicted zones.

The barb reflected a growing perception that the 51-year-old president and other Mexican technocrats had grown so out-of-touch with the masses that they could not respond effectively either to catastrophes or to long-term needs for economic growth and political reform.

While at least thirty-six hours elapsed before most government entities—except some police and fire departments—launched any semblance of a relief program, thousands of private individuals mobilized search brigades, manned bulldozers, set up temporary housing, food distribution centers and medical facilities, and organized emergency transportation, frequently with the help of ham-radio operators, commercial stations, and, later, with volunteers from the United States and other countries. This grass-roots effervescence gave birth to or nourished many of the community groups, women's associations, independent unions, human rights advocates, small political movements, and nongovernmental organizations (NGOs) that abound in Mexico City today.

Just as some have noted that Karl Marx had never touched the warts or smelled the belches of the working class, so too was the case with Citizen President de la Madrid, as designated on official documents. Although he incessantly invoked memories of the 1910 revolution, extolled his government's revolutionary heritage, and served as the PRI's de facto head, the aristocratic chief executive exemplified the economists, accountants, and other professionals who, for fifteen years, had broadened their influence in Mexico's authoritarian regime at the expense of old-line *políticos*. These politicians despaired at the omnipresence in the government of well-educated cosmopolites who had little or no electoral experience, much less an appetite for meeting their constituents up close.

The colorless technocrats lacked either popularity or well-cultivated ties to the people. This may explain their refusal to allow the army to implement fully its 188-page emergency plan in response to *El Grande*, even though the scheme had worked well in other disasters, such as the 1982 eruption of the Chichonal volcano in distant Chiapas state. Reportedly, Mexico City's Mayor Ramón Aguirre Velázquez persuaded the president to limit the armed forces' role in the September tragedy, lest an effective performance in the media-infested capital whet the appetite of the ever-more professional army for greater political involvement. Thus, the military's major function lay in providing security and preventing looting. In so doing, the army occasionally impeded spontaneous civilian rescue ventures, thereby diminishing its prestige—a fact that embittered some generals toward the *técnicos* who had restrained them. At the same time, the navy's reputation sparkled, because after its ministry building collapsed, sweaty, grimy blue-uniformed officers relentlessly hunted for survivors in the ruins of its own and nearby buildings.

Wariness of politicians meant that even more than a week after the earthquake, no one in de la Madrid's entourage had even contacted Fidel Velázquez about drawing trade unionists into the anti-disaster effort. More curiously, the technocrats reacted uncharacteristically to the increasingly ugly mood of uprooted earthquake victims toward a government they saw as indifferent to their misery. Lacking a politician's feel for the situation at hand, the president and his aides sought to mimic the most dramatic political stroke of the last half-century. Imitating Lázaro Cárdenas's wildly popular seizure of seventeen foreign oil firms in 1938, they expropriated 625 acres of disaster-stricken property to build new housing, schools, and parks.

But in contrast to the late beloved leader's unambiguous initiative, the *técnicos* produced an expropriation decree hastily conceived and unartfully drafted. Hence, the enthusiasm for what at first seemed a bold move soon gave way to greater confusion and discontent. Verified reports that politicians and their friends had built many of the collapsed edifices, apparently cutting corners with building materials and construction standards, only fueled popular ire. Observers remained incredulous over the collapse of the National Medical Center of IMSS, Latin America's largest and most sophisticated hospital, which presidents from Avila Camacho to López Mateos had funded. Articles by two journalists typified the charges. They claimed that Guillermo Carrillo Arena, head of the Urban Development Ministry (SEDUE), had approved construction plans for the Juárez Hospital, which fell like a house of cards during the cataclysm. How, they asked, did a government official like Carrillo Arena accumulate the 15 billion peso fortune set forth on his government disclosure statement? The opposition called for the resignations of the mayor and SEDUE chief. The plummeting confidence in the government came to the surface in accelerating capital flight, as the peso—which stood at 384 to the dollar on September 18—traded at 500 to 1 by late November.

Ultimately, SEDUE, under new leadership, launched a well-financed disaster relief program, but even this effort failed to loft the regime's standing, according to a poll published in *Excélsior*. The paper reported that only 37 percent of city residents considered the administration's crisis performance as "excellent" or "good"—better than positive evaluations of congressmen at 17 percent; political parties at 20 percent; and the police at 30 percent.

These figures compared poorly with favorable ratings of 98 percent and 93 percent, respectively, for the behavior of "other countries" supplying aid, and the "people."

The paralysis of a hegemonic, paternalistic regime soured people on the president and the government-PRI system. Perhaps for the first time since the formation of a dominant ruling party, the proverbial man-in-the-street realized that in a crisis, he could not wait for authorities to safeguard his interests. Far better to rely on himself, his family, his friends, and nascent self-help groups of average citizens. This realization spawned, or expanded the membership and role of, civic organizations, whose importance in Mexican society has grown sharply in recent years.

Election of 1988

After three technocrats in a row, the dinosaurs who roamed Mexico's corporatist sector favored selecting a candidate with political skills, a man who could exchange muscular *abrazos* in union halls and swill *pulque* with peasants on *ejidos*. In the mid-1980s, the nomination seemed up for grabs among several contenders. Grave misgivings by the PRI old guard aside, the imperative for Mexico's next chief executive to handle serious domestic and international economic problems argued for de la Madrid's selection of either Finance Secretary Silva Herzog or SPP Secretary Salinas, with the charismatic finance secretary appearing the odds-on favorite because of his close friendship with the president, at least until early 1986.

Of the two technocrats widely mentioned for the presidency, Silva Herzog boasted a worldwide reputation and counted de la Madrid as one of his five closest friends. After earning a master's degree at Yale, the 51-year-old economist distinguished himself in a career that involved teaching and public service. He crossed swords with CTM leaders when, as INFONAVIT's director-general, he battled the corruption that pervaded this housing agency for workers—action which Echeverría rebuked in his 1975 State of the Nation address. These efforts in no way slowed his ascent in the Finance Ministry where he became secretary in 1982 and, subsequently, *Euromoney* magazine named him "Finance Minister of the Year" for helping Mexico cope with the near-bankruptcy that threatened the country in August 1982. The extremely intelligent, flamboyant cabinet secretary attracted attention not only for his outspoken positions on issues, but because he zoomed around Mexico City's congested streets on a motorcycle. Silva Herzog also stood out because—despite being the son of a famous economist—he had no accumulated wealth or business ties, supported his family on his government income, and had lived in the same home in the middle-class Coyoacán district of Mexico City for more than twenty years.

In 1986, the halving of oil prices to $11.5 per barrel forced the economic cabinet—led by Silva Herzog and Salinas—to meet continually throughout the winter and spring to confront a projected $8 to $10 billion shortfall in revenues. They sought to craft a strategy that would pry more monies out of international financiers without requiring the retrenchments likely to incite widespread social discontent just a year before the next presidential campaign commenced.

Silva Herzog headed the negotiations with U.S. representatives, World Bank officials, and private external creditors. They insisted that Mexico undertake major sacrifices. While talking tough overseas, Silva Herzog suggested borrowing an additional $2 billion abroad, increasing the budget deficit $2 billion, and cutting federal spending by $2 billion—an unpopular move that Salinas as SPP secretary would have to implement—rather than boosting taxes, for which his own Finance Ministry would have borne responsibility. To offset the political impact of projected cuts, Silva Herzog reportedly proposed a ninety-day suspension of $1.6 billion of the $3.6 billion in interest on Mexico's $98 billion debt to foreign creditors, which fell due in the second half of 1986.

Salinas, who increasingly sought to ingratiate himself with de la Madrid, warned that the budget had already been "cut to the bone" and further surgery on social programs would invite instability—a gnawing concern of de la Madrid's because of the Mexico City earthquakes. Silva Herzog continued to push for lower expenditures on the grounds that, although painful, room for more reductions existed. Indeed, "not one federal agency had been closed," he scoffed.[18] Such suggestions served only to sharpen the criticism and backbiting directed toward the finance secretary at home. For example, Salinas and the agriculture secretary—another de la Madrid confidant—persuaded the president to approve higher outlays in the countryside. At one point, de la Madrid pointed at Silva Herzog and ordered him either "to find or invent the money" to pay for these expenditures. While agreeing to follow the president's instructions, Silva Herzog asked that the minutes of the meeting note that the "finance minister opposes this action." He also accused Salinas of placing his presidential ambitions above resolving the economic crisis.

Cabinet sessions proved increasingly tempestuous, and the outspoken Silva Herzog alienated the decorous de la Madrid by "losing his cool," in the words of an observer: "He was completely alone in recent cabinet meetings," said one well-placed source.[19] Meanwhile, the crafty Salinas opposed trimming food and transportation subsidies, as well as other popular programs, on the grounds that such reductions would exacerbate social discord in a country already flailed by a 90 percent inflation rate.

In contrast to Silva Herzog's isolation, Salinas had used his SPP post—which entailed allocating resources to both government agencies and the private sector—to cultivate allies: Some of these players belonged to the president's inner circle. No one proved more important to Salinas's fortunes than Emilio Gamboa Patrón, the private secretary who managed de la Madrid's appointment schedule. Gamboa readily found time for Silva Herzog's detractors and Salinas's supporters to gain access to Mexico's equivalent of the Oval Office, while proponents of the finance secretary and opponents of the SPP head often found their entry blocked. One cabinet member has reflected that within a half-hour of a presentation by Silva Herzog to de la Madrid, Salinas knew both the substance of the initiative as well as the chief executive's reaction to it. The private secretary's pivotal role and tremendous influence within Los Pinos gave rise to the joke that Gamboa himself could not succeed de la Madrid as president because Mexico's constitution prohibits reelection.[20] The politically agile SPP head also deployed the pesos that he controlled to court governors. Although he allocated most revenues in January, Salinas always held back some monies to disburse at mid-year. In this manner, he nurtured political ties state by state. Specifically, Salinas catered to the desire of governors to cut the ribbons opening international airports in their key cities. Twenty-four new airports—four international; twenty national—began operation between 1982 and 1990. In any case, much to the dismay of the Finance Ministry, SPP authorized such airports in venues as diverse as Piedras Negras (Coahuila), Tlaxcala (Tlaxcala), Toluca (Mexico state), and Puebla (Puebla).

Other evidence existed of Salinas's extraordinary facility at alliance-building. In the opinion of an insider who insisted on anonymity, he and Government Secretary Bartlett, another presidential aspirant, agreed to an informal nonaggression pact—that is, they would avoid attacking each other and one would back the other in the event that either dropped out of contention. Apparently, Bartlett had no such understanding with other contenders. For example, eight days after Mexico City Mayor Aguirre Velázquez made an amorous phone call to a young lady, the politician's wife received a tape-recording of the conversation, probably through the good offices of the Government Ministry that regularly conducts wire-taps throughout the country. Although not actively cooperating with Salinas, Aguirre Velázquez and Energy Secretary Alfredo del Mazo relished the prospect of the finance secretary's falling on his face. In addition, Salinas managed to bring into the cabinet members of his own political team like Manuel Camacho Solís, whom de la Madrid appointed SEDUE chief to oversee reconstruction work following the catastrophic earthquakes in Mexico City.

The SPP secretary also used his post to forge links with present and future billionaires, destined to enlarge their bank accounts and stock portfolios during his presidency. He went out of his way to court the business community, still wary over the 1982 bank nationalization and Salinas's imperious, hard-nosed manner. He emphasized his commitment to fighting inflation, selling off more state firms, reducing the federal deficit, encouraging investment, and enlarging the role of the private sector at the expense of corporatist organizations. This rhetoric helped him recruit such entrepreneurs as Claudio X. González, Roberto González, Roberto Hernández, Manuel Espinosa Iglesias, Bernardo Quintana, Carlos Slim, and other captains of industry. Needless to say, as head of SPP, Salinas could also help his business allies compete effectively for airport construction, agricultural projects, and other ventures authorized by his ministry. Carlos Hank González provided inestimable assistance to Salinas through his vast network of business contacts and his political acumen, revealed in his aphorism: "A politician who is poor is a poor politician."

Salinas and his cohorts persuaded the chief executive that Silva Herzog had become an apologist for and defender of the IMF, and had remained insufficiently aware of the domestic repercussions of IMF proposals, which included holding the GDP deficit to 5 percent rather than the 12 percent anticipated in mid-1986.

As Salinas toiled incessantly to cultivate de la Madrid, Silva Herzog—a loner by nature—neglected to pull together his scattered supporters, mostly intellectuals without baronial clout. Several factors accounted for this failure. The finance secretary's hubris, his exceptional intellect, and his extraordinarily engaging personality meant that he often outshone the colorless president, who—in consultation with key members of the revolutionary family— would ultimately select his successor. As David Garner of the *Financial Times* has noted, "[t]he only star in an opaque sky, [Silva Herzog's] real crime was to seem to eclipse Mr. de la Madrid in a tradition which demands that all glory reflect on one's superiors." The finance secretary's incessant foreign obligations further harmed his prospects, for "he spent too much time abroad negotiating with bankers and not enough on backstairs political chat."[21]

In the upshot of the donnybrook over budget cuts, Silva Herzog submitted his "irrevocable resignation," an action that so infuriated de la Madrid, long a close friend of the finance secretary's, that he wrote out in long hand a page-one editorial for *El Nacional*, the government-published newspaper, excoriating Silva Herzog for his lack of "team work . . . [and] loyalty in discharging his functions and adhering to the policies of the Executive." The president selected, as the new finance secretary, Gustavo Petricioli Iturbide, 57, a long-time friend of the president with whom Salinas enjoyed excellent relations. By this point, everyone recognized the SPP secretary as the conductor of economic policy, to whom the affable Petricioli played an emphatic second fiddle.

Silva Herzog's departure carried several consequences: It set the stage for a reasonable compromise with the IMF and international bankers, many of whom had previously feared that the ambitious Salinas might drive a harder bargain than the deposed finance secretary; it removed from the presidential sweepstakes the technocratic front-runner to succeed de la Madrid; and it enabled Salinas, previously an aggressive champion of state planning, to fashion for Mexico a liberal economic policy as attractive to the private sector as it was scorned by the PRI's sectoral interests.

Born in 1948 to a politically active family in Nuevo León, the diminutive, balding Salinas earned three degrees from Harvard University, to which de la Madrid had written him a letter of recommendation. His brains and penchant for hard work ensured a meteoric rise in both the ministries of Finance and Planning and Budget. Soon after de la Madrid obtained the PRI's nomination, he appointed Salinas head of the Institute for Social, Political and Economics Studies, the party's think-tank where he crafted the *Basic Plan for Government: 1982–88*. The president rewarded the "atomic ant"—as associates nicknamed the 34-year-old Salinas because of his self-discipline, energy, and perseverance—with the SPP post. The youthful cabinet secretary told friends of his satisfaction at reaching the cabinet while his father, secretary of industry and commerce under López Mateos, and mother were still alive. Passed over for the presidency in 1964, Raúl Salinas Lozano had succumbed to alcoholism and later, according to a disputed report by his private secretary, became a key figure in narcotics dealing.[22] Organized labor's animus toward Salinas sprang from his elimination of special benefits for the Oil Workers' Union and his rejection of ISI in favor of free-market economics in the mid-1980s.

In Salinas, de la Madrid found a trusted associate who would appoint members of the outgoing chief executive's team including Gamboa and Beteta, to key posts in the next administration. In addition, the recent convert to the magic of the marketplace showed enthusiasm for continuing Mexico's *perestroika*. Finally, although a Johnny-come-lately to neoliberalism, Salinas won de la Madrid's admiration for his bare-knuckles attacks on statists within the PRI itself.

In October 1986, products of the corporatist system—headed by former-PRI President Porfirio Muñoz Ledo and ex-Michoacán Governor Cuauhtémoc Cárdenas Solórzano—formed the Democratic Current (CD). These activists championed intraparty "democracy" and decried the use of the *dedazo* to select the PRI's next presidential nominee. Such altruistic positions concealed the CD's real goal—namely, to challenge the growing influence of the technocrats who were rapidly overshadowing the party's traditional elements. In this pursuit, the Democratic Current openly campaigned for Cárdenas's selection as the PRI standard-bearer—an action that violated the rule of the game by which the incumbent selects his successor. When de la Madrid named Salinas, Cárdenas accepted the nomination of the small PARM, which eventually cast its lot with several leftist parties to form the Democratic Front for National Reconstruction (FDN). In reaction to this "violation" of party statutes, the PRI expelled Cárdenas, Muñoz Ledo, and other key figures in the Democratic Current.

To counter the CD's charges of authoritarianism, in August 1987 the PRI released the names of six "distinguished members of the Party" whom the National Executive Committee's president had heard mentioned while examining the body politic—a process called *"auscultación"*—in a nationwide trip. In addition to Salinas, this list of presidential prospects included Energy Secretary del Mazo, Manuel Bartlett, Aguirre Velázquez, and two lesser lights, Attorney General Sergio García Ramírez, and Education Secretary Miguel González Avelar. Presumably, *priístas* could scrutinize the credentials of each man and listen to his policy statements and somehow—vicariously, perhaps—participate in the final selection.

The CTM, key members of the army, and governors of several states, including México, Nuevo León, Sonora, Sinaloa, Colima, and Tabasco, favored del Mazo. Born into a politically prominent family in Mexico state in 1943, del Mazo had studied finance and banking, heading a bank at age 26. He left the private sector when de la Madrid, then a middle-level official, offered him the vice presidency of the National Banking and Securities Commission. He soon won the backing of Don Fidel to head the Workers' Bank, serving from 1979 to 1981. As discussed in Chapter 2, the CTM leader and PRI President Gustavo Carvajal—another key member of the Mexico state *camarilla* that del Mazo's father had once headed—backed the young man for governor of their state, a post that his father formerly held. In 1986, President de la Madrid invited del Mazo to leave the governor's palace in Toluca to join the cabinet as secretary of energy, mines, and government industries. Observers touted this posting as a stepping-stone to Los Pinos, and del Mazo presided over lavish caviar-laden luncheons, celebrating his political mobility and broadening his network of friends. Del Mazo's close connections to de la Madrid's family—especially to the chief executive's son, Federico, for whom he served as godfather—only enhanced his prospects. The president had allegedly referred to the movie-star handsome del Mazo as "the younger brother I never had."[23] The energy secretary's modest international economic credentials aside, he seemed like the man best suited to manage the escalating social ferment of unemployment, discontent among the working and middle classes over the economic crisis, and demands for a democratic opening pressed ever more vigorously by the PAN. Ultimately, the austere de la Madrid—whose *abrazos* sought to keep the recipients at a distance—frowned on the sybaritic social events that del Mazo hosted to advance his candidacy.

After del Mazo, hard-core corporatists preferred Bartlett, who like Salinas and del Mazo was a so-called "puppy of the revolution" (*"cachoro de la revolución"*) inasmuch as his father had been governor of Tabasco nearly two decades after the "junior" Bartlett was born in Puebla in 1936. Before earning degrees from universities in Mexico and abroad, Bartlett organized the PRI's Revolutionary Youth Movement along the lines of the Spanish

Falange—a harbinger of his hard-line policy toward political foes. He combined party activism with a succession of bureaucratic posts until de la Madrid appointed him as political advisor at SPP, general coordinator of his presidential campaign, PRI secretary-general, and government secretary in 1982. The politically inexperienced chief executive relied heavily on the tough, manipulative Bartlett to smother mounting political agitation, as collapsing oil prices plunged the country into prolonged stagflation, and electoral fraud sparked surging opposition to the Tammany-Hall-style regime.

Aguirre Velázquez, 51, stood as a third choice of Mexico's traditional politicians. As mayor, Aguirre Velázquez developed close ties to CTM competitors in the labor movement—specifically, the CROC, the CROM, and the Federation of Goods and Services Unions (FESEBES), organized by Francisco Hernández Juárez, the young, dynamic head of the Telephone Workers' Union. The most down-to-earth of the six, Aguirre Velázquez won praise for his fiestas held at his home in the Coyoacán section of the capital or in his native village, San Felipe Torres Mochas. Of the corpulent, fun-loving backslapper, it was said that in lieu of bodyguards, he traveled with mariachis.[24]

Reportedly, Salinas finished third in an informal survey of the 500 *priístas* who constitute the party's "cupola." Among the top government officials and party leaders, only 94 ranked Salinas their first choice for the presidency, far behind del Mazo (167) and Bartlett (148). He made an especially weak showing among governors (11) and labor leaders.[25]

Why the pantomime of six distinguished contenders if de la Madrid had set his sights on Salinas as the man most likely to continue the economic opening? In addition to attempting—albeit feebly—to repudiate Cárdenas's and Muñoz Ledo's diatribes against the PRI's closed, secret, and undemocratic selection method, the floating of a half-dozen names represented an attempt to demonstrate to all sectors of the PRI that someone of their ilk was still worthy of the presidency, even as Los Pinos increasingly turned its back on the party's traditional values.

The July 1988 presidential contest proved a landmark in the evolution of the corporatist system. After a protracted delay, electoral officials awarded the victory to Salinas (50.47 percent), defeating Cárdenas (30.9 percent), Clouthier (16.71 percent), and two minor-party candidates. Even though Salinas emerged as the official winner, he received the fewest votes of any PRI presidential nominee in history. Meanwhile, Cárdenas made a remarkable showing, especially in Mexico City, among shantytown dwellers nationwide, on communal farms, and in some labor enclaves. This tour de force helped him capture the capital's city hall nine years later. Don Fidel and most CTM unions went through the motions of supporting Salinas. La Quina and the Oil Workers, however, made no secret of their enthusiasm for Cárdenas, to whom the STPRM allegedly made a substantial donation.

Table 3.1   **Profile of Relative Competitivity of Direct-Election Districts in the Chamber of Deputies**

Source: Federico Berrueto Pruneda, "1994: Nueva Geografía Electoral, *Voz y Voto* 21 (September 1994): 36.

Profile of Districts	1988	1991	1994
Hegemonic	55 (18.33%)	76 (25.33%)	0 (0.00%)
Dominant	77 (25.67%)	130 (43.33%)	85 (28.33%)
Competitive	41 (13.67%)	68 (22.67%)	107 (35.67%)
Very Competitive	127 (42.33%)	26 (8.67%)	108 (36.00%)

- **Hegemonic:** The difference between the PRI and its closest competitor exceeds 60% of the votes cast.
- **Dominant:** The difference varies between 30% and 60%.
- **Competitive:** The difference varies between 15% and 30%.
- **Very Competitive:** The difference falls below 15%.

In classic corporatist fashion, the unanticipated avalanche of ballots for the FDN candidate slowed the vote-count to a crawl while PRI alchemists manipulated the outcome. No party stalwart questioned the imperative for a Salinas triumph. Rather, the dispute centered on his victory tally: Technocrats argued for a credibly low margin, while veteran *políticos* favored a landslide, lest a strong performance embolden Cárdenas to run again in 1994. The former group carried the day, and Salinas emerged with just over half of the votes cast. As a result of these machinations, 74 percent of respondents to a *Los Angeles Times* poll doubted the legitimacy of Salinas's victory.[26]

In what many observers considered a fairer count, Mexico's Federal Electoral Institute conferred on the PRI only 260 places in the 500-member Chamber of Deputies, with the remaining seats captured by the PAN (101), and the four pro-Cárdenas parties (139). Later, defections from the *cardenista* ranks swelled the PRI total to 263 seats. For the first time, the opposition broke the PRI stranglehold on the 64-member Senate as the PAN and the *cardenistas* won two seats apiece. Table 3.1 reveals the mounting competitiveness of districts in the lower chamber.

Conclusion

De la Madrid's term, culminating in the 1988 election, had several profound consequences for Mexico's executive branch and its corporatist system. Ironically, even within the PRI, longtime members broke the rules of the game that honored each chief executive's right to choose his successor, and the obligation of all party leaders to back the nominee, whatever their opinion of him. Not only did Hernández Galicia overtly favor Cárdenas, but the Democratic Current turned thumbs down on the *dedazo*, leading to their exodus from the party.

Second, the potent opposition vote in Mexico City—complemented by a high abstention rate—suggested that de la Madrid's and the government's incompetence in the face of *El Grande* had cost the regime support in a metropolitan area whose citizens cast one in every four votes nationwide. The earthquakes gave rise to civic organizations committed to diversity, voluntary participation, and pluralism at the expense of uniformity, authoritarianism, and corporatism.

Third, even though he finished behind Salinas and Cárdenas in the election, Clouthier proved both a skilled campaigner and an adroit recruiter of pugnacious members of the northern business community to the PAN banner. In the late 1990s, these men and women contributed greatly to the most effective challenge to Mexico's traditional system.

Fourth, public contempt of corporatist leaders escalated, as technocratic administrations showed themselves every bit as corrupt as their predecessors. Beteta's exit from Pemex signaled the last step in an anti-corruption minuet performed by Presidents Echeverría, López Portillo, and de la Madrid: Though during the presidential campaign, the PRI candidate turned the air blue with promises to conduct a hammer and tongs attack on wrongdoing, once ensconced in Los Pinos, he merely jailed a few highly visible outsiders. Before leaving office, he forgot about cleaning up the political system, while personally taking advantage of the *Año del Hidalgo*.[27]

Fifth, the marginalization of each corporatist sector became clear in both de la Madrid's quest to deepen the economic opening he had initiated through a Salinas presidency, and the very nomination of Salinas, whom many traditional overlords regarded as an antichrist.

Finally, Mexico's growing dependence on international capital and consumer markets represented a latter-day meteor, whose impact would transfigure the domestic environment, threatening the extinction of the corporatist dinosaurs who had once rapaciously dominated the political and economic landscape.

Notes

1. Riding, *Distant Neighbors: A Portrait of the Mexicans* (New York: Alfred A. Knopf, 1985): p. 66.
2. Lorenzo Meyer, "El gran obstaculo," *El norte*, October 29, 1992, p. 2-A.
3. Frank Tannenbaum, *Mexico: The Struggle for Peace and Bread* (New York: Knopf, 1950), pp. 81–82.

4. Edwin Lieuwen, *Arms and Politics in Latin America* (Rev. ed.; New York: Praeger, 1965), p. 104.

5. Lieuwen, *Arms and Politics in Latin America*, p. 108.

6. Philip, *The Presidency in Mexican Politics*, p. 183.

7. This section benefits from Robert E. Scott, *Mexican Government in Transition* (Rev. ed.: Urbana, Ill: University of Illinois Press, 1964): pp. 213–215; and L. Vincent Padgett, *The Mexican Political System* (Boston: Houghton Mifflin, 1966), pp. 137–139.

8. For an analysis of the "Pendulum Effect," see Martin C. Needler, *Politics and Society in Mexico* (Albuquerque: University of New Mexico Press, 1971), pp. 46–49.

9. Donald Mabry, *Mexico's Acción Nacional: A Catholic Alternative to Revolution* (Syracuse, N.Y.: Syracuse University Press, 1973), pp. 56–57.

10. Middlebrook, *The Paradox of Revolution*, p. 296.

11. Quoted in "Mexico: Tethered Watchdog," *Latin America Political Report*, October 14, 1977, p. 317.

12. Rodolfo Guzmán, La reforma política fortalecerá al pri, coincide la oposición," *Proceso*, December 21, 1977, p. 21; and Stephen D. Morris, *Political Reformism in Mexico: An Overview of Contemporary Mexican Politics* (Boulder, Co.: Lynne Rienner, 1995), p. 183.

13. Quoted in "Mexico: Backlash Victim," *Latin America Political Report*, October 7, 1977, p. 308.

14. Interview with Ambassador Jesús Silva Herzog Flores, Washington, D.C., December 13, 1996.

15. Steve Frazier, "Labor Czar: Mexico Oil Workers Have Powerful Leader in Hernández Galicia," *Wall Street Journal*, January 20, 1984, p. 1.

16. Pinchetti, "Chihuahua: de la ira a la cerrazón," *Proceso*, July 21, 1986, p. 13.

17. *Unomásuno*, July 13, 1986, pp. 1, 9; cited in Dennis M. Hanaratty, "Church-State Relations in Mexico in the 1980s," October 1986 (mimeo.), pp. 15–16; George W. Grayson, *The Church in Contemporary Mexico* (Washington, D.C.: Center for Strategic & International Studies, 1992), pp. 58–61; and Jaime Pérez Mendoza, "Por petición de bartlett el vaticano ordenó que hubiera misas en chihuahua," *Proceso*, August 4, 1986, pp. 6–13.

18. Interview with Ambassador Jesús Silva Herzog Flores, Washington, D.C., June 28, 1996.

19. Quoted in Eric Berg, "Experts Expect Debt Pact Soon between Mexico and IMF," *New York Times*, June 19, 1986, p. D-6.

20. Alfonso Zárate, *Los usos del poder* (Mexico City: Raya en el Agua, 1995), p. 151.

21. Gardner, "De la Madrid Ponders a Successor," *Financial Times*, March 10, 1987, p. 6.

22. Magdalena Ruiz Pelayo quoted in Sam Dillon and Christine Bierderman, "Secretary to Mexican Patriarch Discloses Links to Drug Barons, *New York Times*, February 26, 1997, pp. A-1, A-6.

23. It is highly questionable that the sober, patrician, hyperbole-averse chief executive made this comment, which has become part of Mexico's political folklore.

24. Zárate, *Los usos del poder*, p. 165.

25. Other "precandidates" were Education Secretary Miguel González Avelar (49), Aguirre Velázquez (23), and Attorney General Sergio García Ramírez (19); see, Elías Chávez, "Sólo 20% de la cúpula governante jugaba por salinas," *Proceso*, October 19, 1987, pp. 12– 15. The name of Silva Herzog, who had burned his bridges with de la Madrid, did not appear on the informal ballot.

26. Marjorie Miller, "Mexico Likes Salinas but Is Split over PRI" *Los Angeles Times*, August 20, 1989; pp.1,6; fewer than 25 percent of the respondents believed that Salinas had actually triumphed in the 1988 contest.

27. In his syndicated column, Jack Anderson alleged that de la Madrid salted away $13 to $14 million in a Swiss bank during his first four months in office; he also reported that de la Madrid's "take" during his presidency was at least $162 million. See, Anderson, "Mexico Makes its Presidents Millionaires," *Washington Post*, May 15, 1984, p. C-15. Such allegations aside, de la Madrid left office hounded by fewer charges of venality than did his predecessor or successor.

4
—
Salinas Confronts the Corporatist System

Introduction

Although few Mexican presidents in the twentieth century have begun their terms under more inauspicious circumstances than did Salinas, the atomic ant soon began to challenge, and then dismantle, the country's traditional, authoritarian, closed, corporatist system even as he explored creating a personally focused neo-corporatist structure. Salinas, at best the third choice of party regulars for the PRI nomination, took office as dark clouds of suspicion boiled over his disputed election. Observers doubted that he would enjoy a political honeymoon, much less implement his platform of economic and political modernization trumpeted during a year-long campaign.

Yet, within a few months of his inauguration, Salinas began to impose technocratic solutions on complex problems despite opposition from the country's most predatory dinosaurs. What accounts for the short- and medium-term success of a chief executive who commenced his tenure under the most forbidding circumstances since the Great Depression?

The explanation benefits from Ellen K. Trimberger's theory of "elite" revolutions, as applied to Mexico by Miguel

Angel Centeno.[1] Key elements include: (1) centralization of power in state institutions promoting the desired change; (2) domination of these institutions by technically specialized bureaucrats, who pursued a homogenous policy keyed on the optimal use of resources and the "preservation of system stability"; (3) the maintenance of elite cohesion through teams known as *camarillas;* and (4) a favorable international context in which the reformist elites could attain their objectives.

First, during the 1970s and, especially, the 1980s, presidents had concentrated power in the planning and financial areas of the bureaucracy. Salinas, as observed in Chapter 3, not only emerged from this labyrinthine sector, but as secretary of planning and budget he had mastered its powers and recruited much of its personnel. Second, this technocratic elite—considered by many as "new *científicos*" reminiscent of Díaz's positivist advisers in the nineteenth century—exhibited remarkable cohesion. The Salinas-led team committed itself to a single goal—namely, supplanting ISI, statism, and corporatism with a neoliberal economic policy. So convinced were they of the exhaustion of the state intervention model and the need for a market-oriented strategy that they reinterpreted the 1910 revolution to conform to their objective. Third, many of its members had studied economics and related subjects abroad, worked together in SPP, the Finance Ministry, or the Central Bank, and belonged to the same or interlocking *camarillas*, called by Professor Roderic Camp "the cement of the Mexican political system." Finally, Ronald Reagan, Margaret Thatcher, Felipe González, and other advocates of the magic of the marketplace commanded the global stage even as Soviet and other Eastern European proponents of state planning fell on their faces. The international environment proved warm, nurturing, and inviting for Salinas and his cohorts who not only talked the game of liberal reforms but moved vigorously to put them in place.

Attack on La Quina and Other Corporatists

A Mexican adage holds that "it's more important to be strong than right." Salinas exhibited no love lost for organized labor, which proved more of a liability than an asset in the 1988 election. By launching an army-police blitzkrieg attack on his nemesis Hernández Galicia and fellow leaders of the hugely corrupt Oil Workers' Union within six weeks of taking office, the new chief executive showed how he could be strong and right at the same time. As a result, his public approval standing shot up overnight as citizens who had once considered him a wimp began to talk in terms of the *"hombre fuerte"* (strongman) who inhabits the presidential palace. "He's gained the respect of the people—totally," exclaimed a middle-class businessman previously cool to the new national leader.

Although claiming to have voted for Salinas, whom he detested, La Quina, the *petroleros'* de facto chief, had openly passed the word during the presidential contest that union members were free to cast ballots for Cárdenas, who ran strongly in oil centers. Reportedly, the *petroleros* also contributed to the war chest of Cárdenas, whose revered father had nationalized the industry a half-century before.

These disloyal acts infuriated the new president as did Hernández Galicia's sneering insolence and the eagerness of the Oil Workers' seven-member delegation to embarrass the PRI in Congress. As alluded to, the STPRM[2] delegation hounded Mario Ramón Beteta, a Salinas ally, out of the director-generalship of Pemex by accusing him of having embezzled $49 million in a 1985 tanker-leasing deal. In fact, Beteta had strenuously fought corruption that involved using vessels, owned by a recently jailed La Quina confidant, to ship Mexican oil for union profit.

The straw that broke the camel's back involved a visit that La Quina and his henchmen made to Salinas in early 1989. After offering a pro-forma New Year's greeting and pledging their support in efforts to renegotiate the external debt, the union leaders insisted that they would continue to pursue the prosecution of Beteta, the ex-Pemex secretary-general then serving as governor of Mexico state. Upon leaving the meeting, the usually taciturn La Quina told reporters: "We are not making accusations for the sake of it; when we make charges, it is because we have proof."

Just a week before his arrest, Hernández Galicia excoriated the idea of reorganizing Pemex, declaring that if the government tries to transfer even the smallest part of the oil industry to private hands, domestic or foreign, the oil union will go out on strike.

The feisty young president quietly listened to such threats. In response, however, he dispatched federal police and army units conveyed by Hercules transports from Mexico City to La Quina's home in a middle-class suburb of Ciudad Madero on January 10. Following a bazooka shot that blew a hole in the side of his house and a brief gunfight with bodyguards, the troops stormed the dwelling, captured Hernández Galicia, who had just finished his morning bath, and whisked him off shirtless to a Mexico City prison. Subsequently, other units found—many observers believe planted—a cache of weapons in La Quina's house. The authorities claimed to have discovered 200 Uzi submachine guns, 19 other high-caliber weapons, and 25,000 rounds of 9 mm shells. Some 53 union stalwarts from around the country joined the STPRM leader behind bars. The federal prosecutor arraigned La Quina on charges of resisting arrest, illegal weapons possession, arms smuggling, and "qualified" homicide. Authorities also lodged charges of tax fraud against union-controlled companies. In mid-1997, Hernández Galicia remained in the Reclusorio Oriente prison, seeking an early release from his ultimate sentence of eleven years and nine months. The STPRM leader's arrest sparked a march by 10,000 *petroleros* in front of the National Palace. Many motorists took seriously the demonstrators' warning— *"Sin La Quina, no habrá gasolina"* ("Without La Quina, there will be no gasoline")—and rushed to gas stations to stock up. After the protest in Mexico City and shrill words from union hotheads in Ciudad Madero, peace returned to the heavily guarded Pemex installations.

Far from promoting the democratization and independence of the Oil Workers, the coup against La Quina enabled the government to assert control over the rambunctious union. After the incarceration of the "petroleum mafia," as journalists labeled them, the government flew "Professor" Sebastián Guzmán Cabrera and his bodyguards to Mexico City to meet with the labor secretary. Guzmán Cabrera, an extremely wealthy former associate of Hernández Galicia's who had crossed swords with his boss, endured charges of job-selling and misusing union funds, and was forced into retirement in 1987. As early as 1971, his detractors had accused Guzmán Cabrera —whom novelist Elena Poniatowska described as La Quina's moral twin brother—of hawking 464 oil-field jobs at $240 each.[3] The session in the Labor Ministry produced a new STPRM chief. Blas Chumacero, 83, the ailing second-in-command to the CTM's Fidel Velázquez, publicly rejected Guzmán's selection. "Let's be clear," he said, "that the CTM is not at the service of the government. . . . He [Guzmán Cabrera] cannot be rehabilitated by labor minister Arsenio Farell. He is retired, and it is up to the union and himself to decide if he returns. But from there to his becoming secretary-general of the oilworkers there is a long distance."

Chumacero's admonition notwithstanding, Salinas and Farell nimbly covered the long distance. Now, with the STPRM under leadership amenable to the imperatives of increased productivity, modernization, and worker flexibility, Pemex Director-General Francisco Rojas Gutiérrez moved to slash the featherbedded workforce, eliminate union perquisites, sign service contracts with American firms to drill production wells using non-Mexican crews, and refashion the monopoly.

Salinas's decisive action made clear that a resuscitated presidency would exercise all of the power at its disposal to implement the structural changes deemed crucial to Mexico's economic advancement. At the same time, he made it clear to organized labor that it should not resist the continued sacrifices and belt-tightening inherent in his liberalization program. The business community and international bankers learned that the president, backed to the hilt by the armed forces, was determined to manage events rather than allow them to overtake him. Above all, the intrepid chief executive shed the image of an egg-headed technocrat for that of a formidable leader whom the public and power brokers alike would have to respect even if they did not like him and his market-focused program. "Who says this president doesn't wear long pants?" said a former campaign aide.

Salinas did not confine his attack on labor to the Oil Workers. He also ousted another powerful *cacique*, Carlos Jonguitud Barrios, who had headed the SNTE. Whereas the STPRM had opposed Salinas's election, the National Educational Workers had thrown their weight behind the PRI nominee early and enthusiastically. Jonguitud's sin was not disloyalty, but inability to control large numbers of malcontents within his 1.2 million member union. In early 1989, Education Secretary Manuel Bartlett offered the restive teachers wage and benefit increases that would boost their compensation 31 percent above its 1982 level even as the number of students per class had grown. Headed by the CNTE dissident faction of the union, some 500,000 demonstrators responded to this offer by taking to the streets of the capital. One of their favorite chants poked fun at Salinas's baldness: *"Dejemos el salón, por culpa del pelón."* ("It's Baldy's fault that we left the classroom.") For his failure to preserve intraunion discipline, Jonguitud's head rolled: First, the president's press office announced his retirement from the SNTE; then the media began divulging his assets, including a home with an eight-car garage in an elegant section of the city and another in Acapulco. Elba Esther Gordillo, a Salinas ally, assumed control of the union. Although much more dynamic than Guzmán Cabrera, she signed an agreement with the Education Ministry to decentralize the country's public school system, a move that—if implemented—would diminish the leverage of the national union by requiring individual locals to negotiate directly with state governments over salaries and working conditions.

As further evidence of his crackdown on trade unions, in 1991 Salinas deployed security forces to remove strikers from the Modelo Brewery, and took over the port facilities at Veracruz from the previously untouchable longshoremen's union. As a result of these actions, "the 'official' labor movement fell into a weaker political and economic position in the early 1990s than at any time since the late 1920s and early 1930s."[4]

To demonstrate even-handedness in swinging the *mano dura* (strong hand), the chief executive also took aim at venal businessmen. His prime target was Eduardo Legorreta Chauvet, the head of *Operadora de Bolsa*, the country's largest brokerage house. In February 1989, authorities charged Legorreta and three other executives with illegal activities during the 1987 crash of the Mexican stock market, which wiped out many small, middle-class investors overnight. Legorreta and his family boasted a name synonymous with banking in their country just as Rothschild is in Europe and Rockefeller in the United States. Moreover, they had backed Salinas's candidacy. Still, his arrest and imprisonment in the same penal facility that held La Quina transmitted the message that no one should hold himself above the law. His jailers released Legorreta after a year-and-a-half behind bars, while Hernández Galicia languished in the penitentiary's infirmary.

Broadened *Perestroika*[5]

Once he had established himself as national *jefe*, the youthful chief executive moved to broaden the economic opening begun during de la Madrid's *sexenio*. He sold the state-owned airline, telephone company, and steel mills; reprivatized the banking system that López Portillo had nationalized seven years before; launched a reform of *ejidos* to permit holders to sell, divide, or rent out their land to boost output; and reorganized Pemex along business lines.

Even though Salinas had yet to present a blueprint for linking his country with the global economic system, his enthusiasm for market principles and his readiness to pay interest on Mexico's mammoth external debt garnered him respect and trust among international lenders. Salinas's Mexico earned the distinction of becoming the first beneficiary of the 1989 Brady Plan, initiated by Washington to reduce Latin America's commercial bank obligations.

While pro-U.S. in outlook, Salinas sought to diversify the economic ties of his country, which historically had conducted more than two-thirds of its foreign trade with its northern neighbor. To this end, he jetted to Western Europe in early 1990 to meet with leaders of the twelve-nation European Community, now the European Union. Although then British Prime Minister Thatcher encouraged his efforts, the other hosts graciously conveyed a disheartening message: "We admire your market-oriented venture to open and modernize Mexico's hidebound economy, but Eastern Europe will be the target of our capital investment, finance, and commercial activities."

This polite rebuff reinforced Salinas's belief that Mexico must find other dynamic partners to avoid becoming a stagnant backwater as trading blocs emerged in Western Europe, in the Pacific Rim, and between the United States and Canada. Washington proved an obvious choice. Location, tradition, and a spider web of economic ties pointed Salinas northward. Also, he noted that the U.S.-Canada Free Trade Agreement of 1988 had stimulated bilateral trade and attracted investor attention to Canada. Although lukewarm to a U.S.-Mexico accord during his first year in office, Salinas reasoned that a bilateral deal might redound to his nation's benefit.

Thus, in February 1990, Salinas took the bold initiative of inquiring if President George Bush still favored the U.S.-Mexican free-trade pact that he had endorsed during his presidential campaign. A green light from Washington opened the door for negotiations. The Canadians, who felt compelled for the sake of national interests to become part of any continent-wide commercial arrangement, also joined the parleys. Fourteen months of tedious bargaining preceded the unveiling of a North American Free Trade Agreement. Ultimately approved by the U.S. Congress in November 1993, NAFTA gave rise to the largest market in the world, with some 370 million consumers producing more than $6.5 trillion in goods and services annually.

In addition to its geographic scope, this pact not only covers manufactured items but also agriculture, services, transportation, banking and investment, as well as such intellectual property as copyrights, trademarks, and computer software. Moreover, the "side deals," which constitute part of the free-trade package demanded by the Clinton administration, stipulated that the three signatories enforce their own environmental and labor statutes (i.e., child welfare, minimum wage, and workplace health and safety) lest they incur sanctions.

Ultimately, NAFTA required the rewriting of laws that covered twenty-two sectors of Mexico's economy. Amid such an upheaval, only 25 percent or so of the population might be expected to benefit from the pact in the short- to medium-term. How could Salinas maintain the support of—or, at least, avoid alienating—the majority of shantytown dwellers and poor campesinos for whom the accord was irrelevant?

The president astutely employed three tools to convey to the downtrodden that, profound change aside, he had not forgotten them even as he weakened labor unions, peasant organizations, and other corporatist structures. Specifically, he cultivated the armed forces, the Roman Catholic Church, and participants in the National Solidarity Program.

Salinas lost no opportunity to ingratiate himself with the military, many of whose members reportedly voted for opposition candidates in 1988.[6] He attended their ceremonies, praised their unflinching "loyalty" to the state, and satisfied most of their budgetary demands. In addition, he tended to discount the involvement of the armed forces in drug-trafficking, although so blatant and ubiquitous were criminal activities by sailors and their officers that the commander-in-chief had no choice but to replace Navy Secretary Mauricio Schleske Sánchez. Authorities discovered that the admiral owned two homes in Houston's Galleria section valued at $700,000—a sum equal to his total salary for forty years. Despite Schleske's and the navy's apparent involvement in narcotics trading, the president allowed the cabinet member to resign for "family reasons."

Nearly thirty months after moving out of Los Pinos and compelled by events to live as a political outcast in Ireland, Salinas continued to herald the military's prowess, possibly as part of an effort to revive his sagging political fortunes. In response to an article about alleged narcotrafficking involving his former private secretary and two generals, the ex-president dispatched a late-May 1997 message to the newspaper *Reforma*. He averred that: "The Mexican Army and Air Force are irreproachable institutions. Their honor shields them from slander."

While in office, Salinas sought improved relations with another traditional institution. During his campaign, he began a rapprochement with the Roman Catholic Church, long a bête noire of the PRI because of its intimacy with Porfirio Díaz in the last century and its opposition to the revolution that catalyzed the overthrow of the dictator. Salinas gained passage of legislation to amend the most objectionable anticlerical provisions of the 1917 Constitution. In addition, he renewed diplomatic relations with the Vatican, severed in 1857. And he warmly greeted Pope John Paul II when the pontiff visited Mexico in 1990. As a progressive, Salinas considered anticlericalism as outmoded as a droopy Pancho Villa mustache. Internationally, he wanted to convey an image of his nation as forward-looking and tolerant. And if the atheistic Soviet Union could send an ambassador to the Holy See as President Mikhail S. Gorbachev had done in late 1989, why could not an overwhelmingly Catholic nation like Mexico make peace with the Vatican? Like any shrewd politician, Salinas was also on the hunt for domestic allies. He realized the importance of traditional institutions to preserve national cohesion during a period of fundamental change. For example, the European countries that boasted the greatest stability as they evolved from conservative, agrarian control in the nineteenth century to liberal, middle-class leadership in the twentieth century were those nations that maintained the monarchy as a symbol of national identification, pride, and unity. Mexico had no king but it did boast a president deft at propitiating established institutions, while creating a new one that would reach out to the poor and dispossessed.

Salinas's most impressive contact with the masses came through the National Solidarity Program (Pronasol), commonly called "Solidarity." This antipoverty initiative germinated from interviews that Salinas carried out in the countryside while preparing his Harvard doctoral thesis in the mid-1970s. In analyzing the linkage between public spending and political support, his research convinced him that social give-away programs imposed by Mexico City bureaucrats generated sparse long-range backing for the regime if local leaders acquired no stake in the initiative and if they and their neighbors neither participated in identifying the needs nor made any contribution of their own to accomplishing desired goals.[7]

Chalco, a dried-up lake twenty-five miles from Mexico City where 500,000 people live in hovels connected by muddy, meandering roads strewn with garbage and sewage, represented Solidarity's biggest showcase and challenge. During his 1990 visit to Mexico, Pope John Paul II brought Pronasol to Chalco, where a chapel marks the spot on which he offered a mass for the multitudes, and where deracinated campesinos had flocked to the capital to seek work. The pontiff helped legitimate a project whose name evoked images of the democratization movement that the Polish pope backed in his home country. The government pumped enormous resources into providing clinics, kindergartens, utilities, potable water, free milk, and tortillas.

A community desiring to take part in the program could contact Pronasol directly. The agency would then dispatch a representative to an assembly open to all local residents. Eventually, the people elected a board of directors, set their priorities, and decided whether they would match the govern-ment's contribution to, say, a school building, either with pesos or their own labor—"sweat capital." Once, coordinator Benito A. Collantes Martínez ex-plained, "desk-bound bureaucrats in Mexico City made the decision whether an Indian village in faraway Oaxaca state needed a clinic, a school, or a paved road." Now, "local folks determine not only what they need most but how they will get it."

From his research, Salinas reasoned that grass-roots leadership "had been neglected as a policy instrument that enhances the efficiency of public works and augments support for the system." Indeed, paternalistic schemes gener-ated contempt for outside authorities, who often squandered or pocketed funds appropriated for development purposes. To avoid these rake-offs of the billions of dollars earmarked for Pronasol, Salinas stipulated that its person-nel work directly with community leaders, many of whom learned how to ferret out waste in budgets.

The disbursement of funds from Mexico City directly to beneficiaries meant the bypassing of state governors, local PRI officials, CTM stalwarts, and other traditional corporatist big shots, even though huge outlays poured into PRD strongholds. Chalco resident Rosa Díaz Carrillo recalls that when vouchers for free milk were handed out, she was told to vote for the PRI. Yet Salinas designed the initiative to foster a new-style corporatism—with a con-stituency of 100,000 local committees indebted to the chief executive who had improved their lives. As one analyst noted: "Pronasol point[ed] the way to a kind of neo-corporatism which could modernize clientelism by giving it roots not only in the trade unions, as in the past, but also at the territorial level and by giving political weight to the new social actors who have emerged from the neighbourhood associations."[8] Salinas devoted Thursdays and Fridays to cutting ribbons for projects of the heavily publicized Pronasol program. As the importance of his party's corporatist segments declined, he cultivated this new power base in case he decided to revamp the PRI—Sali-nas actively explored founding a "Solidarity Party"—or seek reelection as chief executive in 2000, perhaps with the wealth that his family accumulated during his administration. In the 1994 presidential contest, he planned to promote the candidacy of a loyalist and the cabinet member responsible for Solidarity.

Further Blows to Traditional Corporatism

While Pronasol tended to weaken the PRI's CNC in the countryside and the CTM in urban areas, other international and national trends dealt a blow to Mexico's historic corporatist labor movement. Like most countries, the ser-vice component of Mexico's economy grew faster than its agricultural and manufacturing counterparts. A combination of factors—anemic pay, low skill levels, high turnover, decentralization, and the predominance of young people—make it especially difficult to unionize this sector. For its part, the CTM has shown little interest in enlisting workers in this area, possibly fearing that service employees might rebel against authoritarian rule if brought into the official fold.

Similarly, Fidel Velázquez devoted few resources to recruiting employees in the 2,000 *maquiladora* assembly plants concentrated just south of the border with the United States. The explanations for failure to mount organizing activities in the service arena generally apply to *maquiladoras*. In addition, most of the factory workers are young women with no union background, who may have children or parents to support, and a social life to pursue. As a result, they perceive little or no advantage to affiliating with and paying dues to a labor organization. Many such employees come from the countryside, don't know their rights, hesitate to stand up to macho male bosses, or fear being fired. "Others work in small shops or factories which have an ephemeral existence; Mexican workers call them *golondrinas* or swallows because they may fly away at any moment."[9]

The harsh stands of cabinet members also weakened the CTM. Labor Secretary Farell proved a formidable bargainer on trade-union issues. Less forbidding personally, but still a powerful force to be reckoned with, was Finance Secretary Pedro Aspe. In early 1990, for example, Aspe arranged to have lunch with Agipito González Cavazos, the labor movement's grizzled patriarch in Matamoros and a foe of the Salinas modernization agenda. After a long, chummy lunch, the treasury official said, "Don Agipito, unlike youngsters nowadays, you probably began working when you were 15 or 16."

"Hombre, I started when I was 13!" grunted the swag-bellied leader.

"Let's see," said the suddenly serious Aspe, "you are now 75; Why then hasn't your name ever appeared on the tax register?" Upon the cabinet member's advice, González Cavazos temporarily retired rather than join La Quina in the Reclusorio Oriente.

González Cavazos, Don Fidel, and Hernández Galicia came to power in a different age, when money, muscle, and mastery of the political game brought prestige, power, and positions of public trust. Under Salinas, the PRI sought to recast its image. After all, critics of NAFTA, an initiative deemed crucial to consolidating the local *perestroika*, excoriated the accord as a "pact with a dictatorship." U.S. Senator Daniel Patrick Moynihan even hurled the epithet "Leninist" at the Mexican state. To counter such invective, Salinas passèd the word to the PRI to nominate candidates who could win on their merits, without recourse to vote-rigging alchemists. Some twenty-two labor candidates had suffered defeat in 1988, including Mexico City's multimillionaire union sachem Gamboa Pascoe, who lost a bid for the Senate to PRD candidates. As a sop to organized labor, Salinas had approved Emilio M. González, 75, one of six CTM alternate secretaries-general, as Senate majority leader. However, the chief executive directed PRI President Luis Donaldo Colosio Murieta to seek out well-educated and articulate men and women who could impress voters on the hustings and through the media. This innovation in recruitment advantaged the CNOP at the expense of the party's labor and peasant components, which could offer few attractive candidates. As a result, union representation in the Chamber of Deputies and the Senate continued to decline as popular sector members attained 70 percent of nominations.

The advanced age of Don Fidel, who turned 89 four months after Salinas took office, contributed to the CTM's debilitation. Velázquez cast a jaundiced eye on tying salary levels to higher productivity and greater quality control—elements regarded as crucial to modernizing Mexico's economy. The technocratic cabinet members reacted to the octogenarian's intractability by cultivating other labor leaders in tune with Salinas's economic strategy. This search took them outside Vallarta 8, the bunker-like, seven-story CTM headquarters overlooking the Monument to the Revolution, because Velázquez had hand-picked the confederation's second- and third-echelon officials, and none was inclined to break with the organization's top dog, especially when he spent most of his time snarling and baring his teeth.

Hernández Juárez of the Telephone Workers (STRM) emerged as the most attractive new trade-union chief. In 1977, the youthful leader took control of the STRM's executive committee. Since then, his 51,750 members have continually reelected him to the union's main post. He gained national prominence when Salinas privatized the state-owned telephone company (Telmex), execrated for featherbedding and abominable service. Rather than fulminate against the sell-off, Hernández Juárez—encouraged by Los Pinos—engaged Telmex in protracted negotiations. The talks spawned an accord whereby the union took advantage of a low-interest government loan to purchase 4.4 percent of the company's equity, and management pledged to preserve most union jobs. The explosion in price of Telmex stock converted the Telephone Workers from an impecunious to an immensely prosperous organization, which provides outstanding benefits for its workers.

For its part, the STRM accepted more flexible work rules and agreed to tie salary increases to improved output and enhanced quality of service. Salinas identified the 1989 pact as "a model of successful worker-management cooperation (*concertación*)," in the words of Mexico expert Kevin J. Middlebrook.[10]

Even though a member of the Labor Congress, the STRM has remained outside the hidebound CTM. In 1990, Hernández Juárez sought to challenge Don Fidel's confederation by forming his own labor body, the Federation of Goods and Services Unions or FESEBES. Under Hernández Juárez's watchful eye, FESEBES aggressively targeted industries with well-educated workers attentive to the imperatives of quality, productivity, training, cutting-edge technology, and worker involvement in decision making if Mexico were ever to resume sustained economic growth. During its first six years of existence, FESEBES signed up eight affiliates in the transportation, electric-power generation, and film and television sectors. Hernández Juárez also recognized the importance of recruiting younger workers, especially women, employed either in retail establishments or in *maquiladoras.*

Hernández Juárez became Salinas's fair-haired boy in the union movement when the STRM leader helped resolve a conflict that pitted rank-and-file auto workers against their leaders and Volkswagen's management at the company's Puebla plant. The new pro-industry contract allowed the German automaker substantially more flexibility in organizing production, allocating workers among different departments, and hiring and firing employees.

Hernández Juárez won accolades for his labor diplomacy. The Volkswagen union demonstrated its appreciation by bringing its 10,000 members into FESEBES. The Labor Ministry followed suit by granting FESEBES official registration—a status that Velázquez had blocked for more than two years as Leonardo "La Güera" Rodríguez Alcaine, a tough-as-nails aspirant for the CTM throne, slammed Hernández Juárez and his comrades as "witches' apprentices." In 1993, Salinas invited the *telefonista* to observe the May 1 Labor Day parade next to him from the presidential balcony, a spot customarily reserved for Don Fidel.

Hernández Juárez has evinced skill in coalition building. His most powerful comrade was then Esther Gordillo, 51, who followed Jonguitud as head of the SNTE and another acutely ambitious and capable labor leader and PRI activist. Other allies include Pedro B. Castillo (SME Electrical Workers), Enrique A. Aguilar Borrego (Bank Workers), and Antonio Rosado García (Social Security Employees).

Salinas, Farell, and Mexico City Mayor Manuel Camacho actively courted Hernández Juárez whose relations with Don Fidel soured as the STRM secretary-general garnered more stature and publicity. Still, FESEBES's membership—a mere 115,300—paled in comparison to the several million men and women who belong to CTM affiliates. Thus, as the August 1994 presidential election approached, Salinas began to hold Hernández Juárez at arm's length while he opportunistically embraced Don Fidel, importuning him to mobilize the CTM faithful behind PRI nominee Ernesto Zedillo. Although useful for symbolic purposes, the veteran labor leader saw his influence plummet. He had evolved from initiating policies, to enjoying a veto over them, to being advised in advance of their implementation, to reading about them in newspapers.

Velázquez and his colleagues paid lip service to backing the ruling party's standard-bearer, but labor leaders could stir little enthusiasm for another Ivy-League-educated Ph.D. whose passion for market-focused reforms would threaten the jobs of even more working people. In the process, they revealed their declining influence as players in the Mexican political game.

While cultivating new labor leaders constituted a direct attack on old-guard corporatists, Salinas employed more oblique methods to reduce their power. At his behest, the PRI's fourteenth assembly in 1990 diminished the sectors' representation to only one-fifth of the 8,600 voting delegates, cut the number of secretariats within the National Executive Committee to promote efficiency, and made affiliation with the party "individual and free." The last item meant that trade unionists and campesinos could join the party as individuals, not collectively through their CTM- or CNC-linked organization as had been the case since Lázaro Cárdenas's time. In addition, the assembly created a National Political Council and thirty-two state-level councils to direct the party; both bodies enhanced the decision-making weight of well-educated, middle-class *priístas* and diminished that of the corporatists.

Furthermore, the delegates acted to democratize candidate selection in accord with Salinas's desire to win elections honestly rather than falsifying the outcome—a practice that besmirched Mexico's image in the United States. Proponents of change recommended *consultas a la base*, which would require prospective candidates (except for the presidency) to muster the backing of directive bodies of organizations or a certain percentage of voters at the district level to obtain the party's nomination. These reforms contributed to a fall in sectoral standard-bearers: The complement of labor nominees dropped from 75 (1988) to 54 (1991); the peasant nominees fell from 58 to 48 during the same period. "These reductions made way for an increase in the number of candidates from the popular sector, particularly those in the federal and state governments tied to the Salinas team and members of the local business community."[11]

Two years later at its fifteenth assembly, PRI reformists instituted additional changes. Salinas had called for a "refounding" of the party based on his program of "social liberalism." This ideology, which stood in contrast to the "revolutionary nationalism" espoused by traditionalists, would provide an alternative to state capital and libertarianism. The "solidaristic state" would encourage private initiative, while combating monopolies and strengthening the safety net protecting the disadvantaged in society. The restructuring entailed substituting the party's three traditional sectors with the Popular Territorial Movement (MPT), the National Citizens Front (FNC), and Union Movement (MS), and the Worker-Peasant Pact (POC).

As "the political and social arm of the party," the MPT would organize networks among shantytown residents, Solidarity committees, and other grass-roots constituencies. For its part, the FNC would reach out to professionals, environmentalists, civic associations, and similar groups as part of "a program of political attention to the middle classes of the country." Party President Genaro Borrego Estrada envisaged MS as incorporating FESEBES and other new trade-union movements into the PRI's traditional labor sector. "The idea," according to Borrego, "is to create it without affecting or originating confrontations with the Labor Congress and the strong leadership of Fidel Velázquez."[12] Finally, the Worker-Peasant Pact would spawn new enterprises involving workers and campesinos.

The inertia of habitual chicanery combined with the animus of the corporatists to frustrate these reforms. Party leaders selected "unity candidates" rather than involve the rank-and-file in nominations. Even when the party president encouraged a *consulta a la base* in the Colima gubernatorial election in 1991, the experiment boomeranged. Used to practicing electoral trickery, the unsuccessful PRI contender for the nomination cried "fraud" after losing the intraparty face-off. Thus, charges of foul play, which usually flooded the air after the general election, arose earlier in the electoral season and spurred party disunity. Decisions by the hierarchy gave rise to 90 percent of the legislative candidates in 1991 and the vast majority of the twelve gubernatorial nominees in 1992. "Even the official policy of recognizing dissident currents in the party was overshadowed by the practice of quieting them and allowing them no input into party affairs."[13] The sectors led by Don Fidel reasserted themselves even more at the 1993 party assembly. Not only did they succeed in reversing many of the earlier changes, they spearheaded the replacement of reformer Borrego with Fernando Ortiz Arana, 49, a legislative leader from Querétaro state with links to the party's young militants who privately manifest skepticism or downright opposition to a political opening.

The old guard's brief rebound aside, Salinas had managed to disorient the PRI with his on-again, off-again reforms, which generated a profound identity crisis within the party. The president exacerbated the confusion with overtures to long-standing enemies of the revolutionary family. He had instigated a rapprochement with the hated Roman Catholic Church; he was negotiating a pact with the aggressive *gringos* that would integrate the Mexican and U.S. economies; and, perhaps worst of all, he forged an entente with the National Action Party, long the PRI's political nemesis.

Salinas's flirtation with the PAN began early in his administration. In August 1989, he recognized the defeat of his party's nominee at the hands of *panista* Ernesto Ruffo Appel in Baja California, marking the first time that an opposition candidate had captured a governorship since Calles instituted the ruling party sixty years earlier. In 1990, the president paved the way for another PAN stalwart, Carlos Medina Plascencia, to take over the Guanajuato statehouse in lieu of a PRI candidate whose triumph excited charges of fraud. Two years later, the president gave his blessing to the victory of Barrio Terrazas in Chihuahua, exactly six years after the businessman-turned-PAN candidate had lost the governorship amid brazen PRI-engineered fraud. All told, by the time Salinas left office, 12.8 million Mexicans constituting 15.8 percent of the national population, lived under PAN-controlled state or local governments.

Several reasons underlay Salinas's cultivation of a party long detested by the PRI. First, the chief executive, for whom high-tech computer thievery may have served as his key to victory, realized the need to brighten his country's image in the United States. Indeed, approval of NAFTA hung in the balance until a year before Salinas left office. What could be a more artful public relations gambit than allowing an opposition party to capture the governorship of a major state contiguous to San Diego? Besides, stealing the Baja California contest would have sparked sit-ins, demonstrations, bridge blockages, and other protests in a large state that receives widespread attention from the American media. Second, Salinas needed some non-PRI votes to gain congressional approval of his domestic program. He correctly perceived that center-right, pro-business National Action offered the best ally on such controversial measures as revising the electoral laws, selling off state companies, reforming the *ejido*, and reestablishing relations with the Roman Catholic Church. Many of these policies were abhorrent to the *ex-priístas* running the PRD, who had cut their political teeth on statism, anticlericalism, and corporatism.

Third, the PAN's dominant faction looked favorably on political *concertación* as a means to win more elections and broaden the party's base—considerations that augured well for their fulfilling agreements entered into with the revolutionary party. In fact, the leadership's decision to collaborate with Salinas spurred the exodus of several prominent figures in the party's conservative Catholic wing that deeply distrusted the PRI.[14] On the other hand, feuds over personalities, ideology, and strategy convulsed the Democratic Revolutionary Party (PRD), which often resembled a Mideast bazaar more than a coherent political organization.

Fourth, the ever more diverse and pragmatic PAN National Executive Committee comprehended that alliances on issues of concern to it were crucial to advancing its cause. Although not naive about the pitfalls of making common cause with the PRI, it loathed the PRD, comprised of the PAN's two historic enemies: the nationalists who had bolted the PRI and the old left.

Finally, the chief executive regarded the PAN as far less of a threat than the PRD whose foremost leader, Cuauhtémoc Cárdenas, had given the PRI the scare of its political life in 1988. Salinas and his advisors reasoned that the left might attract a large number of followers, particularly during the economic and social dislocations occasioned by NAFTA. In contrast, they perceived that the middle-class PAN, with little organized support outside urban areas, would never amass more than 20 to 25 percent of the vote nationwide to constitute a serious challenge to the PRI. As it turned out, both Salinas and Cárdenas overestimated the left's strength at least in the short- to medium-run. Many of the votes received by the five-party FDN in 1988 were cast against the PRI rather than in favor of Cárdenas and the nationalist-statist platform on which he stood. Cárdenas had hoped that militants from the five organizations that lined up behind his presidential candidacy would join the PRD. In fact, the right-of-center PARM and the opportunistic Party of the Cardenist Front for National Reconstruction (PFCRN)—traditional *"paleros"* or PRI satellites—insisted on maintaining their autonomy and identity. Further, Salinas's virulent hostility to the PRD leadership, many of whom had forged the Democratic Current in 1986, militated against cooperation with his administration.

While conciliatory toward the PAN, Salinas turned heaven and earth to cripple the PRD. He despised its leaders, feared its proselytizing potential, and deplored its shrill opposition to economic liberalization. Thus, he used the Solidarity program to lessen its grass-roots appeal, unleashed *alquimistas* against PRD candidates, and coopted some of the party's most promising intellectuals. The PRD reported that upwards of 300 members were killed under peculiar circumstances during the first five years of Salinas's tenure.

PRI stalwarts applauded this intransigence toward the PRD, but they, as well as moderate *priístas*, were aghast at Salinas's concession of offices that their candidates had actually won, according to observers and public-opinion polls. Several examples illustrate this point. On August 18, 1991, former Mexico City Mayor Aguirre Velázquez apparently captured a majority of votes to attain the governorship of his native state of Guanajuato in a three-way race sullied by charges of irregularities. Enraged over the outcome on election day, runner-up Vicente Fox Quesada of the PAN fomented a "second round"—not of voting but of agitation, designed to win through demonstrations what could not be achieved at the ballot box. "It has been a terrible fraud," he told a reporter. "We are going out to the streets to fight." Escalating protests and incessant charges of vote-tampering prompted Salinas, through Government Secretary Fernando Gutiérrez Barrios, a fierce dinosaur, to phone Aguirre Velázquez. "I have bad news," the cabinet member told the governor-elect, "the president wants you to step aside. Please come to Los Pinos." Aguirre Velázquez replied that his removal was a "bad idea," that his experience in Mexico City would be useful in Guanajuato, that he had no political ambitious beyond the governorship, and that he had prevailed in the election. He even offered to have a "public count of the votes in the main square of León," the state capital.

Gutiérrez Barrios persisted, saying that "because of public relations in Mexico and abroad—as well as promises to the PAN—he should step down."[15] Although Aguirre Velázquez did not meet with Salinas, he obeyed and became the first living governor-elect to fail to take the oath of office. The jettisoned *priísta* justified his action on the grounds that: "The threat of violence and intolerance are lurking over Guanajuato. We cannot let the great democratic and constructive thrust that opened new horizons for the people of Guanajuato . . . be cut short." The thickset *bon vivant* went on to accuse Fox of "trying to seize, through blackmail and violence, a government that he knows he has not won through votes." He also lambasted the losing

PRD candidate Muñoz Ledo for "sowing distrust and terror within this process and seeking only to gain personal political benefits."

In Aguirre Velázquez's place, Salinas installed as "interim" governor Medina, a moderate *panista* and mayor of León, in a move to marginalize the populist, hard-charging Fox who might have used the governorship as a springboard for a presidential candidacy. Local PRI militants protested the displacement of their nominee by occupying seven mayors' offices in the state. They vented their spleen on the president, "Salinas, listen: we are struggling for the sovereignty of Guanajuato; we reject the imposition [of Medina]." Signs and placards reiterated the message: "*¡El pueblo votó, Salinas negoció!*" ("The people voted and Salinas negotiated"!) Ultimately, a delegation of enraged party activists met with Gutiérrez Barrios to request that Aguirre Velázquez's victory be respected. These demands fell on deaf ears.

Although allowed to occupy the governorship of San Luis Potosí for two weeks, Fausto Zapata suffered the same fate as Aguirre in September 1991. Salvador Nava, the rival of the PRI governor, galvanized a coalition embracing conservative members of the PAN and leftists within the PRD to contend that Zapata owed his victory to fraud. Rather than make their charges to PRI-controlled state electoral authorities, they extemporaneously presented them to Salinas, PRI President Colosio, and Government Secretary Gutiérrez Barrios on the day of Zapata's inauguration. Meanwhile, Nava's forces continued their noisy protests outside the state's government palace. On October 9, Salinas summoned Zapata to Mexico City; the next day, the governor informed the state legislature of his "unilateral decision" to resign—with Gonzalo Martínez Corbalá, a veteran of the PRI's left wing and Salinas's political mentor taking over until new elections could be held. Much to the dismay of party loyalists who had rejected the notion that the state was "ungovernable" and reiterated their "faith" in Zapata, the chief executive sought another sacrificial lamb to demonstrate his commitment to democracy. "Tell us how to explain this to our people," groused América Wong, a PRI leader in the city of San Luis Potosí, "how are we going to tell them that their vote no longer counts, that all was a hoax (*vacilada*), that they were just pulling our leg."

Equally as disheartening to PRI regulars was the treatment suffered by Eduardo Villaseñor Peña, the party's candidate for governor of the western state of Michoacán in mid-1992. Although a 46-year-old pork and banking millionaire, the jowly Villaseñor's lack of a university education and plodding oratory seemed to be drawbacks as he faced an attractive, seasoned opponent from the PRD. But PRI-sponsored polls conducted early in the year found that *michoacanos* were fed up with professional politicians and wanted just such an "outsider" as their state's next chief executive. The selection of Villaseñor reaffirmed Salinas's courtship of the business community, as well as his appeals to the PAN, which Villaseñor's father had helped found. In addition,

Villaseñor's wealth and access to donations from businessmen obviated the need for the covert injection of funds into his campaign accounts, which he promised to make public after the race.

Villaseñor emerged from the protracted campaign with 53 percent of the ballots cast to bury his PRD opponent (36 percent)—a Cárdenas protégé—and three also-rans. Even before the results were broadcast, the PRD began crying foul despite the finding of every major poll—including those published in the highly respected *El Norte* newspaper and *Este País* magazine—predicting a PRI landslide.

Failing to win on election day, the PRD launched the now-*de rigueur* "second round" of marches, demonstrations, and sit-ins in government offices in Morelia, the state capital. Such civil disobedience did not prevent Salinas's flying in to administer the oath of office to Villaseñor in mid-September, even though PRD protesters prevented the businessman-turned-politician from entering his executive office. As tensions rose in the state, at least six PRD members died amid suspicious conditions. Three weeks later, however, the president yanked the rug out from under the freshly minted state executive. At the chief executive's behest, Villaseñor requested a "leave of absence," paving the way for the president to name a PRI old hand as interim governor. Apparently, the president wanted to avoid facing the stark choice between political chaos and the use of force because of the consequences of either outcome for the NAFTA debate. Indeed, the day after Villaseñor stepped aside, Salinas traveled to San Antonio to join President Bush and Canadian Prime Minister Brian Mulroney as their trade ministers initialed the final text of the commercial agreement. Still, the episode left the local PRI flabbergasted. "Why even nominate candidates if Mexico City's going to boot them after they win fair and square," was the complaint that bubbled through the local party headquarters. Others groused about "rewarding" the opposition's recourse to antidemocratic behavior. Borrego said that "we do not share Eduardo Villaseñor's personal decision [to step down], although we respect and understand his wanting to guarantee public peace and preserve a full state of law."

All told, Salinas replaced sixteen governors, the most in modern memory. In several cases, he moved incumbents to the cabinet or other important posts. More often, he ousted individuals because of political expedience or their inability to maintain order in their states. Table 4.1 compares Salinas's actions to those of his predecessors.

1994 Presidential Campaign

Salinas sought to "modernize" the electoral laws in response to a guerrilla movement in Chiapas and in anticipation of the 1994 presidential contests. In October 1990, the Congress passed comprehensive legislation that estab-

Table 4.1*   Governors Removed by Presidents,
              1934–1997

*Sources: George Philip, *The Presidency in Mexican
Politics* (New York: St. Martin's Press,
1992); and Roderic Ai Camp, *Mexican
Political Biographies 1935–1993* (Austin:
University of Texas Press, 1995).

Administration	No. of Governors Removed
Cárdenas (1934–40)	15
Avila Camacho (1940–46)	2
Miguel Alemán (1946–52)	9
Ruiz Cortines (1952–58)	4
López Mateos (1958–64)	6
Díaz Ordaz (1964–70)	5
Echeverría (1970–76)	5
López Portillo (1976–82)	1
De la Madrid (1982–88)	2
Salinas (1988–94)	16
Zedillo (1994–present)	2

lished the semiautonomous Federal Electoral Institute (IFE) to conduct all federal elections. The IFE completely revised the voter registration list, undertook a vigorous registration campaign, and trained teams of private electoral observers for all voting sites. Such observers could collect and count ballots and immediately disseminate election results. The new law also created a Federal Electoral Tribunal (TFE) to hear complaints of voting irregularities. The mid-1991 congressional elections, the first held under the 1990 reform, appeared cleaner than previous contests. Turnout, which reached only 50 percent three years before, rose to 65.3 percent.

Still, continued cries of foul play and the increasing use of post-election protests gave rise to even more changes. Congress created a new body, the IFE's General Council, which would have the final say over federal legislative elections. It also eliminated the so-called governability clause whereby previously the party obtaining 35 percent of the national vote in deputy elections was guaranteed a majority in the Chamber of Deputies. Under no circumstances would one party be allowed to hold more than 315 seats in the lower house, ten short of the number required to approve a constitutional change—a fact important to Salinas's overtures to the PAN. The number of Senate seats per state was expanded from two to four, with the runner-up party in each state ensured one of those seats. The opposition, which then held only three of sixty-four seats, could count on at least a quarter of the 128 seats in the enlarged upper house. Other reforms included imposing spending limits on candidates for all offices, ensuring equal access for all parties to commercial media, and abolishing—effective December 1999—the constitutional provision that both parents of presidential candidates must have been born in Mexico.

In 1994, the country witnessed still more changes as the PRI, PAN, and PRD signed the Pact for Peace, Justice, and Democracy. Among the innovations were the requirement that six citizen councillors with no party affiliation sit on the IFE's twelve-member General Council; the authorization of observers and "international visitors" to monitor the August 1994 elections; the nationwide use of ballot boxes that are transparent and voting booths that guarantee privacy; and a renewed commitment to issue counterfeit-proof voter cards to all eligible citizens.

Such changes notwithstanding, Salinas employed the customary *dedazo* to select the first PRI candidate who would seek the presidency under the new rules. His choice was the mustachioed Colosio, 43, a native of the small town of Magdalena de Kino, Sonora, a hour-and-a-half drive from the U.S. border. In contrast to Salinas, de la Madrid, and every other Mexican president since 1970, Colosio had fought in the trenches of elective politics before seeking the presidency, having served in the Chamber of Deputies and the Senate. In fact, he won his Senate seat while managing Salinas's presidential campaign. Further, he had distinguished himself as head of the PRI where he quietly emerged as a combination ideological architect, gatekeeper, drill sergeant, and envoy to other parties. He diminished the cloud over Salinas's election by leading the governing party to a convincing victory in the 1991 legislative contests. Next, the extroverted Colosio, who had previous experience in SPP, became secretary of urban development and ecology in 1992 and, with the name change of the ministry, secretary of social development. In this cabinet post, he oversaw the extremely popular and emphatically political Solidarity initiative. While Salinas would be cutting ribbons to inaugurate new projects and exchanging *abrazos* with gap-toothed peasants, Colosio would stand or sit among the people, forging contacts with community leaders who could assist in his race for Los Pinos. Of course, Salinas's early and emphatic endorsement diminished the imperative for Colosio to assemble a large team. The deft politician, who also held an M.A. in regional planning from the University of Pennsylvania, strongly backed Salinas's market-oriented reforms. Young, dynamic, fun-loving, attractive, sentimental, cosmopolitan, politically experienced, and possessed of strong supporters, Colosio won praise as a leader who could implement the sweeping provisions of NAFTA while managing the social and political turmoil implicit in root-and-branch economic reform.

As 1993 drew to a close, Salinas basked in his accomplishments. During the previous five years, he had rekindled economic growth, slashed inflation, sold off hundreds of state firms, attracted billions of dollars in private investment, and activated market forces in a once-suffocating statist economy. He had laid the foundation for the next chief executive to expand political pluralism and competition. Two factors seemed to ensure that the country would remain on the course that he had charted: the signing of NAFTA and the selection of Colosio. The president was "batting a thousand," according to Federico Estévez, an astute Mexico City professor.

Indeed, the incumbent seemed to be doing better than the heir apparent who, upon being tapped for the nomination, found himself upstaged by Manuel Camacho Solís. Rather than endorsing Salinas's choice as the rules of the game required, the spurned Mexico City mayor expressed disappointment and said, "I had hoped for the nomination"—a statement that suggested he would continue to pursue the presidency. Camacho Solís also conveyed his disappointment by resigning as Mexico City's mayor. Nevertheless, to avoid reprisals against him and his team, the ambitious politician agreed to an "institutional" solution. He entered the cabinet as foreign secretary: This post kept him on the PRI/Salinas team, but provided a refuge from involvement in domestic politics in general and Colosio's campaign in particular.

1994 and the Looming Crisis

Early in 1994, Salinas became the target of a rebel uprising that further eclipsed Colosio's bid for the presidency. On January 1, the Zapatista National Liberation Army (EZLN), led by the ski-masked Subcomandante Marcos and several hundred Indian rebels, sprang to the public's eye. They seized San Cristóbal de las Casas and a half-dozen other towns in the river-rich, dirt-poor southern state of Chiapas, which lies cheek-by-jowl with Guatemala. In their "Declaration of the Lacandona Jungle," the insurgents asserted:

> We are the product of 500 years of struggle . . . . But today we say, enough! We are the heirs of the true forgers of our nationality; we the dispossessed are millions and we call on all our brothers to join this call as the only way to avoid dying of hunger under the insatiable ambition of a dictatorship of more than 70 years headed by a clique of traitors . . . .[16]

At first Salinas dispatched the army to suppress the EZLN, most of whose poorly armed soldiers were Mayan Indians. Press reports put the number of dead in the twelve days of fighting at 150. The Zapatistas claimed to have killed at least twenty-seven army troops, while suffering nine deaths and twelve comrades lost in action.

The government soon shifted to the political arena. It fired the local director of state police and prisons, who was linked to kidnappings arising from Chiapan land conflicts that had ignited the uprising. The power-hungry

Camacho Solís immediately took advantage of the rebellion. He informed Salinas that, as foreign secretary, he could not endorse a crack-down on the insurgents—a position that, if publicized, could have embarrassed Los Pinos by suggesting disunity in the government. The rebuffed presidential candidate also importuned the chief executive to give him a role in Chiapas. In late January, Salinas, whom Camacho Solís had over a barrel, agreed to shift his former confidant from foreign secretary to "peace commissioner." This highly visible position kept alive his ambition either to supplant the PRI nominee or pursue the presidency under another party's banner.

Upon assuming his new responsibilities, Camacho Solís emphasized that the PRI and seven other parties had endorsed a package of electoral reforms that would address many of the rebels' grievances. These measures created an independent authority to supervise campaigns and elections, prohibited the use of government resources by any party, and established an office to prosecute "electoral crimes." The proposals also stipulated fair treatment of all parties by the Mexican media, the recognition of the role of domestic and foreign observers in the August national elections, and the reduction of graft and sleaze in political campaigns. Nevertheless, the EZLN remained unconvinced, while opposition parties castigated the PRI for breaking previous pledges to halt political fraud and abuse. "It is a daily struggle of political pressure to break down this monolithic political system," stated PAN leader Cecilia Romero.

Salinas, to his credit, spurned a scorched-earth policy in Chiapas in favor of negotiations. He realized that the army would have difficulty quelling the rebels in a state partly blanketed by a rain forest. U.S. Ambassador James R. Jones, who drew on his experience as chief-of-staff in the Johnson White House in the late 1960s, strongly advised against military action to quell a grass-roots uprising. Slaughtering peasants and EZLN soldiers, he argued, would evoke bitter memories of Vietnam and harm Mexico's image abroad, while generating sympathy for the insurgents at home. Worse still, protracted conflict would scare off more parochial American investors, who had just begun to comprehend the opportunities offered by Mexico.

The flamboyant Zapatistas commanded worldwide attention. After the five-year run of the uncharismatic Salinas—known for his type-A personality—and a supporting cast of Ivy League economists, planners, and other number-crunching technocrats, Marcos drew the press to Chiapas with the allure of secret rendezvous, blindfolds, multiple vehicle transfers, and poems as passwords. The *San Francisco Chronicle, Der Spiegel, Cambio 16, Le Figaro, Vanity Fair, 60 Minutes,* and scores of other media dispatched journalists to tap into the romance of the world's "first postmodern guerrilla leader," as the *New York Times* described him. At the same time, Marcos relied heavily on the Internet to transmit EZLN pronouncements and his own poetic musings.

Theatrical flourishes aside, Marcos acquitted himself as much a realist as a romantic. He disclaimed pursuit of a military victory, comprehending that his guerrilla troupe could not defeat government troops that quickly encircled them. "No, the political system can't be the product of war," he averred. Rather, "the purpose of war is to open up space in the political arena so that people can really have a choice."

Marcos quickly acquired the status of a folk hero on university campuses, in shantytowns, and in coffee houses. Even well-heeled cosmopolites acclaimed Marcos and his entourage. During a performance of Verdi's potently political *Nabuco*, an excited aficionado in the second balcony of the Bellas Artes auditorium shouted at the top of his lungs, "¡Qué Vivan los Zapatistas!" From below, the elegantly coiffed and handsomely dressed audience responded, "¡Qué Vivan!"[17]

Salinas, through his special negotiator, tried to strike a deal with the EZLN in discussions that dragged on during 1994, and then continued during the Zedillo administration. As these talks progressed, it became clear that the guerrillas represented a thorn in the side but not a dagger in the heart of the Mexican regime. Several factors distinguished Chiapas from other areas of the nation: the dense concentration of Indians, the presence of tens of thousands of Guatemalan immigrants, the grinding poverty, the tradition of egregiously crooked political leadership, and the endorsement of the rebellion by Samuel Ruiz García, the outspoken bishop of San Cristóbal.

Ruiz, Mexico's most prominent devotee of Liberation Theology, led a group of Catholics striving to empower the poor to face poverty, injustice, and violence. Rather than relying on prayer, charity, and other traditional means to oppose misery and inequality, some liberation theologians emphasize political action—even violence—to change elite-manipulated political, social, and economic systems that exploited the "have nots." Since 1960, Bishop Ruiz had sought to raise the consciousness of both the seminarians who trained in his diocese and the indigenous population of Chiapas. While he admitted to hailing from outside of the state, Subcomandante Marcos betrayed the influence of Liberation Theology in his speeches and writings. In August 1995 the Vatican exhibited its displeasure with the 71-year-old Ruiz by naming a coadjutor bishop to take over his most important functions. The newcomer wound up defending the poor, inveighing against government policies, and more often than not aligning himself with Ruiz.

Marcos and his players enjoyed only a few months in the limelight. The army surrounded their rain-forest enclave. The government renounced repression for protracted parleys conducted by—in the subcomandante's words—a regime backed by "the same hard-liners who subterraneously encourage sabotage of the peace process by the big land owners and businessmen." And EZLN enthusiasts in Mexico City cafes shifted their gaze from the Lacondona to their Visa cards when interest rates soared to 90 percent amid a 6.9 percent fall in gross domestic product and 55 percent inflation in 1995. To diminish his appeal, the government identified Marcos as Rafael Sebastián Guillén Vicente, 37, a prize-winning sociology student and son of an upper-middle-class proprietor of furniture stores in Tampico. By early 1996, *"el Sub"* and his company voiced their readiness to abandon guerrilla theatrics for the more legitimate stage of traditional politics, even as Salinas's successor, Ernesto Zedillo Ponce de León, poured huge quantities of aid into Chiapas. Yet negotiators for the two sides had failed to strike a deal by mid-1997.

Just as the Chiapan situation began to cool, other events complicated the political picture. In mid-March 1994, kidnappers seized Alfredo Harp Helú, one of the country's wealthiest businessmen. Then on March 23, Mario Aburto Martínez, a 23-year-old mechanic, allegedly fired two bullets into Colosio's head and abdomen. This act horrified a nation unaccustomed to the murder of national politicians. The assassination left Salinas shaken and sparked a highly publicized donnybrook within the PRI to choose Colosio's successor. After a bitter four-day struggle, Salinas and reformers within the ruling party triumphed over old-line stalwarts. The result was the selection of the Yale-trained Zedillo, a brainy, market-oriented economist who in two cabinet posts had enthusiastically impelled the government's liberalization program and decentralized a woefully inadequate educational system. Even though born into a lower-middle-class family, he displayed none of the common touch cultivated by the martyred Colosio. He seemed much more relaxed while debating exchange rates with bankers and policy wonks than slapping backs in union halls. Zedillo had served as the titular head of Colosio's campaign; however, the candidate's confidants devised strategy, while professional politicians attended to tactics. As the PRI's presidential quest resumed with a new standard-bearer, the Bolsa, Mexico's jittery stock market, fell 14 percent below its January 1 level.

The technocratic Zedillo took to campaigning like a fish to hot sand. He appeared wooden and self-conscious when emphasizing the need to broaden Mexico's economic liberalization and continue the Solidarity program launched by Salinas. In addition, he seemed ill at ease when promising to achieve true separation of powers in a system where judges and legislators often acted like lapdogs of *señor presidente*.

In May 1994, PAN candidate Diego Fernández de Cevallos—called "Jefe Diego" or Sir Diego because of his prominence and haughty bearing as leader of his party's legislative faction[18]—took advantage of his own oratorical prowess to savage Zedillo and PRD nominee Cárdenas in a televised debate—the first in Mexican history—that attracted 38 million viewers. Even as he subscribed to many of the PRI's economic proposals—the PAN rode high on the free-enterprise express before the PRI jumped aboard—Fernán-

Table 4.2   Distribution of Income in Mexico by Deciles

Source: Instituto Nacional de Estadística, Geografía e Informática (1994);
published in *El Financiero*, May 3, 1997, p. 38.

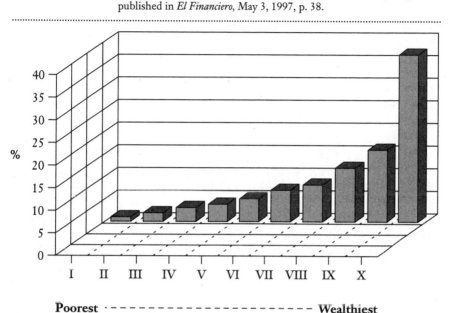

dez de Cevallos flailed the brainy Zedillo for the PRI's legacy of vote-stealing
and authoritarianism. "We know that you've been a good boy and gotten
high grades, but in terms of democracy, we sincerely believe you fail." Jefe
Diego noted that "I am here because millions of men and women of the PAN
freely elected me as their nominee." In contrast, he added "you, Zedillo, owe
your candidacy to two tragedies: Colosio's death and the *dedazo*." At the same
time, the 53-year-old lawyer blasted the phlegmatic, uninspiring Cárdenas,
whom he despised, as a self-promoting, do-nothing governor when he ran
Michoacán state from 1980 to 1986.

Jefe Diego's hands-down victory in the debate vaulted him from obscurity
to contender status. He grabbed the imagination of millions of Mexicans who
thirsted for change from the PRI. *"Peleador"* (fighter), *"gallo"* (rooster), *"cara
nueva"* (new face)—these were some of the terms applied to the unconventional, quick-witted attorney. Some polls even showed him running neck-and-
neck with the bland, foundering Zedillo, while Cárdenas's ratings tumbled.

Fernández de Cevallos's strong showing did energize the PRI campaign;
its candidate improved his performance on the stump and the fear generated
by assassinations and a guerrilla insurgency convinced many voters to opt for
continuity over change. As a result, Zedillo managed to win the relatively

clean August 21 contest, which brought 77.7 percent of the electorate to the polls. Still, the PRI candidate benefited from virtually unlimited resources, a better get-out-the-vote apparatus than his opponents, and markedly more coverage on government-influenced TV networks. Cárdenas excoriated the results as "fraudulent," but the PAN, whose campaign slogan was "For a Mexico without Lies," conceded defeat even as it submitted more than 13,000 formal complaints of electoral irregularities. For its part, the Civic Alliance, an amalgam of nongovernmental organizations that blanketed the country with observers, identified 215 improprieties that disfigured the election. The unexpectedly strong challenge to the PRI persuaded even more investors to shift their resources to the United States, where rising interest rates proved attractive.

Capital flight accelerated in September. This month also witnessed the murder of Francisco Ruiz Massieu, an ally and ex-brother-in-law of Salinas, former governor of Guerrero state, and the PRI's secretary-general. The killing fed grist to the mill of conspiracy theorists who speculated that everyone from the president to narcotraffickers to pro-statist PRI dinosaurs had engineered the Colosio and Ruiz Massieu assassinations. Just as the political outlook darkened, the Finance Ministry began disguising the sharp expansion of the money supply arising from credits extended by NAFIN, Banco Rural, Banco Obrero, Bancomex, and other state-controlled banks—a development that belied claims of prudent financial management. In a move to restore confidence, the government accelerated its issuance of short-term, dollar-denominated bonds (*tesobonos*) at handsome rates.

Conclusion

On December 1, 1994, hundreds of foreign dignitaries and business leaders hobnobbed with local notables at the inauguration of Mexico's eightieth chief executive, Ernesto Zedillo. After donning the red, white, and green presidential sash, the 43-year-old economist committed himself to broadening the market-focused reforms championed by his predecessor. Outgoing President Salinas, leaving office as the most popular leader in contemporary Mexican history, beamed approval of his protégé's endorsement of economic liberalization.

Although this was Zedillo's day to shine, observers heaped praise on Salinas whom they expected would depart Mexico City for a prestigious international post, possibly as head of the newly created World Trade Organization in Geneva. Little did Mexicans realize the fate that would beset their country within a few weeks of Zedillo's swearing-in: A sharp peso devaluation would precipitate the worst economic crisis in modern memory; authorities would imprison the ex-president's brother Raúl on charges of orchestrating Ruiz Massieu's murder; and Salinas himself would embark on a pathetic hunger strike before leaving Mexico for a self-imposed exile on March 11, 1995. These events turned the erstwhile chief executive from hero to villain.

Salinas left the shaky corporatist system that he had inherited on the verge of collapse without creating new institutions. First, his arbitrary and capricious manipulation of the PRI, its candidates, and office-holders had further reduced the influence of the party, already weakened by the defection of the Democratic Current in 1987. His disdain for the PRI manifested itself in a thinly veiled flirtation with creating a new Solidarity party based on the myriad of Pronasol committees throughout the country.

Second, not only did he undermine the PRI, he lofted the star of the PAN. Although his candidacy faded toward the end of the campaign, Fernández de Cevallos demonstrated that his party could garner sufficient support outside the middle class to crash through a ceiling of one-quarter of the national vote. In contrast to the PRD, which has an affinity for the constituencies—if not the leaders—of trade unions and peasant confederations, the PAN seeks the dismantlement of corporatist organizations. Unwittingly, the former chief executive also helped the PRD, which soon exploited its role as both martyr and "we-told-you-so" critic of Salinas.

Third, Salinas's replacing La Quina with a puppet combined with his courtship of Hernández Juárez and FESEBES further diminished the power of Don Fidel and the CTM. Meanwhile, Mexican workers saw their paychecks shrink by one-third in the 1988–1994 *sexenio* at a time when *Forbes* magazine reported that the number of billionaires in the country shot up to twenty-four, many of whom owed their fortunes to the Salinas administration.

Fourth, Salinas left the country in the hands of a technocrat, who lacked political know-how, a *camarilla*, a base in the PRI, rapport with average people, and a vision of the country's future. The outgoing chief executive prepared only one man to succeed him. While Colosio might have attempted to breathe new life into the corporatist movement at least until the neoliberal economic model took root, Zedillo barely concealed his hostility toward the party's traditional structures.

Fifth, Salinas's failure to make difficult economic decisions before leaving office left his neophyte successor with a heavily overvalued peso whose devaluation wreaked havoc on the country. The collapse of the peso and the ensuing economic "Time of Troubles" discredited Salinas and the entire *nomenklatura* who had run Mexico during most of the twentieth century.

Finally, although enfeebling the corporatist system, Salinas bequeathed no viable alternative. For all his braggadocio about delivering "an improved democracy" and "strengthening the citizenry's participation" in a modernized regime, he made a mockery of the electoral process by ousting elected governors as if they were scullery maids and messenger boys.

Arguably, his *perestroika* policies would enlarge the middle class—a powerful advocate for "political sophistication and democratic choice"; decentralize economic activities, which "inevitably diminishes the ability of the state to manipulate economic resources as a tool of political control"; generate demands for greater choices in the political sphere to match those in the economic marketplace; and, by slashing the size of government, decrease opportunities for sticky-fingered bureaucrats to exact *mordidas*.[19]

Demands for openness did mushroom throughout the 1988–1994 period. Yet, by converting so many state monopolies to private monopolies and participating in, or winking at, the alleged appropriation of public monies by his brother Raúl and other insiders, Salinas deprived the government of resources needed to address social needs and ensure the legitimacy of the political system passed onto Zedillo.

Notes

1. Trimberger's classic study is *Revolution from Above: Military Bureaucrats and Development in Japan, Turkey, Egypt, and Peru* (New Brunswick, N.J.: Transaction Publishers, 1978); Centeno's is *Democracy within Reason: Technocratic Revolution in Mexico*, pp. 39–41.

2. For several years in the 1980s, the union changed its name to the Revolutionary Oil Workers' Union of the Mexican Republic (Sindicato Revolucionario de los Trabajadores Petroleros de la República Mexicana—SRTPRM). To avoid even greater confusion in a book already swimming in an alphabet soup of organizations, the author has consistently used STPRM.

3. Russell, *Mexico under Salinas*, (Austin, TX: Mexico Resource Center, 1994), p.11

4. Middlebrook, *The Paradox of Revolution*, p. 298.

5. The first part of this section draws heavily on George W. Grayson, "Mexico: Embattled Neighbor," *Great Decisions* (New York: Foreign Policy Association, 1996), p. 24.

6. One survey of ten voting places in Mexico City where many members and their families cast ballots found the PRI nominee garnering 3,771 votes compared to 3,411 for Cárdenas, 592 for Clouthier, and 98 for minor-party candidates; see *Proceso*, July 18, 1988, p. 11.

7. Carlos Salinas de Gortari, *Producción y participación: política en el campo* (Mexico City: Fondo de Cultura Económica, 1987).

8. Jaime Marques-Pereira, PRONASOL: Mexico's Bid to Fight Poverty," *UNESCO Courier* (March 1995): 25.

9. Dan LaBotz, "Manufacturing Poverty: The Maquiladorization of Mexico," *Multinational Monitor* (May 1993): 20–21.

10. Middlebrook, *The Paradox of Revolution*, p. 296.

11. Stephen D. Morris, *Political Reformism in Mexico: An Overview of Contemporary Mexican Politics* (Boulder, CO: Lynne Reinner, 1995), p. 93.

12. Quoted in *La Jornada*, June 24, 1992, pp. 1, 11.

13. Morris, *Political Reformism in Mexico*, p. 94.

14. On October 7, 1992, nine members of the Democratic and Doctrinaire Forum bolted the party. Those withdrawing included two former party presidents and presidential candidates, two ex-secretaries general, and Pablo Emilio Madero, nephew of the instigator of the Mexican revolution; see, Russell, *Mexico under Salinas*, p. 388.

15. Later Salinas offered Aguirre Velázquez "an ambassadorship or some other post." The ex-mayor said that the only position he would like was the presidency of the PRI, which Salinas was not prepared to bestow; interview with Ramón Aguirre Velázquez, Mexico City, June 17, 1996.

16. *Shadows of Tender Mercy: The Letters and Communiqués of Subcomandante Marcos and the Zapatista Army of National Liberation* (New York: Monthly Review Press, 1995), pp. 51–52.

17. Katzenberger, *First World Ha Ha Ha!*, p.87

18. PRI hardliners in the Chamber of Deputies sarcastically coined this sobriquet because Fernández de Cevallos wielded such great influence over legislation in the 1988-91 period that he sometimes seemed in charge of a body that the revolutionary party had grown accustomed to treating as its private preserve.

19. For the most developed presentation of this thesis, see Sidney Weintraub and M. Delal Baer, "The Interplay between Economic and Political Opening: The Sequence in Mexico," *The Washington Quarterly* 15, No. 2 (Spring 1992):187 201; and "El dilema liberal," *Vuelta*, No. 191 (October 1992), pp. 70–71.

5
—

Zedillo and the Corporatist Challenge: Conflict between Economic and Political Reform

Zedillo: The Accidental President

It should hardly come as a surprise to find that the chief executive who has moved sedulously to steer Mexico from its corporatist past reached the office over an unconventional path. Zedillo proved an aberration in Mexico's political system, where most prominent politicians have emerged from the social and economic elites, often with political roots in Mexico City and a family tree adorned with fathers, grandfathers, and uncles who held key political posts. In contrast, Mexico's last president of the twentieth century grew up in a lower-middle-class family near the U.S. border. The second of six children, Ernesto Zedillo Ponce de León was born in Mexico City on December 27, 1951.

Around Zedillo's third birthday, his family moved from the capital to Mexicali, Baja California. His father Rodolfo worked as an electrician in movie theaters in Mexicali. His mother Marta Alicia was a candy vendor at the neighborhood cinema and worked as a secretary at the city hall. Later, while employed in the Baja California state bureaucracy, she sold jewelry to earn extra pesos. Although of modest means, this tall, attractive, hard-working lady instilled discipline, self-respect, and the importance of education in her five children, all of whom attended college. Zedillo's chemistry teacher recalled the fruits of his mother's efforts, appreciating the "fact that a student came to school with a clean, ironed uniform, obeyed the rules, showed that the family was concerned about that kind of thing—that there was order, discipline."[1]

Noted for excellence, his "18 *de Marzo*" public junior high school challenged students academically and treated them equally whether they came from rich, middle-class, or poor homes, as did Zedillo, who shined shoes and collected scrap metal to supplement the family's income. "He got used to the idea that it's possible to live without social distinctions and that good public education is a way to offer opportunity to all social classes," stated a longtime friend of the president.[2] At 18 *de Marzo*, he ran track, participated in the student council, wrote for the school newspaper, and served as a member of the honor guard. On Sundays, he was an altar boy at San Antonio Church.

Upon graduating in 1966, Zedillo followed his brother to Mexico City to study at the public National Polytechnic Institute (IPN), created by Lázaro Cárdenas to permit the children of average families to complete high school and college in one institution. While a marginal participant in the protests that preceded the Tlatelolco massacre of October 1968, the bearded young Zedillo dedicated himself to completing the IPN's rigorous five-year curriculum in three years, even though he worked part-time as an accounting assistant at the Bank of the Army and Navy. "He put all his effort into earning his Ph.D.," says historian Lorenzo Meyer. "That was his moment of glory. A Ph.D. is an amazing achievement for someone from his background. If it was the logical, normal thing for Salinas, it was almost impossible for Zedillo to achieve." He did find time to join the PRI in 1971; two years later, while teaching at IPN, he married one of his students, Nilda Patricia.

Zedillo studied briefly at the University of Bradford in England. Later, a Mexican government scholarship allowed him to transfer to Yale, where he completed doctoral training in economics. Upon leaving New Haven in 1974, he landed a post as assistant manager for economic and financial research at the nation's prestigious Central Bank.

In the 1980s, the Mexican economy reeled from the effects of a huge foreign debt amid plummeting oil prices: Zedillo headed a national Trust Fund for Hedging against Exchange Risks to help large corporations restructure their external debt. Observers credited this mechanism—known as FICORCA—with keeping many Mexican firms solvent during an extremely difficult time. "It was really ingenious," said Deborah Riner, chief economist at the American Chamber of Commerce in Mexico City. "The private sector would have gone under without it."

In 1987, Zedillo moved to a subcabinet post in the Ministry of Planning and Budget, then headed by Salinas. When his boss ascended to the presidency in 1988, Zedillo rose to the top at SPP. During his tenure, the talented young technocrat helped prepare four federal budgets, a national plan for so-cioeconomic development, and the Solidarity program. All told, he succeeded in boosting social spending by 50 percent, while paving the way for budget surpluses.

In 1993, as a result of fusing SPP with the Finance Ministry, Salinas dispatched Zedillo to take charge of the Education Ministry, another assignment crucial to Mexico's future. Zedillo sparked a national controversy by introducing new grade school texts, the original versions of which contained factual errors and proved politically incorrect. Before being edited, they painted a reasonably sympathetic picture of dictator Porfirio Díaz and highlighted the army's role in repressing the Tlatelolco protest. This embarrassment aside, the energetic Zedillo managed to extract limited pay-for-performance concessions from the powerful, demonstration-prone teachers' union; won the SNTE's support for vesting administration of the nation's educational system in Mexico's thirty-one state governments, thus obviating a nationwide teachers' strike; completed a modest curriculum revision; and stressed job training and continuing education.

Photographs show the often-dour cabinet secretary smiling broadly at the unveiling of Colosio as the PRI's 1994 presidential nominee. Although Salinas himself mentioned the education secretary as one of a half-dozen or so prospects to ascend to the presidency, the reclusive Zedillo, hardly known outside the Mexico City bureaucracy, realized that service as finance secretary or elsewhere in the inner circle of Colosio—with whom he enjoyed a productive rapport—would give him six years to learn the political ropes, develop crucial contacts, and otherwise lay the groundwork for any bid for Los Pinos he might later essay.

From the cabinet, Zedillo moved to Colosio's campaign. Neither a member of the candidate's close-knit entourage nor a grand strategist, Zedillo concentrated on media questions, especially where and how best to use television advertisements. The candidate's assassination placed the PRI in a quandary: Mexico's Constitution prohibits anyone from running who has served in a senior government post six months before the election, and Salinas encountered overwhelming opposition to a possible amendment slashing the out-of-office period to three months. Consequently, most incumbent cabinet members and governors were eliminated from consideration. Party elders from Querétaro, San Luis Potosí, Sonora, and other states faxed and telephoned PRI national headquarters to urge the selection of party president Ortiz Arana as Colosio's replacement. Concerned about the exodus of foreign exchange, Salinas opted for Zedillo the fiscal manager over Ortiz Arana the politician in a move that angered many party veterans. When a PRI official announced the naming of a "unity candidate," a clot of party dissidents yelled catcalls and screamed in unison: "False! Lies!" Partisans bused in for the occasion quickly shouted down the malcontents, even though many of the loyalists could neither pronounce Zedillo's name nor identify their new hero. Dissent quickly dissipated, as the corporatist system's cardinal rule of incumbents selecting successors still remained inviolate. An observer noted that: "Zedillo's leading rival began circling party wagons at 8 a.m. [March 29], vowing to remain faithful to 'our principle . . . and to President Carlos Salinas de Gortari.'"[3]

Zedillo Attacks the Corporatist System

Had the new president's speechwriters conspired for months, they could not have crafted an inaugural address more offensive to the irascible corporatist barons who deplored Zedillo's candidacy, regardless of custom.[4] The first part of the speech contained socially progressive, but largely predictable bromides. Zedillo's comments focused on his campaign slogan "Your Family's Well-Being" and emphasized his determination to improve education, job training, housing, and health services in order "to break the vicious cycle of sickness, ignorance, unemployment, and poverty that entrap many millions of Mexicans." He also pledged to fight crime, including the "intolerable" assaults, kidnappings, and murders plaguing Mexico's homes, streets, and businesses. He cited narcotraffickers as the "greatest threat to national security, the gravest risk to social health, and the bloodiest source of violence."

Appeals to nationalism, patriotism, and sovereignty aside, the last half of the address brought heartburn to the old guard. He stressed that "Mexico must be a country of laws," in which "the Constitution and the legal order derived from it enjoy full observance," serving notice to PRI dinosaurs and plutocrats alike. In view of the uncertainty surrounding adherence to the law, rising insecurity, and the frequent violation of human rights, he proposed that: "We undertake deep and genuine reform of institutions charged with ensuring justice, [because] it is here that incompetence, corruption, and institutional breakdown are more frequent and pose the greater threat to personal security." To make good on this commitment, Zedillo vowed that his first submission to Congress would be a constitutional reform to strengthen the judicial system, augment its independence, and enhance its administration and enforcement—a promise that he made good on!

Although Zedillo had captured the presidency in the cleanest national contest in Mexican history, the election's victor himself expressed qualms over the integrity of the electoral process, whose "democratic advances remained insufficient." Thus, the moment had arrived, he asserted, that all parties, political organizations, and civic groups devote themselves to Mexico's "integral democratization," flinging down the gauntlet at Mexico's mossbacks by threatening their traditional implement of social control. Constructing this "new democracy" would entail improving ties between citizens and their government, embarking upon a "new federalism" that would empower states and cities in their relations with the central regime, and adopting a modern ethical code for political contenders. Zedillo also called for a "better balanced" power relationship between the presidency and other branches of government, as well as the implementation of a "definitive electoral reform," including close scrutiny of political-party financing; limits on campaign expenditures; fair access to the news media for all parties; and full autonomy for electoral authorities. In Zedillo's words, "Mexico demands a reform which, based on the broadest political consensus, will eradicate the suspicion, recrimination and distrust that mar the electoral process." Members of his administration quickly received their first standing order: "Government is not the place to amass wealth. . . . Those who aspire to do so should leave my government and pay strict attention to the law."

To the amazement of veteran *priístas*, Zedillo—who during the final weeks of his campaign had declaimed the need "to put a healthy distance between the PRI and the government"—announced that, while remaining a party militant, he would treat opposition groups on an equal footing with the ruling party. The new chief executive forswore intervening in "whatever form" with the PRI's internal life, indicating he planned to cut the Gordian knot that had long identified Mexico as a corporatist party-state, which lavished government resources—from cash to warm bodies to the use of vehicles and copy machines—on the PRI and its nominees. After the speech, Zedillo and his aides astonished grizzled *políticos* by implying that he would renounce the *dedazo*—the same tradition that had vaulted him from bureaucratic obscurity to national leadership and arguably the system's most potent tool to preserve discipline among ambitious politicians, whose opposition to the incumbent could terminate their chances of reaching Los Pinos.

PRI stalwarts took umbrage at Zedillo's early acts in office. Acknowledging that Zedillo might want to submit himself to the confines of the law, many veteran politicians nonetheless found his position as naive as they did threatening. An outsider who boasted several confidants but no real political team or kitchen cabinet, the new president selected his cabinet with three objectives in mind: continuing economic modernization, rewarding politicians who had made possible his victory, and giving credibility to his commitment to political reform. As a result, he conferred most ministerial portfolios on technocrats, many of whom had served under Salinas. He brought only three senior PRI *políticos* into cabinet posts—Santiago Oñate Laborde (Labor), Silvia Hernández Enríquez (Tourism), and ex-party president Ignacio Pichardo Pagaza (Energy). And Zedillo elected to display his reformist credentials by naming as attorney general a member of the PAN. His first choice Fernández de Cevallos turned down the offer, but recommended Fernando Antonio Lozano Gracia, Jefe Diego's protégé and successor as head of the PAN's legislative faction, who got the presidential nod. In this key position, said PRI malcontents, a PAN zealot could embark upon a political witch-hunt in the guise of combating corruption and apprehending the killers of Colosio and Ruiz Massieu, so disrupting the PRI's subtle political and social balance. Diehards also blanched at Zedillo's selection of Julia Carabias Lillo as fisheries and environmental secretary. The 42-year-old scientist had political experience in the left-wing Popular Action Movement (MAP), as well as the United Socialist Party of Mexico (PSUM), one of several organizations that merged into Cárdenas's Democratic Revolutionary Party. In addition, she helped found the leftist UNAM Workers' Union.

During his first week in office, Zedillo met with opposition-party leaders. As if to further insult the injured dinosaurs, he stamped his seal of approval on the choice of a PAN legislator, Juan Antonio García Villa, to chair the committee with oversight responsibility for federal expenditures—*Comisión de Vigilancia de la Contaduría Mayor de Hacienda.*

This action revealed Zedillo's desire to strengthen Congress, long maligned as "presidential messenger boys," (*"mandaderos de presidentes"*), "yes men" (*"levantadedos"*), and a presidential echo chamber (*"caja de resonacia del presidente"*). When convenient, Los Pinos showed unprecedented respect for legislators by submitting drafts of bills to them for comment before introduction; consulting lawmakers on budgetary issues; empowering the Senate to name Supreme Court justices and approve the president's nominee for attorney general; and taking seriously congressional initiatives on crime, changes in the government of Mexico City, and other grass-roots issues. Of course, earlier electoral reforms gave Congress the right to select the IFE's citizen councillors. The anticipated increase in the number of PAN and PRD deputies at the expense of the PRI would magnify the influence, assertiveness, and visibility of the 500-member Chamber. Still, several factors—low public prestige, inadequate staffing, a small budget, and the prohibition on reelection which increases their dependence on the president for future career opportunities—ensure the continued weakness of the legislative branch compared to the executive.

The president followed through on pledges to promote judicial reform through constitutional amendments introduced soon after he took office. These initiatives reduced the number of Supreme Court justices from twenty-six to eleven; required two-thirds' Senate approval for judicial appointments, in lieu of presidential nomination alone; replaced life tenure for judges with fifteen-year terms, subject to congressional impeachment; created a federal judicial council to handle court administration and financial management; established professional criteria for selecting lower-court judges; and provided for supervision and oversight of these judges. During the first half of the Zedillo administration, these changes had little impact on the administration of justice in lower courts where corruption and the lack of professionalism abound. While Zedillo's own actions gave warning of changes in Mexico's politics from the inside, subsequent days would demonstrate the country's vulnerability to the global economic system.

The Christmas Crisis

The celebrations surrounding Zedillo's inauguration constituted the calm before the storm. Three weeks after taking office, the new chief executive confronted a challenge much graver than disaffected PRI war horses, as the peso went into a tailspin. Caesars and generals returning to Imperial Rome following military conquests assigned husky-voiced young men to jog alongside their chariots. As frenzied crowds cheered themselves hoarse for the exultant heroes, the runners would scream into their ears, "You are not a god, you are not a god." Regrettably, Mexico's new president had designated nobody to provide a similar reality check to his finance secretary, Jaime Serra Puche. Despite the well-distributed talent in Salinas's cabinet, the handsome, intelligent Serra Puche quickly rose to prominence. As commerce secretary from 1988 to 1994, Serra Puche—a Yale-educated technocrat like Zedillo—had spearheaded the negotiation and ratification of the free-trade pact with the United States and Canada. A tour de force with NAFTA, combined with close ties to Zedillo, landed Serra Puche the coveted finance post. No sooner had the 43-year-old minister taken his oath than pundits began touting him for the presidency, even though Zedillo's term ran to the year 2000.

The arrogant Serra Puche spurned advice on dealing with the financial community from his immediate predecessor, Pedro Aspe; vouchsafed the peso's stability to foreign visitors at Zedillo's inauguration; and two weeks later, predicted a 4 percent rise in GDP for the upcoming year, assuring Congress that Mexico would "grow with stability." Apparently, he believed that his appointment would ensure market confidence, facilitating a gradual adjustment of a national economy bedeviled by a $28 billion trade deficit and hemorrhaging of foreign exchange reserves.

Serra Puche's cocksureness notwithstanding, the Mexican government had surreptitiously extended vast credits during the preceding year. This expansion in the money supply; a mountain of debt in dollar-denominated treasury bonds (*tesobonos*); the galloping excess of imports over exports; and pesky Zapatista guerrilla adventurism in Chiapas discouraged investment and accentuated speculation against the peso. On December 20, the government decided on a 15 percent increase in the upper limit of the peso's floating range against the dollar. "What we are doing is simply expanding the band to insure that the central bank has the sufficient flexibility to deal with the disturbances that have come forward in the Chiapas conflict," conciliated Serra Puche.

Nonetheless, pressure on a hugely overvalued currency continued to build. On December 22, after publicly vacillating over devaluation for several days, a taciturn Serra Puche announced that the Central Bank would no longer prop up the peso with its meager hard-currency holdings. Once allowed to float freely, the peso fell like a bowling ball dropped from a skyscraper. When the New York-based Standard and Poors Ratings Group held a ninety-minute international conference call that day with investors, operators required a half-hour just to connect all the participants due to the market's frenzied activity.[5] In an attempt to calm the panic over Mexico's bungled economic management, Serra Puche jetted to New York for a pre-Christmas meeting with bankers, portfolio managers, and U.S. Treasury Department officials. In a session described as "disastrous" by some participants, a usually self-assured Serra Puche—used to asking questions, not supplying answers— spent most of his time apologizing for the handling of the peso debacle.

During the NAFTA negotiations, Serra Puche had mastered Washington's inside-the-beltway political culture. To his dismay, he discovered that the nation's capital does not provide a microcosm of the United States. New York's financial community—accustomed to an open line of communication with the trusted and unfailingly attentive Aspe—quickly began to decry Serra Puche as an aloof and excessively ambitious pariah, criticizing him for having clumsily tipped off Mexican businessmen to the devaluation, ignoring their phone calls and faxes, and failing to provide credible data to bankers, portfolio managers, and governments. In December alone, the value of stocks held by U.S. investors plunged from $20 billion to $13.5 billion, while the worth of their peso-denominated securities fell from $15 billion to $12 billion.

In a no-nonsense speech on December 29, Zedillo announced plans to halve the trade shortfall, cut public spending, restrain wage increases, and allow private capital into more sectors of Mexico's economy. At the same time, the chief executive accepted Serra Puche's resignation, quickly replacing him with the owlish but understated Guillermo Ortiz Martínez, who as Salinas's undersecretary of treasury had managed the lucrative reprivatization of Mexico's banks.

On November 20, 1994, Ortiz, 46, recipient of a doctorate in economics from Stanford and a former IMF executive director, had joined Zedillo and Serra Puche in urging devaluation of an undeniably overpriced peso. Aspe turned thumbs down on the request. Similarly, Salinas had rejected this action, as it would have cast a shadow on a term that promised to end up as the most successful *sexenio* in modern history, and possibly thwart his chances to assume a prestigious international post. Within hours of taking office, the slightly built, curly-haired Ortiz Martínez—portrayed by the *New York Times* as the "Dogged Doctor for Mexico's Morass"—burned up the phone lines with calls to investors and American commercial banks like Chase Manhattan.

Factors other than his know-it-all bravado had hastened Serra Puche's fall from grace. First, he only learned that Zedillo would appoint him finance secretary shortly before the inauguration and had little time to prepare for his new assignment, although he certainly knew that he would hold a key portfolio in the new economic cabinet. Second, Serra Puche's strong suit came in cutting commercial deals rather than as architect of broad, invariably public, financial policy. Third, events that moved with lightning speed overtook Serra Puche and Zedillo before either could settle into his new jobs. In two days in December alone, Mexico lost $2 billion in foreign reserves, then hovering around $6 billion. Above all, he inherited a bloated peso from Salinas, who—in accord with the traditional rules of Mexico's political game—should have accelerated the currency's depreciation instead of leaving a time bomb to explode in his successor's face. After all, to maintain the official 3.45 peso–1 dollar exchange rate, Salinas borrowed heavily from abroad and dissipated the dollar reserves. Reportedly, Zedillo's plea that the outgoing president swallow the devaluation pill fell on deaf ears. While U.S. officials expressed concern over deteriorating conditions in 1994, no one grabbed Salinas or Aspe by the lapels and said: "Good heavens, man, you've got to speed-up the devaluation." Washington believed that Salinas and his star-studded cabinet could sail through a bad patch of economic weather, especially since the gifted Zedillo stood poised to take the helm.[6] The one conceivable silver lining from the December catastrophe lay in focusing most of the blame on Serra Puche and Salinas, allowing Zedillo to assume a low profile as he scrambled for credit lines from his North American allies: Only the disenchantment of traditional politicians eclipsed that of the foreign community.

State governors, former PRI presidents, and ex-cabinet members watched apprehensively when, on January 3, 1995, Zedillo went on national television to outline an "Economic Emergency Plan," aimed at attacking the "grave and urgent" crisis bequeathed to him by his predecessor. In an oblique reference to Salinas's promise to elevate Mexico to first world status, Zedillo told his viewers that "we are not a rich country, but a nation with serious needs and shortages. We cannot, therefore, identify ourselves with patterns of consumption in wealthy societies that have already resolved the disparities that still afflict us." Less a grandiose ruler than a stern schoolmaster, Zedillo stressed the need for collective "sacrifices," for his own part vowing that

> I will head a government that will always speak the truth, however hard it may be; a government that will safeguard the general interest over and above the interests of individuals or groups, a government to serve Mexicans, not for anyone's personal success or promotion.

In terms of specifics, Zedillo unveiled a tripartite pact in which organized labor—long used to complying with presidential directives—reluctantly accepted a 7 percent wage cap for the year. While avoiding precise targets, business interests promised to rein in prices and trim profits. In turn, the government agreed to limit increases in state-mandated charges for gasoline, electricity, and basic foodstuffs. The president also reiterated his determination to slash public spending: This would further diminish the boodle available to the PRI. Though Salinas's popularity before he left office buoyed the party's reputation, after the December financial crisis the PRI's standing plummeted along with the value of the peso. Dinosaurs despaired that Zedillo did not take advantage of Mexico's financial troubles to retreat back to the old ways from the political uncertainty emanating from the economic opening and greater Mexican integration with North American neighbors. More of a true believer in free enterprise than Salinas, Zedillo invited private capital to finance ports, railroads, satellite communications systems, and electrical generating plants. A clause in the Emergency Plan also envisioned the "privatization of other public sector companies"—a reference, according to government officials, to the projected sell-off of Pemex's petrochemical facilities, which produce plastics, resins, fertilizers, pesticides, and other items. "In the short run [the decentralization and divestment is] going to be very recessionary," said the highly respected political economist Luis Rubio, "but it's the least bad program under the circumstances."

Clinton to the Rescue

U.S. President Bill Clinton extended a helping hand to his Spanish-speaking ally: Not only did Clinton act in the spirit of NAFTA unity, but he realized that a financial disaster in Mexico would send shock waves throughout the Western Hemisphere, if not throughout the global market. Thus, he proposed that the United States mobilize $40 billion in credits for Mexico's reeling economy. When Congress balked at approving this rescue scheme, the U.S. chief executive took matters into his own hands, working with the U.S. Treasury, the IMF, and leery European governments to craft a $52 billion international aid bailout; the United States pledged $20 billion; the Canadians, $1 billion. In exchange for access to these funds, the Mexican government agreed to furnish timely, accurate economic data to lenders, and to guarantee repayment of the loans with Pemex revenues that would be placed on deposit in New York's Federal Reserve Bank.

Clinton's bold response to the crisis elicited praise from Mexicans, even as they lampooned their own leader. A popular joke at the time commended Zedillo as the only winner of three Nobel prizes: in physics, because he made the peso float; in chemistry, because he transmuted the country into dung; and in literature, because he created *Les Misérables* in nineteen days, a feat that took Victor Hugo nineteen years. Another humorist asked, "What does the Zedillo government have in common with Easter?" The answer: Either can fall in March or April.

In a late February 1995 fight for political survival, Zedillo broke a taboo against incumbents attacking predecessors and their families. In what became a political tragicomedy, he ordered the arrest of Raúl Salinas de Gortari, brother of the former *jefe*, who not only held a key post in the 1988–1994 administration, but also managed the family fortune that had ballooned during the government sell-off of state assets to Salinas friends. Authorities charged Raúl with masterminding the murder of PRI Secretary-General José Francisco Ruiz Massieu, once married to his and Carlos's sister. Absurdly, Carlos Salinas phoned a Mexico City TV station to deny responsibility for Zedillo's "December error" and, later, launched a 44-hour hunger strike, demanding exculpation from any involvement in the Colosio assassination. Once publicly exonerated of the killing, the erstwhile president left the country for self-imposed exile in Ireland, although he continued to send dispatches to the Mexico City media. The arrest of Raúl rekindled the anger that Mexicans across the political spectrum heaped on the ex-president and, indirectly, the PRI. Pedestrians and motorists paraded past Salinas's mansion in the southern area of Mexico City, shouting expletives, honking horns, and otherwise displaying their contempt for a man who had raised their expectations only to prove himself one more *ratero*, or "rat" in local street parlance. A late-February public opinion poll reflected the former chief executive's fall from grace, as more than three out of four respondents favored prosecuting him. During Holy Week 1997, the disdain for Salinas manifested itself again when vendors of Judas dolls—customarily burned at Midnight on Easter Eve to strike a blow against Judas Iscariot in particular and evil in general—did a robust business selling papier-mâché figures of the ex-president, some embellished with fangs and devil's horns. "This kind of open conflict between presidents has not happened in sixty years," noted John J. Bailey of Georgetown University: "Zedillo is fighting back because Salinas is the one who broke the rules first."

These political conflicts delivered a further body blow to the already faltering economy: Continued decline, combined with pressure from Washington to put his country's house in order, forced Zedillo to prepare an even more drastic belt-tightening scheme. To begin with, he persuaded PRI members in Congress to boost from 10 to 15 percent the unpopular value-added tax imposed on consumer purchases. At the same time, he raised the price of gasoline by 35 percent and electricity by 20 percent, with additional monthly increases scheduled for the rest of 1995. Finally, Zedillo slashed the original 1995 budget by 1.6 percent of GDP. These retrenchments alarmed *priístas*, who had to face constituents with whom they'd struck old-fashioned corporatist bargains in gubernatorial and local elections later in the year.

Zedillo's bold moves, complemented by substantial international credits, paid some dividends by spring. Finance Secretary Ortiz managed to redeem the *tesobonos* as they came due. Meanwhile, the devalued peso led to lower prices and boosted demand for Mexican exports, while imports proved too expensive for most Mexicans. The adjustment gave rise to a favorable trade balance with a surplus exceeding $3.7 billion during the first half of 1995. In his September 1 State of the Nation address, a greatly relieved Zedillo proclaimed that Mexico had halted its slide toward insolvency, noting that: "The initial objectives of the adjustment program have been achieved and [t]he threat of financial collapse that existed during the initial months of the year has clearly vanished." The president insisted that once fully in recovery, the economy would grow at 5 percent annually.

To underscore the economic improvements, Zedillo announced the advance payment of $700 million of a $12.5 billion U.S. loan before his trip to Washington in October 1995. The praise that the chief executives showered on each other during the state visit both lofted Zedillo's anemic standing at home and silenced Clinton's critics, who had warned that American taxpayers would never recover the money loaned to Mexico. In fact, Zedillo completed the repayment in early 1997.

Less sanguine about recovery than political grandees, voters vented their spleens on the president and the governing PRI in state elections held throughout 1995. PAN candidates convincingly won the governorships of Jalisco (February), Guanajuato (May) and Baja California Norte (August). In Guanajuato, Vicente Fox, a flamboyant Coca-Cola executive-turned-politician, rolled to a two-to-one landslide over his opponent, marking the PRI's worst recorded defeat at the state level. Only in late May in Yucatán—a state infamous for political fraud—did Víctor Cervera Pacheco, a Tyrannosaurus Rex from the PRI's Jurassic Period, eke out a disputed victory over his PAN opponent, more than anything marking the waning of corporatist politics.

The crisis also gave a fillip to new organizations, created to promote political and economic reform. Among the groups that have come to play a particularly important political role are the Alianza Cívica and El Barzón. The first, created in 1994 by Sergio Aguayo—a well-known academic and president of the Mexican Academy of Human Rights—has assiduously advanced the cause of electoral reform, including the monitoring and evaluation of elections. The second, an outgrowth of the Christmas crisis, serves as a militant advocate for hundreds of thousands of individuals and small businesses plunged into debt because of the sharp economic downturn that attended the peso devaluation.

In the spirit of the public activism generated by the *El Grande* earthquakes, average citizens have shown a much greater readiness to "fight city hall"—whether through groups like the Alianza Cívica and El Barzón or through spontaneous actions. A prime example of the latter unfolded in the mid-1990s when residents of Tepoztlán in Morelos state—assisted by Greenpeace and other environmental activists—thwarted the construction by wealthy investors and their political partners of a lavish golf club, planned community, and resort for affluent tourists in the ecologically sensitive Parque Nacional El Tepozteco. A few years before, the government would have deployed armed forces to quell the demonstrators and advance the project. After prolonged demonstrations, sit-ins, and other highly publicized protests, authorities sat on their hands while the entrepreneurs were forced to abandon the venture.

Labor Shows Age

Even as grumbling among Mexican elites grew louder, on May 1, 1995, labor patriarch Fidel Velázquez figuratively scorched his sausage-sized fingers, even as he snatched Zedillo's political chestnuts from the fire. Upon orders of Don Fidel, neither his CTM nor other major unions participated in Mexico's annual May Day festivities, citing a "lack of resources" to transport and feed the workers. More importantly, however, Velázquez feared that blue-collar marchers—angered by shrinking take-home pay, escalating unemployment, higher taxes, and soaring prices—might have hurled antigovernment catcalls and chants or even missiles at the unpopular chief executive. After all, a sore-head had lobbed a Molotov cocktail toward de la Madrid on May Day 1983.

Two years later, on May 1, 1997, the situation had not improved: The president, high-government officials, the CTM, and labor's official umbrella organization—the Labor Congress—bused in trade unionists to fill the huge National Auditorium rather than risk a march that could discredit the government. Ill-health prevented the now 97-year-old Velázquez from attending a conclave in which disgruntled workers booed and ridiculed Rodríguez Alcaine and other CTM notables who endeavored to address them. Don Fidel's subsequent death on June 21 confronted his interim successor, Rodríguez Alcaine, and veteran labor bosses with the challenge of preventing profound discontent from erupting into large-scale strikes and violence, particularly with an opposition-party mayor elected to occupy the capital's city hall. Still, as indicated in Table 5.1, workers have remained amazingly quiescent through the first half of Zedillo's administration.

Even if "official" unions linked to the PRI remain on good behavior—a big if—radical organizations have begun to challenge the regime whose austerity measures wiped out a million existing jobs in 1995, just as a million young Mexicans entered the labor market. Still, the PRD has proven incapable of occupying the space that the PRI lost among organized workers: Thousands of protesters in 1995 did hoist placards emblazoned with the PRD's yellow-and-black Aztec sun as Cárdenas and leftist-nationalists excoriated the government's "inhumane, anti-worker" policies. However, the PRD found itself riven in this period by internecine battles over personalities, programs, and policies that have traditionally plagued the left, and

Table 5.1   Labor Strike Petitions and Actual Strikes, 1938–1996

*Source: Secretaría del Trabajo y Previsión Social; and Kevin J. Middlebrook,
The Paradox of Revolution: Labor, the State and Authoritarianism in Mexico
(Baltimore: Johns Hopkins University Press, 1995), pp.164–165.

President	Year	Federal Jurisdiction Strike Petitions	Federal Jurisdiction Strikes	Local Jurisdiction Strikes
Cárdenas	1938	140	32	287
	1939	153	35	268
	1940	184	15	342
Ávila Camacho	1941	117	17	125
	1942	133	19	79
	1943	858	569	197
	1944	1,103	734	153
	1945	263	107	113
	1946	NA	24	183
Alemán	1947	NA	13	117
	1948	NA	34	54
	1949	NA	35	55
	1950	NA	28	54
	1951	NA	17	127
	1952	NA	29	84
Ruiz Cortines	1953	NA	20	142
	1954	NA	18	75
	1955	NA	13	122
	1956	NA	10	149
	1957	NA	10	183
	1958	NA	11	729
López Mateos	1959	NA	18	361
	1960	NA	52	325
	1961	NA	42	331
	1962	NA	23	702
	1963	1,244	36	468
	1964	1,532	46	16
Díaz Ordaz	1965	1,127	40	27
	1966	NA	73	18
	1967	1,661	45	33
	1968[1]	145	39	117
	1969	1,361	40	104
	1970	1,512	NA	NA
Echeverría	1971	1,632	36	168
	1972	2,176	33	174

continued

Table 5.1   *Continued*

President	Year	Federal Jurisdiction Strike Petitions	Federal Jurisdiction Strikes	Local Jurisdiction Strikes
Echeverría *(cont.)*	1973	5,557	57	NA
	1974	5,182	55	337
	1975	2,150	84	236
	1976	6,299	107	547
López Portillo	1977	5,033	128	476
	1978	5,572	87	758
	1979	6,021	141	795
	1980	5,757	93	1,339
	1981	6,589	108	1,066
	1982	16,095	675	1,971
de la Madrid	1983	13,536	230	978
	1984	9,052	221	548
	1985	8,754	125	489
	1986	11,579	312	903
	1987	16,141	174	949
	1988	7,730	132	518
Salinas de Gotari	1989	6,806	118	757[2]
	1990	6,395	149	NA
	1991	7,006	136	NA
	1992	6,814	156	NA
	1993	7,531	155	NA
Zedillo	1994	7,490	116	NA
	1995	7,676	96	NA
	1996	7,621	51	NA
	1997[3]	3,213	28	NA

1. Information on federal-jurisdictional petitions may be incomplete.
2. Data on Federal District missing.
3. Through June.

---

failed to organize a trade-union wing that might catalyze labor opposition to Zedillo's cutbacks. In fact, the 1995 rally organizers, whose cynicism extended to all politicians, even refused to permit the PRD's 1994 presidential candidate, Cárdenas, to address the Zócalo audience. For their part, individual PAN candidates clearly attract blue-collar voters, but they reject the old-style centralization and cronyism, and no mechanism exists to link union members to the PAN.

While allowing independent organizations to blow off steam through peaceful protests, the government cracked down on rabble-rousers in 1995. Mexico City's mayor, for example, had recently disbanded the Ruta 100 bus company, whose violence-disposed, pro-Zapatista SUTAUR-100 union served as a potential magnet for anti-regime hotheads. Moreover, the union's radical demands threatened to destabilize the Federal District on the eve of negotiating a collective contract with city employees whose terms were crucial to the capital's finances. Dissolving the firm and charging six union officials with fraud let all union firebrands know that the government would brook little dissent. The crackdown on SUTAUR-100 also sent a warning to its ally, ex-mayor Camacho Solís to watch his political flank when deciding how to advance his political agenda, after Salinas had passed him over for the presidency.

In contrast to the stick used to whack SUTAUR-100, Santiago Oñate, Zedillo's first labor secretary, employed the carrot to defuse labor unrest: As he told a reporter, "a strategic alliance [involving labor, management, and government] . . . could take the form of understandings and struggling for common goals, breaking a pattern that is essentially confrontational, acquiescent, or submissive."

Oñate and his successors assiduously courted the irascible Don Fidel and his curmudgeonly colleagues by including them in decisions related to job programs, price adjustments, and the possible introduction of food stamps. He knew that after Velázquez's retirement—likely when his term ended in 1998—Mexico's labor movement would become more pluralist.

Of course, Don Fidel deserves enormous credit for doing more to preserve his nation's stability than any of the ten PRI chief executives who had worked with him. As mentioned in Chapter 2, the street-smart former dairy worker had discouraged strikes, inoculated most of the labor force against radical ideologies, helped cool inflation by moderating wage demands, thrown his weight behind presidents in a jam, and allowed the PRI to trumpet itself as a "workers' party," despite a real decline in the minimum wage since the Echeverría administration.

But Velázquez gained prominence during the heady days of post-World War II protectionism, when a sky-high wall of tariffs, quotas, and import permits safeguarded domestic industries that proved inefficient, high-cost, and known for goods of indifferent quality. Yet, these monopolies and oligopolies generated immense profits, and trade unionists benefited through officially sanctioned collective contracts, tenure, and weekly pay for forty-eight hours when most worked for less time. In addition, labor recruiters had a field day in a "come back tomorrow" bureaucracy that grew apace with a miasma of procedures, permits, and paperwork.

NAFTA and trade liberalization hit the late Don Fidel and his fellow "dinosaurs" like a meteorite: They claimed that the CT and the CTM had adapted to a changed environment in which raises and benefits depend on higher output, better products, and innovative shop floor techniques. In fact, such concepts remained alien to an old guard accustomed to statism, subsidies, sweetheart contracts, and an expensive, though porous safety net.

No one rivaled Don Fidel in eliciting deference among leaders of the seventy-plus industrial unions and state confederations constituting the CTM. His departure from the national stage delivered yet another blow to the once-formidable union movement, whose influence has plummeted amid the worst recession in modern memory; the decline of smokestack industries; the growth of hard-to-organize service and *maquiladora* sectors; and organized labor's reputation for corruption, violence, and disdain for democracy. The best hope for labor to avoid fragmentation during Mexico's politico-economic transition lies with Juan S. Millán Lizárraga—the head of the Federation of Workers in Sinaloa state and a possible 1998 gubernatorial candidate, who accepts the imperative that organized labor must modernize or watch its clout dissolve. The shrewd, affable 54-year-old economist boasts a quarter-century of CTM activism, but has also initiated parleys with employer groups in hopes of hammering-out a win-win deal: Unions would accept some modifications to Mexico's Bible-thick Federal Labor Code—last revised in 1970—which virtually guarantees costly, cumbersome, and labyrinthine barriers to firms re-assigning, reorganizing, and discharging employees; in return, management and government would seek to restrain job losses, reward improved performance, and most importantly, launch a bold program to give workers the skills needed to prosper in an ever more globalized economy.

As alluded to in Chapter 3, other articulate champions of a "new labor culture" include Hernández Juárez (Telephone Workers) and Gordillo (SNTE Teachers). Hernández Juárez formed the Federation of Goods and Services Unions (FESEBES) in 1990, as then-President Carlos Salinas hoped a new-look confederation could balance the procrustean CTM's influence. While not affiliated with the 115,300-member FESEBES, the talented Gordillo and her huge SNTE have cooperated closely with the maverick federation.

In 1996 and 1997, Hernández Juárez helped fill the CTM-created vacuum in the streets of Mexico City. After Zedillo took office in late 1994, STRM officials joined in "forums" organized by like-minded leaders of other labor organizations—Gordillo, Pedro Castillo, and Joel López Mayrén. Ultimately, participants in these conclaves became the "Forum: Trade Unionism before the Nation" ("El Foro: El Sindicalism ante la Nación") embracing the FESEBES unions plus twelve other organizations, most of which belong to the CT.

Despite Don Fidel's and the CT's edict that its affiliates stay out of the streets on May 1, Hernández Juárez, Gordillo, and other *foristas* flocked into the Federal District's central square. They orchestrated their activities to avoid conflict with those of the more radical *Coordinadora*—an assortment of

PRD activists, SUTAUR-100 bus drivers, university workers, the Trotskyite-leaning Independent Proletarian Movement, small unions, shantytown dwellers, and debtor groups.

Although each leader exhibits intelligence, political acumen, and ambition for power, Millán—thanks to high-level PRI and CTM posts—has developed a professional, working relationship with Hernández Juárez and Gordillo. Any of the three progressives would give new direction to Mexican labor, but Millán alone boasted an excellent rapport with Don Fidel—whom the younger man deeply respected—and a number of other CTM/CT veterans. Millán would offer the best hope of bringing new groups into a revitalized, more democratic Labor Congress, even stretching its tent to cover elements of the *Coordinadora* and peasant organizations.

Such a prospect strikes many traditional bosses as the political equivalent of gargling glass shards. They lust for Don Fidel's mantle, as well as his hammerlock on the CTM and the increasingly diverse CT. Most visibly Rodríguez Alcaine, 78—the tough, vulgar chief of the large, immensely wealthy Electrical Workers Union—drew public censure from Velázquez for his shameless self-promotion.

Also eyeing the succession is José Ramírez Gamero, who joined two other *políticos*—Senator Manuel Cadena and CTM-insider Javier Pineda—as self-selected aides-de-camp to the dying Don Fidel. In 1997, for example, one picked the stogie-chomping curmudgeon up in the morning; another kept him company during his abbreviated office hours; the third drove him home or to meetings. Puckish observers nicknamed Don Fidel "*la pelota*" (the ball), which the scheming factotums passed among themselves in hopes of influencing the changing of the guard.

In the unlikely event that Ramírez Gamero should snatch the brass ring, FESEBES, SNTE, and key public sector unions will make good on threats to bolt the CT to form a separate, competitive labor central. Even the Electrical Workers, Railroad Workers, and STPRM might jump ship. University workers and other leftist bodies would continue on their separate path. The ensuing free-for-all would threaten labor peace, and spur zealots to blast Labor Code-reform and Zedillo's unpopular but essential market-focused changes in a bid to win converts to their respective federations.

Privately, the chief executive declares that he will remain on the sidelines if a donnybrook erupts, and he and the PRI may have no choice but to look on and pray that labor's post-Velázquez evolution takes place so as to facilitate—not frustrate—sustained economic recovery. Millán, who blends political with technocratic traits, offers far more hope to his country's hard-pressed workforce than does Rodríguez Alcaine, for whom the worst corporatist practices are second nature, and innovation and democracy are anathema. Nonetheless, Rodríguez Alcaine's serving as secretary-general on an interim basis after Don Fidel's demise will be necessary to keep the hundreds of CTM dinosaurs in the fold until Millán and other modernizers broaden their support base. Whether Rodríguez Alcaine—smarting from charges of missing pension funds within his own union—will relinquish the leadership after a few months in office seems improbable. Even Ramírez Gamero advocated his election to a full six-year term at the Confederation's National Congress in March 1998, when delegates may reform the organization's statutes to prevent any secretary-general's reelection.

Return to Traditional Politics

In light of the disarray besetting the labor movement and his own precarious position, by mid-1995 Zedillo realized that he could not abandon the old order completely, lest he find himself hopelessly isolated. He bolstered his political team by making important changes in his cabinet and in the PRI. His first move involved appointing Emilio Chuayffet Chemor as government secretary in the place of his closest confidant, Esteban Moctezuma. A 43-year-old attorney, Chuayffet had earned praise from across the party gamut for chairing the Federal Electoral Institute in the early 1990s. He had amassed political capital during Zedillo's tenure in the Education Ministry by helping him repair relations with the military, after textbooks appeared emphasizing the army's role in the Tlatelolco massacre. When invited to join the cabinet, Chuayffet was serving as governor of Mexico state—a venue renowned for the Byzantine politics of the famous Atlacomulco machine— where he had learned the art of coalition building.

In an equally important appointment, Zedillo moved Oñate from the Labor Ministry to the PRI presidency in August 1995. The affable, chain-smoking 46-year-old lawyer replaced *salinista* María de los Angeles Moreno, an economist who presided over a rudderless party once the president, striving to keep a "healthy distance," stopped charting its course. Unlike his technocratic predecessor, Oñate had worked his way through the party ranks, serving as federal deputy; representative in the Assembly of the Federal District; ambassador to the Organization of American States; Salinas's chief-of-staff; and secretary of labor. Although a strong *colosista*, Oñate, like Chuayffet, boasted contacts among all segments of the party—especially with Don Fidel and the CTM, who applauded his "openness" and "willingness to listen" when Oñate headed the Labor Ministry. Oñate moved immediately to strengthen the party's relationship with its strongest corporatist element by recruiting Millán to become the PRI's secretary-general, the party's second-in-command. In addition to the new post, Millán had political experience as a senator (1982–1988); deputy (1991–1994); and head of the PRI in Sinaloa. He had resigned the latter post in late 1989 when the national PRI leadership recognized PAN candidates as the victors in several major municipal elections in his state, which Millán insisted they had not won.[7] A rising star in the CTM, Millán's entry into the party hierarchy reinforced his identification as a possible successor to the enfeebled Velázquez.

The government secretary and the PRI president occasionally lock horns, since both discharge vital political functions that engender turf battles. These disputes tend to be cyclical, flaring out when each man seeks to secure for members of his team nominations for governorships, Senate seats, and deputy slots—a process in which other powerful politicians intervene. While not particularly close personally, Chuayffet and Oñate sought to cooperate, hoping to assist the political neophyte wearing the presidential sash. Zedillo's decision to stand apart from the PRI altered the relationship between the Government Ministry and PRI presidency, inasmuch as both institutions had traditionally attempted to advance the government party's political agenda.

In early 1996, Zedillo added another seasoned politician to his political crew by naming Arsenio Farell as comptroller-general, a watchdog agent for official economic transactions. By placing the seasoned former labor secretary, 75, in this post, the president let the PRI's piratical old guard know they would not have to walk the plank for past plundering, but he expected no mutiny against the current captain.

At first, the PRI's electoral fortunes improved under the Chuayffet-Oñate Farell troika. From Zedillo's inauguration through August 1995, the PAN (43 percent) had run neck and neck with the PRI (43 percent) in the ten state and local contests that took place. Even though performing poorly in the November 1995 elections, the PRI registered a clear 46 percent to 28 percent advantage over the PAN in balloting held in twelve states between mid-1995 and mid-1996.

Gradually, hints at separating his office and his party disappeared from the president's vocabulary, as he assumed an increasingly pragmatic posture. This new stance came through decisively in his reaction to charges of electoral law violations in the southeast state of Tabasco. In November 1994, the PRD screamed foul when its nominee, Andrés Manuel López Obrador, lost the governorship to the PRI's Roberto Madrazo Pintado, 42, whose reformist father had served both as governor of the state and president of the PRI before dying under puzzling circumstances in an airplane accident. López Obrador charged that the PRI had resorted to fraud, intimidation, and an avalanche of cash to prevent his party's capturing its first statehouse.

The populist, dynamic López Obrador took his complaint from Villahermosa, Tabasco's capital, to Mexico City. There, he and hundreds of participants in his "Exodus for National Sovereignty and Dignity" encamped in the Zócalo, using the famous plaza as a staging area for protest marches along traffic-snarled avenues. Before sunrise on June 5, 1995, two secretive men awakened one of López Obrador's operatives with the promise that they had something "very important for the democratic movement in the country."

That something turned out to be sixteen file boxes jammed with ledgers, invoices, check stubs, and receipts that, according to the PRD, proved that Madrazo had spent $70 million to capture the governor's palace.[8]

This sum, more than fifty-eight times the legal ceiling on campaign expenditures in Tabasco ($1.2 million), amounted to nearly double the figure that Zedillo reported spending to win the presidency. In fact, each major American party received only $61.8 million in public funds to wage its presidential campaigns in 1996, and the population of the United States exceeds 150 times that of Tabasco.

The alleged PRI outlays shocked few Mexicans. After all, access to a trove of ill-gotten money has helped the official party dominate the country since 1929. The surprise came in the surfacing of compelling evidence for expenditures made in behalf of Madrazo, once deemed a rising force in the party. "This is a very, very important event," said Santiago Creel, a leading magistrate of the Federal Electoral Institute and later a PAN activist: "This is the first time in the history of the country that there has been evidence of this sort."

Rumors proliferated that senior federal officials—piqued at Madrazo's refusal to step down from the governorship amid earlier cries of fraud—provided the documents to embarrass him. Other theories traced the predawn delivery to old-guard bellyachers eager to ridicule Zedillo's fledgling efforts to promote fair elections, a practice destructive to their corporatist interests. For his part, Madrazo and his allies suggested that the PRD and its allies forged the documents, but the size, scope, and complexity of the material cast doubt on their self-serving hypothesis.

After private urgings for Madrazo to step aside failed, Zedillo accepted the reality of the situation: Should the Tabasco governor ignore a public demand to resign, Zedillo would lose even more credibility. Moreover, mobilizing the coercive powers of the presidency to unseat Madrazo—even if successful—would have given lie to the chief executive's promise to spurn his predecessor's authoritarian methods. Besides, the PRI's support network in the state—fortified by businesses and labor unions—was one of the most militant in the country. Rather than fight them, Zedillo decided to placate Madrazo and a group of other hard-line governors headed by Puebla's Manuel Bartlett. The latter governor had performed as the regime's top alchemist when, as government secretary, he conjured the votes necessary for Salinas to win the presidency. Conciliation took the form of Zedillo's taking time out from a tour of Campeche to pay a brief visit to Madrazo in neighboring Tabasco. Next, in June 1995, the president flew into Villahermosa. On the airport tarmac, he literally and figuratively embraced Madrazo, symbolizing a live-and-let-live policy towards Tabasco's beleaguered chief executive, his confreres, and other hard-boiled governors. Although Madrazo had to vault several more legal hurdles, Zedillo's *abrazo* ensured his absolution. In the process, the reformist chief executive showed that he understood the limits of his authority over the country's Madrazos and Bartletts. In the words of one journalist, "Mexico's state governors—powerful overlords, whose fathers and grandfathers were often governors before them—represented the obvious ballast for the president's unstable ship."[9]

Did, however, the Zedillo–Madrazo rapprochement prompt the diehard state executives to express any change of heart toward revamping the political system? "We [the PRI] gave away seats in Congress to the opposition long before they were strong enough to win on their own," averred Bartlett. "We invented the system of proportional representation. We introduced state financing for all political parties. All this was done courtesy of the PRI. And instead of thanks, what did we get? All out war," he added.

The federal government acted less passively in the case of Rubén Figueroa Alcocer, one of Zedillo's few close friends and governor of the impoverished Pacific coast state of Guerrero, well-known for violence, rebel movements, corruption, and the tourist mecca of Acapulco. In June 1995, seventeen peasants died in a shoot-out with the police, who insisted the campesinos had attacked them in the village of Aguas Blancas. Figueroa backed his law enforcement officers to the hilt, despite allegations they had murdered the small farmers and then planted weapons on them to substantiate the official version of events. "They wanted war, and they got war," Figueroa said of the peasants just after the killings.

A 360-page report by the National Human Rights Commission concluded that senior officials—including the state attorney general—had manipulated or destroyed evidence in the case. The Commission accused state authorities of blocking an independent investigation of the episode, falsifying forensic evidence, and placing the guns at the scene.

Charges and countercharges filled the air until February 1996, when a major television network broadcast unexpurgated video footage of the encounter, leaving no doubt that the police had executed unarmed peasants. Under a long-dormant constitutional provision, Zedillo promptly ordered the Supreme Court to investigate the case, enabling the president to accomplish a legal exit from this political thicket. After a two-month inquiry, the justices concluded that Figueroa and four of his key aides shared culpability for the crime, and urged Federal Attorney General Lozano to initiate action against all five. Surprisingly, he dismissed the findings as "mere opinion" and refused to investigate. Meanwhile, the Chamber of Deputies voted against impeaching Figueroa. Within a few days, however, Zedillo and Chuayffet persuaded the unrepentant governor to request a "leave of absence," although a PRI-backed congressional committee blocked efforts to remove him from office permanently. While inside maneuvering rather than democratic deliberation still determined many outcomes in Mexico, revelations of old-style politics had begun to elicit ire from the public and embarrassment from key government figures.

Old Guard Strikes Back

Just as Zedillo, Finance Secretary Ortiz, and other free marketeers believed they had replaced statism with neoliberalism and extended the olive-branch to traditionalists, all at once Old Mexico—personified by corporatist leader Carlos Romero Deschamps—sprang up to flay the privatization of the nation's secondary petrochemical industry. Escalating attacks on the proposed sell-off has profound implications for this country's long-term development. After the imprisonment of La Quina, the government recruited Professor Guzmán—a retired STPRM leader and La Quina-hater from Minatitlán—to take over the Oil Workers' Union, purging virtually all *quinista* loyalists from key posts. Authorities struck a deal with Guzmán Cabrera and other sympathetic labor officials: The latter renounced their longtime chief and supported management's quest to improve operations via restructuring and downsizing. For its part, the government vouchsafed their union allies' dominance over the STPRM.

When illness forced Guzmán Cabrera to step down in mid-1993, Pemex executives, convinced that they needed a stronger secretary-general to preserve stability in an ever more restive petroleum sector, handed over the union's reins to Romero Deschamps, the redoubtable head of Mexico City's large Local 35, another opportunistic *petrolero* with no current love lost for La Quina, once his ally. Romero Deschamps had caught the eye of former Pemex director-general Rojas (1987–1994), when the local leader had agreed to close Mexico City's pollution-belching Azcapotzalco refinery only after the government conceded to generous severance packages for the 5,000 *petroleros* thrown out of work. Intense preliminary talks with Romero Deschamps allowed Salinas to announce the closure at 11 a.m. on March 18, 1991, and initiate the shutdown before dark, with only pro forma protests.

In return for his loyalty to the team, the PRI even rewarded Romero Deschamps with a senate seat from Hidalgo state, paying $4,000 per month. This quid pro quo enabled foreign-trained technocrats to rule the roost at Pemex. They halved the number of oil workers from 280,000 to 139,022; signed service contracts with U.S. firms to drill in Mexico's most promising new oil zone, Campeche Sound; and reconfigured the sprawling corporation along functional lines. Pemex also spun off air-transport and other peripheral activities; bought into Shell's Deer Park, Texas, refinery; crafted plans for private firms to construct and operate facilities for gas distribution, transportation, and storage; and instituted comprehensive long-range planning at the monopoly.

In the past, Pemex CEOs had measured success by the quantities of hydrocarbons produced, the degree of energy self-sufficiency attained for the nation, and the diversity of the firm's overseas customers. In accord with these objectives, Pemex even dispatched an occasional tanker from a

Caribbean port, via the Panama Canal, to Salina Cruz if this Pacific Coast refinery ran short of crude oil: Never mind that the company would have saved hundreds of thousands of dollars by acquiring a tanker lot in the port of Long Beach, only a few hundred miles away in California. Similarly, managers routed tanker trucks long distances to replenish the supplies of Pemex service stations along the border, when instead the firm could have purchased the gasoline much more cheaply from U.S. distributors in Texas, Arizona, or California. Adrián Lajous Vargas, Pemex's astute director of planning and operations, jettisoned the company's pursuit of volumetric targets, Mexican autarky, and client diversification, striving instead for efficiency, transparency, accountability, and profitability.

Then came the December 1994 crisis that slashed the peso's value: Stung by his denunciation as a "traitor" in provincial union halls, Romero Deschamps' defense of Zedillo's neoliberal reforms began to wane apace with his members' loss of purchasing power, surging unemployment, and soaring prices. Since the dinosaurs roaming most of Mexico's official union sector use spoils and sanctions to ensure discipline among members, the loss of assets to redistribute brought the risk of serious dissent.

In early 1995, traditional top-down control succumbed to rank-and-file agitation: Popular pressure on Romero Deschamps mounted when Pemex began reviving plans to auction off ten petrochemical complexes including sixty-one plants, in hopes of raising some $1.5 billion for exploration and production. After the sale, the facilities' new owners would close many of the older units, consolidate operations, and slash their payrolls. To rub salt in the STPRM's wounds, the Zedillo administration's original scheme called for workers in affected complexes to shift from the Oil Workers' Union to the 25,000-member Chemical and Petrochemical Workers' Union, headed by Gilberto Muñoz Mosqueda, a government ally and another possible successor to CTM chief Velázquez.

Thus, Romero Deschamps began voicing his qualms about the projected sale, targeting his indignation at Lajous, the 53-year-old, Cambridge-trained economist whom Zedillo had promoted to director-general of Pemex at year's end in 1994. Despite encouragement to continue backing reforms, Romero Deschamps began to lash out at changes in the petroleum sector. At the March 18, 1995, commemoration of the fifty-seventh anniversary of the oil industry's nationalization, the barrel-chested senator stressed that the STPRM had undergone "internal cleaning," enjoyed "extraordinary unity," and no longer constituted a "state within the state"—a reference to its status under La Quina. Such "moral authority," stated Romero Deschamps, compelled him to denounce privatizing petrochemicals, contracting out maintenance work, limiting investments in modernizing Pemex facilities, and firing unconscionable numbers of loyal workers. Mouthing the language of free markets, Romero contended that our "experience as oil workers indicates that it's precisely the petrochemical sector that yields products with the greatest value added."[10]

Later in the year, Romero Deschamps and four other union representatives abstained when Pemex's government-controlled, eleven-member board narrowly endorsed privatization in October 1995. His constituents demanded even more aggressiveness from the STPRM chief, who increasingly found himself under the gun from Pablo Pavón Vinales (Minatitlán), Ramón Hernández Toledo (Pajaritos), and other grass-roots union activists. Romero Deschamps perceived that failure to staunchly oppose further layoffs could jeopardize his union leadership. Meanwhile, the PRD—joined by local elements of the PRI and PAN—ignited "anti-desincorporación" protests in the southern Veracruz area, home to 90 percent of the nation's petrochemical production.

At this point, Romero Deschamps confided his dilemma to Don Fidel. He acknowledged Velázquez's desire to help the struggling president. However, Romero concluded that Zedillo's venture would spell the end of his tenure at the STPRM. Arguing that he had his back against a wall and had to fight, Romero asked Don Fidel to empathize with his predicament. Comprehend Velázquez did, and the bulky CTM chief pledged to support his hard-pressed union brother.

On March 18, 1996, Pemex convened its "national dignity day" festivities on an island several hundred miles from Mexico City, aiming to prevent protests against the projected sale of state-owned assets. There, Romero Deschamps excoriated the petrochemical scheme with Zedillo, Lajous, and a dozen cabinet members and governors glumly looking on.

Later in the week, at a conclave of PRI heavyweights in Mexico City, Romero Deschamps quoted Luis Donaldo Colosio, the party's beloved, martyred presidential candidate, asserting that "economic modernization only makes sense when it enhances the welfare of Mexican families." Romero Deschamps decried privatization as an assault on the nation's sovereignty, challenged its constitutionality, and analogized it to a farmer's "selling one of his last productive cows to purchase milk, butter, cheese and yogurt." When asked to express their views on the proposal, the 250 PRI stalwarts in attendance jumped to their feet to give the STPRM leader a prolonged, foot-stomping ovation.

Why did such a modest, sensible proposal blow up like a Unabomber device in the faces of Mexico's best and brightest? First, all STPRM local presidents—even Romero Deschamps' bitterest enemies—fell in behind their secretary-general, whether or not their members worked in petrochemical facilities. They viewed the petrochemical deal as a test case of Pemex's policies, which, if allowed to succeed, would trigger a chain reaction leading to the privatization of refining, distribution, sales, transport, and exploration. Second, trade union leaders from across the spectrum rallied behind the Oil

Workers. Their action sprang not only from animus toward the modern-day mandarins and the market-focused agenda they learned at top American universities, but also because time had begun to run out for the nonagenarian Velázquez, and aspirants to succeed him wanted to appear as champions of the workers, not as puppets of the government or the Seven Sisters. Third, Romero Deschamps played an old corporatist gambit, activating peasant organizations by warning that foreign control over ammonia—the key ingredient in fertilizers—would boost the price of farmers' crucial input, threaten its availability, and undercut Zedillo's "Alliance for the Countryside," designed to improve rural output and welfare.

Fourth, the PRI—with its vocal labor and campesino sectors—weighed in on Romero Deschamps' side, lest opponents in mid-1997 gubernatorial and congressional elections accuse the party that has run Mexico for the last sixty-seven years of facilitating the gringos' "seizure of our nation's black-gold patrimony." The contests would hold particular significance because, for the first time, voters would directly elect Mexico City's mayor—with the winner well-positioned to vie for the presidency in the year 2000. On September 22, 1996, 4,423 delegates to the PRI's National Assembly vehemently had turned thumbs-down on the petrochemical privatization, disregarding technocrats' efforts to forestall a vote. "The PRI reiterates its historic compromise to '*el petróleo*' and all . . . hydrocarbons as property of the Nation," decreed a unanimously adopted resolution.[11]

Fifth, while large corporations had vacillated on this issue, small-scale producers of plastics, paints, and solvents groused about the plan, fearful that in a competitive market they could no longer count on special treatment from the old-boy network at Pemex. Sixth, as mentioned earlier, the petroleum industry remains a powerful symbol of national unity, at easy reach for politicians eager to arouse public anger against an administration scorned by foes as more sympathetic to Yankee investors than to Mexican workers.

Finally, and most importantly, the STPRM spurned an exclusively fist-in-the-face approach by complementing its nationalistic alarums with a challenge using the technocrats' own weapon, legal principles. To begin with, they argued that in 1985 the government—once known for expropriating peasants' property willy-nilly—erected a portion of the Cosoleacaque complex—the first petrochemical facility scheduled for the auction block—on a former *ejido*. Apparently, the technocrats overlooked the legal obligation to return this land to its campesino owners once its use changed from "public" to "private" benefit. In addition, while Mexican statutes permit private ownership of secondary petrochemical holdings, a number of the plants destined for sale also turn out one or more of the eight primary petrochemicals, which only Pemex can produce under existing law. In yet another faux pas, on November 14, 1995, the Energy Ministry announced the bidding process with respect to properties "for the production of secondary petrochemicals that now belong to Pemex-Petroquímica"—one of the monopoly's four quasi-independent units created by Lajous three years earlier: However, the corporate holding company failed to transfer Cosoleacaque's title to its subsidiary until December 12, 1995, apparently invalidating the offer.[12]

In the PRI's heyday, a powerful president would have thrown caution to the wind, swept these "technicalities" under the rug, and done as he pleased without a second thought. But the opinion leaders and average citizens—who cheered after Salinas assured them that government divestiture of its holdings would slash inflation, lower prices, give consumers more choices, and propel economic growth—now associated privatization with Mexico's worst recession in modern memory and the ubiquitous, toxic intrigues of the disgraced ex-president's family.

Lajous and the Energy Ministry found themselves saddled with a legal framework vulnerable to attack by foes of the transaction, including many Pemex insiders who eagerly supplied ammunition to Romero Deschamps and his fellow naysayers. Even La Quina entered the fray: By showering the media with money and granting interviews from his comfortable infirmary room in prison, Hernández Galicia emphasized his credentials as an "avowed nationalist," "defender of the national patrimony," "opponent of decreased expenditures at Pemex," and "political prisoner" of Carlos Salinas, who larded the state company with "*pitufos*" or bureaucratic smurfs. La Quina proudly pointed to letters from thirteen governors, received in prison, lauding the STPRM's donation of roads in their states.[13]

In Ciudad Madero, the Second of August Movement, named for La Quina's birthday, sprang to life to lobby for the release of its hero, depicted as a sick, enervated martyr who wanted nothing more than to spend the remainder of his life quietly with his "family." Needless to say, Romero Deschamps doubted La Quina's feebleness, and preferred that the longtime boss remain a guest of the state lest, as a free man, he add to the STPRM leader's intramural headaches.

While most observers believed that the PRI Assembly's action had laid the issue to rest, the strong-willed Zedillo refused to yield. Not only did he seek to save face after suffering a stinging rebuke from his own party; he also wanted to signal to the investment community a resolve to stay the privatization course. He concocted and steamrolled through Congress a measure under which Pemex could divest itself of up to 49 percent of existing secondary petrochemical complexes, while retaining majority control. This plan allowed private firms to attain 100 percent ownership of any new plants they constructed. Romero Deschamps beamed a Cheshire cat grin when voting for the so-called "privatization lite" legislation, realizing that only a vastly scaled-back sell-off would transpire in an industry fraught with labor, legal, maintenance, and environmental challenges.

Conclusion

"What-ifs" abound in analyzing Zedillo's efforts to leverage his technocratic skills to modernize a Mexico that has functioned on the same governing model for almost five centuries. Although ever more subject to change, Mexico still relies upon the patterns of corporatism woven into its history and politics for social stability. For example, what if Salinas had chosen the politically adroit Ortiz Arana to replace Colosio? Might not the selection of a parochial politician rather than a cosmopolitan economist have concerned the U.S. government and private investors so much that Salinas would have had no choice but to devalue the peso before leaving office? What if Zedillo had kept Aspe in the Finance Ministry at least for a transitional period? Would not such an appointment have ensured a more orderly devaluation of the peso, even if accomplished early on Zedillo's watch? What if Serra Puche had borrowed Aspe's Rolodex and immediately opened communications with New York bankers and creditors? Could the new finance secretary have prevented the orgy of investors unloading pesos?

Hypothetical questions aside—and despite his reformist zeal—Zedillo inherited an intensely troubled economy, and promptly made the worst out of a bad situation. The new cabinet's arrogance, inexperience, and lack of political bases reinforced the weaknesses of an accidental president. Although the Salinas family drama diverted attention from the chief executive's own travails, the public itched for revenge against the Ivy League-educated eggheads who had promised economic salvation, but instead provided a hell-on-earth—replete with mounting inflation, surging unemployment, and shrinking paychecks. While the old guard harbored serious misgivings about Salinas, they also feared him as a ruthless in-fighter, surrounded by a big, loyal team, who had managed to revive a moribund economy. In addition, his plethora of "free-trade agreements," "privatizations," and "market-oriented policies" brought accolades from both local elites *and* international observers, appealing to Mexican nationalism. While the PAN scored some questionable victories, the PRI's popularity rose in keeping with that of the chief executive, and Salinas did not make wholesale threats against most PRI bosses' positions. In contrast, Zedillo lacked political savvy, counted on one hand his walk-through-fire allies, and had failed at his alleged strength—managing the economy, at least during his first two years in office.

The recruitment of Chuayffet, Oñate, and Farell helped to calm some hackles raised by grass-roots opposition to the economic disaster. Yet for Madrazo, Bartlett, and other corporatist bullies, Zedillo's Mexico seemed a sun-drenched beach where they could kick political sand in the face of the professorial president, a ninety-pound weakling. With the emergence of the petrochemicals issue, the muscle-bound Romero Deschamps leaped into the fray with a vengeance.

Figure 5.1   Salinas's Actions and their Impact on the Zedillo Administration

Source: Oscar Aguilar Asencio, Professor of Political Science, *IberoAmerican University*, Mexico City

Salinas	Zedillo
Inaugurated during a crisis of legitimacy	Assumed power enjoying substantial legitimacy
Inherited a political and economic crisis	Accomplished the transition smoothly
Selected a cohesive and balanced governing team	Inherited a governing team from his predecessor for want of his own *camarilla*
Rapidly enhanced his legitimacy (*Quinazo*)	Lost political capital quickly (December 1994 peso crisis)
Broadened his room to maneuver, thereby accentuating his control and firm-handedness	Reduced rapidly his room to maneuver, breeding uncertainty
Established the presidency as the center of power and decision making	Diminished presidential powers by renouncing such metaconstitutional faculties as the *dedazo*
Controlled the governors	Promoted a "New Federalism," allowing conflicts to overflow their traditional channels of control
Redefined strategies and alliances (PRI and PAN vs. PRD)—with increasing links between the government and the church, big business, and the media.	Overcame political polarization: reproachment with PRD amid tensions with the PAN and elements of the business community
Fashioned a clear image	Suffered from a negative image until the July 6, 1997, elections
Solved electoral disputes pragmatically	Diminished electoral conflicts
Devised a national security doctrine that warded off attacks on his economic program and promoted policies that would transcend his *sexenio*	Projected no vision of national security
Advanced a social policy that increased political legitimacy, social control, and electoral support (Pronasol)	Advanced no social policy
Promoted "trust" and "understanding" as basis of Mexico's relationship with the United States.	Witnessed strained relations with the U.S. because of drug and immigration issues highlighted during Clinton-Dole presidential campaign
Presided over a cabinet characterized by counterweights (Camacho Solís vs. Gutiérrez Barrios and Córdoba Montoya; Aspe vs. Zedillo and Ortiz Martínez)	Named a cabinet without counterweights composed largely of members who lack political clout
Synchronized relations between financial and political operators	Failed to synchronize political and financial operations

As portrayed in Figure 5.1, Zedillo's presidency bore little similarity to that of his predecessor. It can be argued that Salinas lost the election, but won the presidency—thanks to the *quinazo*, a top-notch balanced team, a crisp image, the centralization of decision making within Los Pinos, a coherent vision of Mexico's future, and legitimacy derived from linkages to the military, the church, the business community, the media, and—above all—the masses via Pronasol. In contrast, Zedillo defeated Fernández de Cevallos and Cárdenas fair and square. Yet, by mid-term he appeared to have lost—or failed to have won—the presidency for a number of reasons. The peso debacle knocked him for a loop; he assembled a cabinet long on degrees but short on political experience and significant constituencies; he weakened the presidency by sharing power with other branches and renouncing such "metaconstitutional" prerogatives as the *dedazo;* he projected an ambiguous image; and he scuttled Pronasol without replacing it with a new social policy.

In sum, Zedillo focused on macroeconomic policies, leaving it to Government Secretary Chuayffet to fashion the political keystone of his administration—namely, sweeping electoral reforms, designed to renew the legitimacy of the political system and hasten its evolution from corporatism to pluralism. The final chapter assesses his progress in accomplishing this daunting task.

Notes

1. Austreberto Silva, quoted in Sam Quiñones and Thomas Catán, "The Unknown President," *Mexican Business* (November 1996): 48.
2. Leticia Maldonado, quoted in Quiñones and Catán, "The Unknown President," p. 48.
3. "Candidate is Selected after Division in Party," *Washington Post*, March 30, 1994, p. A-1.
4. For the full text, see Ernesto Zedillo, "Queremos una patria en paz," *Reforma*, December 2, 1994, pp. 61–71.
5. Tod Robberson, "Key Official Forced Out in Mexico," *Washington Post*, December 30, 1994, p. A-1.
6. Tod Robberson, "Political Arrest Jars Long Tradition," *Washington Post*, March 2, 1995, p. A-24.
7. Interview Juan S. Millán L., PRI Secretary-General, Mexico City, August 1, 1996.
8. Guadalupe Irízar, "Revelan millonaria campaña de madero," *Reforma*, June 10, 1995, p. 4-A.
9. Leslie Crawford and Daniel Dombey, "Isolated Zedillo Trades Policy for Friends," *Financial Times*, July 11, 1996.

10. Carlos Romero Deschamps, *Discurso: lvii aniversario de la expropiación petrolera, 18 de marzo de 1995* (Mexico City: STPRM, 1995).

11. "El disenso interno," *Reforma*, September 25, 1996.

12. Fernando Ortega Pizarro, "El proceso de privatización de la petroquímica viola límites jurídicos, territoriales y jurisdiccionales, *Proceso*, May 27, 1996, pp. 6–11.

13. Miguel Reyes Razo, "Fue cuento; ni apoyé a del mazo ni ccs era mi gallo: la quina, *Excélsior*, September 11, 1996, pp. 1-A and 10-A.

6

Mexico's Prospects

Introduction

During the nearly five centuries that have elapsed since the arrival of Cortés, politics in Mexico have been shaped by a distinctive social and political outlook, a vision of the natural order of society and the state that I have called, following scholarly usage, corporatism: namely, a sociopolitical system organized on the basis of functional groups rather than individualism or "one man, one vote"; it tends to be top-down, mercantilist, statist, and authoritarian; a mechanism for controlling change and keeping interest groups in line. It is usually anti-liberal, anti-pluralist, and anti-free enterprise.

From the colonial era to the present, Mexican society has witnessed many profound economic and technological transformations, periodic political instability, major and minor civil and international wars, and, at the beginning of this century, one of the world's greatest revolutions. As a result of these upheavals, key political actors have been transformed or displaced while new ones have entered the scene. Yet a singular focus on these often tumultuous changes masks an underlying continuity: the persistence of an inclusive but sharply differentiated and hierarchical conception of society

in which the holders of state power reserve to themselves the right to selectively organize, sanction, discipline, deny, or even destroy competing societal
interests. The Mexican revolution, important and far-reaching as it was, did
not really challenge this figural model. Rather, as earlier chapters have
shown, it confirmed and institutionalized corporatism as a strategy of both
gradual change and social control.

The six decades that followed the revolution witnessed a degree of stability that was unparalleled in Latin America. Miraculously, that stability has
survived nearly intact the brutal economic downturns of the 1980s and 1990s.
Yet proliferating signs of fundamental disorder—assassinations of high-level
political figures, armed insurgencies in the south, rising crime and insecurity
in the urban centers, Croesus-rich drug cartels, a fractured but increasingly
sophisticated and formidable opposition, and open splits within the PRI itself—are now everywhere to be seen.

Partly owing to the success of the PRI's corporatist strategy, Mexicans
have only rarely looked beyond their boundaries for assistance or succor.
Staunchly, often arrogantly nationalist, Mexico remained a world unto itself.
Even Mexico's foreign trade was guided by the inward focus of the import
substitution industrial model. With the extended economic crisis that began
in August 1982, however, Mexico's external orientation has been utterly revised. The debt crisis, never adequately resolved, ushered in a now fifteen-
year period of progressive domestic economic reform and external opening
that has slowly but inexorably eroded the underpinnings of the Mexican system. The failure of a series of attempts at ever deeper economic transformation to produce a robust revitalization of real per-capita economic growth;
the decision, under highly visible foreign tutelage and encouragement, to
rely ever more on the market mechanism as basic distributor of goods and
arbiter of incomes; and the eagerness of recent presidents to open up ever
wider sectors of the Mexican market and financial system to international investment and influence—all have laid bare Mexico's economic and political
vulnerabilities.

In true corporatist fashion, the principal agent of control in this story has
been the government-party amalgam. The party functions both as a vast patronage mechanism and a device for linking many interest groups to the system, although the mounting number of unrepresented organizations,
institutions, and individuals has diminished the regime's legitimacy. The remarkable tranquility amid economic convulsions confirms the unique powers
that the central government still wields in Mexico. But it also reflects the continuing influence of the corporatist image. Subaltern social groups no less
than the elites continue to look to the peak of the political pyramid as the
locus of legitimate social decision making and action. No other feature of
Mexico's political history or contemporary landscape better explains the relative tranquility of the past decade and a half. Yet today Mexico's political lead-

ership, still dominated by the PRI, confronts a dilemma as challenging and portentous as any in its history. They must decide what posture to assume when confronted by necessary economic restructuring and the forced relaxation of political control.

Proponents of electoral reform frequently compare the Mexican experience to that of Spain a generation before,[1] drawing an implicit analogy between the PRI-government regime and Generalissimo Francisco Franco's dictatorship—which *El Caudillo* ruled with an iron hand after taking power in 1939, only gradually softening his authoritarianism in the years before his death in late 1975. These electoral reformers compare President Zedillo with Prime Minister Adolfo Suárez González, whom King Juan Carlos designated to take the reins of the first post-Franco government. Like Zedillo, the inexperienced Suárez confronted grave economic problems, attacks from guerrilla organizations, and plotting by disgruntled right-wing defenders of the *franquista* autocracy: The negotiation of electoral reforms among Mexico's three major parties—along with the tiny Labor Party—resembled the Suárez-impelled Law for Political Reform that disbanded Franco's Falange and legalized the Communist Party, as Spain evolved from corporatism into a competitive and pluralistic parliamentary monarchy. To secure this transition, the King and Suárez had to stand firm against threats from diehard Falangists, known as the "Bunker," roughly the Castillian version of Mexico's dinosaurs.[2]

As discussed later in this chapter, the premise of this comparison has proved erroneous and the outcome of the Mexican experiment has given rise to a polity that looks less like Spain after Franco than the post-Chernenko Soviet Union—with the discrediting of established political institutions and the unleashing of social forces that threaten the regime's durability.

Zedillo's Gambit

In his inaugural address Zedillo called for electoral law revisions as part of an overall Reform of the State. As described by the president on December 1, 1994, this "definitive reform" would embrace such elements as the fair financing of political parties, limits on campaign expenditures, access to the mass media for all contenders, and the full autonomy of electoral organs. "Electoral democracy must cease to be the focus of political debate and the precipitant of rancor and division," Zedillo declaimed.[3] Reforms would also revamp the judicial system, diminish *presidentialismo* by conferring greater power on the judicial and legislative branches, reconfigure relations between the federal government and those at the state and local level, and combat the corruption that pervaded the bureaucracy.

The country's evolution from corporatism to pluralism promised many advantages, according to the new chief executive: First, it would promote national unity, guaranteeing "a stable and uneventful transition to both a developed economy and a strong democracy." Second, the transformation would enhance both the rule of law and the legitimacy of state institutions. Third, governmental reform would spur economic and social progress and vice-versa, allowing Mexico to "take full advantage of the changing global economy."

In mid-January 1995, the leaders of Mexico's four largest, most influential political parties met in Los Pinos. There with Government Secretary Moctezuma, they signed "Compromises for a National Political Accord," immediately hailed as a "landmark agreement," to initiate Zedillo's proposed electoral-law revisions. Signatories hoped that in addition to facilitating cooperation on election matters, the compact would calm financial markets. In turn, this would help achieve congressional approval of the Clinton administration's multibillion-dollar rescue package, facing criticism that Mexico's economic problems followed principally from sixty-five years of single-party hegemony.

Zedillo also argued that serious negotiations might persuade the PRD to abandon strikes against Madrazo's disputed election as Tabasco's governor in late 1994. Supporters of losing candidate López Obrador complemented these work stoppages by blockading roads leading to refineries and drilling sites in that oil-endowed southeastern state. To entice the PRD to the bargaining table, government officials promised to hold new elections in both Tabasco and Chiapas within twenty-four months. In the latter state, the PRD declared a "rebel government in transition," while joining the Zapatistas in demanding the removal of PRI governor Eduardo Robledo.

The agreement to craft a definitive electoral reform launched a jerky, eighteen-month roller-coaster ride with the four participating teams—each headed by their party presidents. The negotiators alternatively sat on their hands, threatened to sabotage the tracks, threw on the brakes, or even leapt out of the car. The ink had barely dried on the electoral accord when the "Tabasco mutiny" broke out: An irate Madrazo mobilized thousands of *priísta* supporters to urge Zedillo to rescind any call for new Tabasco elections that would require Madrazo's leaving office three years early. "I am with you," the besieged governor told a protest rally staged by club-wielding militants, who used buses, cars, and cargo trucks to seal off Villahermosa, as federal highway police stood by idly. Zedillo's subsequent trips to the state capital reassured Madrazo that he could complete his term despite festering charges of hyper-campaign spending. While appeasing the *madrazistas*, the chief executive's action drove the PRD from the negotiating table as they decried "yet another act of PRI fraud."

Such actions contributed to Secretary Moctezuma's difficulty in advancing the talks. Only when able politician and bargainer par excellence Chuayffet replaced him in early July 1995 did the discussions begin to gain momentum. Not surprisingly, the PAN withdrew from the deliberations—twice: once to object to alleged gross irregularities in Yucatán's May 1995 state elections and, again, to underscore assertions of vote manipulation in the municipalities of Huejotzingo, Puebla. The second boycott lasted from February to late May 1996, persuading many observers that only three parties would subscribe to any final agreement. Felipe Calderón's election as the PAN's new president—and reversal of the Huejotzingo results in favor of the *panista* candidate—drew them back into the talks.

Several hours before the midnight signing ceremony at Los Pinos, the PRD representative balked at endorsing the document because it proscribed the reelection of current citizen councillors to the autonomous Federal Electoral Institute—a move that betokened the PRI's animus towards several incumbents they perceived as hostile to their party. Only assurances from Chuayffet and the PRI's congressional leadership about revisiting this issue when crafting implementing legislation convinced Muñoz Ledo to sign the accord so as "not to frustrate the democratic advance of the country."

On July 25, the negotiators announced they had hammered out an agreement, which is summarized in Table 6.1.

Many key provisions attacked the PRI's corporatist mechanisms: notably, the requirement for "individual" rather than "collective" party membership; shifting the IFE presidency from the government secretary to a councillor chosen by Congress; reducing from 315 to 300, the number of members a single party could elect to the Chamber of Deputies; and selecting one-quarter of the Senate by proportional representation.

In addition, the reforms made it possible for Mexicans overseas to vote in the next presidential contest. Opposition parties anticipated that expatriates—having lived in democratic societies like the United States and enjoying economic opportunities unavailable at home—would cast their ballots against the PRI. Further, under this plan the Federal District would have a popularly elected mayor, in lieu of a presidential appointee. The capital's chief executive manages a sprawling city administration providing more than 100,000 jobs to the party faithful. Opportunities for party fundraising or individual bribe-taking abound in a Kafkaesque bureaucracy, often requiring an entrepreneur to obtain two-dozen signatures just to open a fast-food restaurant or other small enterprise. The city's three separate law enforcement agencies have attained a worldwide reputation for exacting *mordidas* for trumped-up charges or protecting drug dealers while supposedly safeguarding the public. In 1994 Zedillo garnered 42.5 percent of the vote in the D.F. Nonetheless, Salinas (27.3 percent) and the PRI lost badly there in 1988, and public opinion surveys throughout 1997 showed either the PRD, the PAN, or both outpolling the PRI. Popular election of the D.F.'s mayor would yield a powerful anti-PRI vote because of dire economic conditions and a soaring crime rate in the capital area. The new mayor would occupy the country's second-most

Table 6.1   Electoral Reform Adopted by Congress, August 1996

*Source: "Reformas electorales a 18 artículos de la constitución," *El economista*,
July 26, 1996, p. 31

Category	Provisions
Presidency	*Eliminates government secretary as president of IFE *Stipulates direct election of "governor of Federal Electoral Institute (IFE) and Federal District (D.F.), governor will appoint D.F.'s attorney general
Congress	*Selects the nine councillors composing IFE *Names the president of the IFE
Judiciary	*Incorporates into the national judiciary the Federal Electoral Tribunal, which declares the validity of all elections *Vests ultimate review of electoral disputes in Supreme Court of Justice of the Nation (SCJN) *Creates a new form of injunction (*amparo*) to safeguard political rights
Institutional Revolutionary Party	*Requires affiliation with parties to be individual, not collective *Provides for greater public than private campaign financing *Distributes 70 percent of public funds to parties proportional to their representation in the Chamber of Deputies—with 30 percent disbursed equally to parties *Regulates access of candidates to the media *Reduces from 315 to 300 the maximum number of seats that any party can hold in the 500-member Chamber of Deputies *Establishes the election of 32 members of the 128-seat Senate by proportional representation *Calls for the direct election of "delegates"—or borough presidents—in the year 2000

powerful position—with standing comparable to that of New York City's, Chicago's, and Los Angeles's mayors combined. Immediately upon entering office he would appear on everyone's short list of likely contenders for the 2000 presidential contest. In addition, reforms stipulate that, in the 2000 elections, citizens would directly elect the heads of the capital's *delegaciones* or boroughs, the number of which will increase from sixteen to twenty-one.

The PRI did manage to take revenge on a renegade party member who had broken the rules of presidential succession. They supported language—initially offered by the PAN—to bar anyone who had ever served in an elective or appointive capacity as D.F. mayor from standing for election as the city's chief executive. Although the provision affected a half-dozen other war horses, the PRI savored blocking a run by Camacho Solís, the mayor named by Salinas, who had publicly groused over losing the PRI's 1994 presidential nomination to Colosio; Camacho Solís had resigned from the PRI in hopes of forming a center-left anti-PRI coalition or gaining another party's nomination for the top spot in city hall.

Chuayffet and Oñate agreed to these and other compromises because they wanted to deliver an electoral reform on which Zedillo had staked his reputation. The PRI gave ground on questions of other parties' access to the mass media, as well as the amount and transparency of campaign financing. For their part, the PAN, PRD, and PT could not secure an agreement on authorizing ballot initiatives and referenda. Also, the PAN and the PRD failed to gain standing for individual citizens to challenge the findings of electoral tribunals. Nor could its political competitors prevent the PRI's employing red, white, and green—the colors on Mexico's flag—on its party logo and materials.

Still, each of the four parties had achieved some of their priorities. PRI leaders had broadly supported Zedillo's quest for "definitive" electoral reform. The PAN succeeded in requiring individual party memberships and attaining the vote for Mexicans abroad. The PRD helped dispel its radical obstructionist image by negotiating in good faith to improve the electoral system. Finally, despite winning less than 3 percent of the ballots cast in the 1994 presidential election, the PT had demonstrated its legitimacy as an equal of the three major parties at the bargaining table.

Predictably, Zedillo drew the most satisfaction from the reforms. After participating in the accord's signing as a "witness of honor," the president asserted that "today we are taking an irreversible and decisive step toward constructing full democratic development," as Mexico moved into a new century. Spokesmen for opposition parties concurred. "The document signed by the party leaders represents one of the greatest contributions to our political system in recent years. It is an initiative without precedence that requires the support of all of society to achieve its goals," gushed usually taciturn Attorney General Lozano.

Outgoing PRD president Muñoz Ledo took pride in the accord not only for its substance, but because his role in the negotiations had burnished his credibility as a national figure who might seek the mayor's seat in Mexico City, the presidency, or both: "We have fulfilled our responsibility [and] must act quickly to ensure that hunger and despair don't win the race against politics," he said. "The time is brief to apply the reform; citizens demand credible action from . . . political actors; we can respond neither ambiguously nor by violating our promises." Labor Party President Alberto Anaya Gutiérrez added: "This is the most transcendental reform of the nation in modern times."

In mid-1996, the legislative leadership convened an extraordinary session of Congress to take up this legislation. Several considerations underlay the urgency of addressing the electoral initiatives. On August 3, the moderate Muñoz Ledo would turn over the PRD's reins to López Obrador, the articulate, anti-Madrazo rabble-rouser from Tabasco who had agreed to the constitutional revisions, but expressed little enthusiasm for them. In addition, Zedillo hoped to highlight electoral reform in his State of the Nation speech, planned for September 1: "Since Zedillo made political reform one of the main points of his campaign in 1994, it was important for the . . . agreement to be reached before his second address," commented political analyst Juan Pablo González.[4] Finally, its authors wanted to have the changes in place for the thirteen state, local, and federal contests that jammed the 1997 electoral calendar.

The Chamber of Deputies took only four hours to debate and pass changes to eighteen articles of the constitution. Even though some of their delegation decried the proposals as the "first step toward ceding power to the opposition," labor members grudgingly joined their colleagues in delivering a unanimous vote in favor of the plan. "This agreement shows a different side of political parties," emphasized PRI Deputy Jorge Moreno Collado, noting that "rather than political reform talks falling apart, the nation's parties have put their partisan interests aside for the good of the nation."

Senators followed the deputies' lead, approving the reform package with no dissent. PRI senators praised Zedillo and Chuayffet for their respective roles in spurring and brokering the compromise. Ortiz Arana, president of the body and the PRI heavyweight who had thrown his support to Zedillo after Colosio's assassination, lauded the chief executive's vision and praised the initiative as the start of a new relationship between Mexico's political parties. With an eye on rebel movements in Chiapas and Guerrero and the poverty that precipitated them, Ortiz Arana added:

> These are times of democracy, both as a means of government and as a social agreement. These reforms are the mechanism which will allow us to confront the threats that are being posed to social harmony. These reforms will change the configuration of the parties and strengthen Mexican politics.

The PAN's Senate leader, Gabriel Jiménez Remus, said: "Cleaning up Mexican politics is complex but very necessary. There can be no further delays. Electoral reform is the first step but there is still a very long way to go before we see an integrated reform of the state." PRD senators concurred with the *panistas* that they would leave issues—such as determining the basis for proportionally selecting one-quarter of the Senate—for subsequent implementing legislation. A PRD senator from Guerrero, Félix Salgado, called for accepting the reforms in good faith but warned: "We're moving ahead. But we're moving ahead with the same people, the same false democrats who have made a habit of fixing elections in the past." Salgado's PRD colleague from Tabasco, Auldárico Hernández, conveyed even sharper skepticism: "Laws come and laws go," he said,

> Many of the elements in the reform package are very good but these must be accomplished. I have my doubts that these will be completely fulfilled. Even if 60 percent of the proposals are achieved that will be a huge advance but looking around and seeing the number of local political power barons, or caciques, it is clear to see there will [be] no change until they are forced out.

Misgivings and Second Thoughts

Later in the year, Senators Salgado's and Hernández's reservations proved prescient, as electoral reverses diminished the readiness of an already reluctant PRI to champion sweeping changes. As expected, Zedillo lauded the electoral reforms during his State of the Nation address on September 1, but embedded references to the changes amid invective showered on the violent, newly emerged People's Revolutionary Army (ERP), which he vowed to pursue with "the full force of the law."

"Just when we are progressing toward real democracy . . . we will not accept the emergence of outdated and bloody incidents of violence," Zedillo contended in what observers called the most effective speech of his administration to date. Still, dissent lay near at hand. In contrast to Zedillo's excoriation of the ERP, PRD Deputy Marco Rascón detracted from the dignity of the ceremony by donning a rubber pig's mask and hoisting placards ridiculing the chief executive's policies: "Long live the market economy!" proclaimed one poster, signed by "The Rich."

Three weeks later, even while deploring "neoliberalism" and "technocrats," PRI delegates paid lip service to the innovations at the party's seventeenth National Assembly. In November, however, PRI candidates lost ground in three states, giving credence to the view—voiced by PRI labor deputies in mid-summer— that the spade of electoral reform could dig the party's grave. The governing party suffered its most embarrassing loss in Mexico state, which wraps around three-quarters of Mexico City and captures a microcosm of the country, embracing urban, suburban, small-town, and rural areas. The PRI did manage to retain control of the state legislature

(30 to 15), capture at least pluralities in more than half of the municipalities (72 of 122), and win the mayoralty of Toluca, the capital, and Ecatepec, the state's second largest city. Still, the PRD attained the mayor's office in Nezahualcóyotl, a teeming settlement of 1.2 million shanty-dwellers adjacent to the Mexico City airport. The PAN did even better, scoring victories in four huge working- and middle-class municipalities: Naucalpan, Tlalnepantla, Atizapán, and Cuautitlán Izcalli. All told, the PRI polled 38.1 percent of the ballots, down from 46.4 percent in 1994; the PAN increased its presence to 30.9 percent, up from 25.6 percent; and the PRD witnessed its share of the vote rise from 18.1 percent to 22.2 percent. While the PRI had entered the fray controlling jurisdictions encompassing almost 97 percent of the state's 12.5 million residents, after the contests PRI mayors governed only 50 percent of the population, or 6 million citizens.[5]

Several reasons made the electoral rebuff an especially bitter pill for the PRI to swallow. First, the revolutionary party enjoys one of its best organizations in Mexico state, the spawning ground of Fidel Velázquez, Rodríguez Alcaine, Hank González, Mario Ramón Beteta, Alfredo del Mazo, and other political muckymucks. Second, even though a product of the state's political machine, Government Secretary Chuayffet could not deliver his own bailiwick. Third, Mexico state is the largest of the country's thirty-one states, boasting thirty-eight members in the Chamber of Deputies. Finally, some *priístas* feared that the outcome could foreshadow the mid-1997 vote in Mexico City: The state melds into the capital; its residents fall into the same media market as the *capitalinos*; and concern about jobs, salaries, public safety, and pollution pervade the entire metropolitan area. In each of the major municipalities contiguous to Mexico City, the PRI's percentage fell twenty points, and respondents to a post-election survey conducted by the newspaper *Reforma* cited poor personal economic conditions as the principal reason for desertions from the ruling party.[6]

To add insult to the PRI's political injury, the opposition also made headway in the northern state of Coahuila, birthplace to early twentieth-century revolutionary heroes Madero and Carranza. For the first time in history, the opposition broke the ruling party's vise-like hold on the state legislature, picking up half of its thirty-two seats. The PRI held on to the mayors' offices of Piedras Negras, San Pedro, and Matamoros, but the PAN swept to victory in the state's four most populous cities—Saltillo, the capital, and Torreón, Monclova, and Frontera. The PRI suffered only a slight decline in its overall vote compared to 1994 (45.4 percent), while the PAN registered a 23.1 percent gain increasing to 34.9 percent overall.

A similar pattern prevailed in the small state of Hidalgo—once the world's biggest source of silver—which lies fifty miles northwest of Mexico City. The PRI held on to seventy-four of eighty-four municipalities, including the capital, Pachuga. Still, it lost the important refining center of Tula, long a union town, to the PRD and the picturesque Apan to the PT.

The Party Reacts

One week after the PRI misfortunes in local elections, Government Secretary Chuayffet, Chamber of Deputies Majority Leader Humberto Roque Villanueva, and other party stalwarts reversed ground on Zedillo's "irreversible" electoral plan. The turnabout took place in Congress, where PRI legislators—egged on by deputies and senators from the CTM—broke ranks with their PAN, PRD, and PT colleagues over the all-party deal forged in mid-summer. They justified their stance on grounds that inability to concur on state funding for political parties—the PRI sought a $278 million cap; the opposition backed $125 million—relieved the ruling party of its obligation to support the entire package. In two days, the PRI bloc steamrolled a watered-down reform package through the Chamber by a 282 to 142 vote, with only one PRI deputy defecting. Similarly the Senate voted strictly along partisan lines. Among the most important of the sixteen changes were:

- Reimposing the higher level of public funding;

- Raising the ceiling on private campaign contributions by $12.5 million—10 percent higher than the agreed maximum of 10 percent of the funding received from the state;

- Changing excess campaign spending from a criminal to an "administrative" penalty, except in cases of money laundering;

- Eliminating safeguards against any party's capturing a majority in Congress with less than 50 percent of the vote (Accomplishing this change necessitated limiting the number of "common candidates"—those backed by two or more parties—from 160 to 100 in the Chamber and from 34 to 20 in the Senate);

- Reducing from 40 to 30 percent the amount of media coverage distributed equally among parties, while increasing from 60 to 70 percent the media time allocated according to a party's electoral strength;

- Prohibiting parties from forming coalitions for the D.F. mayor's race; and

- Sharply restricting coalition-building in other contests.[7]

The PRI's fear over losing the mayor's office in Mexico City and relinquishing control of the Chamber of Deputies lay at the heart of their hobbling reforms. Both addicted to and adept at disbursing funds for political advantage, the ruling party wanted to enter the election cycle with a bulging treasury, even if it meant additional resources for competitors. Thanks to the changes wrought by Humberto Roque and Chuayffet, the federal government would dole out funds to parties as follows: PRI ($109 million); PAN ($65 million); PRD ($48.5 million); and PT ($23.2 million). The ruling party hiked the limit on private contributions, secure in the knowledge that it could tap more resources than its adversaries, especially from the business community and affluent individuals whose wealth derives from their ties to the PRI.

In the aftermath of what analysts called a "fast-track" vote in both houses, the governing party became the target of mordant criticism. "The PRI has shown its true face," said Santiago Creel, a former IFE official who played an important intermediary role in the negotiations, adding "[i]t does not want to compete fairly." PRD President López Obrador offered an even harsher assessment: "Now we know that change in Mexico is not going to come through legal reforms. It's going to come from the mobilization and votes of the people." In the words of PAN president Calderón, "This reform is not deep or durable and it doesn't guarantee us a democratic regime. We risk returning to fraudulent and questionable elections." When asked whether the PAN would reject the additional $65 million funding available under the modified plan, the party's secretary-general said that decision would be made by the party's National Council. Ultimately, the determination for taking the monies was left up to the appropriate party organization: the National Council spurned funds for its legislative candidates while the Mexico City PAN accepted the financing of the July 1997 elections in the capital.

Did corporatists rebel against Zedillo, or did he acquiesce in the sweeping changes? Apparently, simmering discontent over the reform bubbled to the surface while the president was traveling in South America. Majority Leader Roque—a PRI apparatchik respected among his legislative colleagues and generally a dependable backer for Los Pinos—decided that he had better stay at the head of the party's corporatist activists rather than find himself trampled by a rank-and-file enraged by the party's recent electoral setbacks. He euphemistically termed the modifications to the reform a "catharsis" rather than a rebellion, reflecting the "full unity of *priísmo*."

"We imposed on ourselves two conditions," he averred, "not to change . . . absolutely anything in the Constitution, and not to contradict anything in the political philosophy articulated by Ernesto Zedillo." For his part, Chuayffet blessed the revisions, perhaps in an attempt to ingratiate himself with the party's more traditional elements and to enhance his chances for attaining the PRI's presidential nomination in 2000.

The President Regroups

Zedillo unconvincingly denied that PRI lawmakers had blindsided him during its deliberations over what, he reiterated, would constitute the definitive electoral reform of his *sexenio*. Further, the president even resorted to machismo when he emphasized that the opposition should take up any grievances with him, not the PRI, because he altered the public financing provisos for "state reasons," designed to thwart wrongdoers: "If we don't want democracies corrupted by criminal interests, including organized crime," he said, " . . . we must take a very important step to ensure . . . sufficient financing and expenditures for political parties." He dismissed sarcastic assertions that the reform had been perverted, inasmuch as the IFE and other electoral tribunals maintained the autonomy so cherished by the four parties. As for the PRI's loyalty, he said: "I'm obliged to say immodestly that the party's record of support for me [and] my government, even in decisions considered unpopular in the short term, has been extraordinary." He lavished special praise on his *priísta* brethren in the legislature.

Such plaudits aside, local Jeremiahs began warning darkly about even more devastating defeats in store for the PRI. In 1997, the nation's increasingly cynical voters would select 1,300 officials, including federal legislators, as well as governors in six states besides Mexico City's mayor. In the face of such prophesies, Zedillo did not hesitate to lock arms with party regulars, lest PAN and PRD victories turn him into a lame duck and consign the PRI to has-been status. The rapprochement actually began in September, when Zedillo dispatched ex-Government Secretary Moctezuma—his political alter ego—to the PRI, as "technical secretary" to the party's policymaking National Political Council. In November, even as he continued consultations with state executives, the president added five governors to the PRI's council to expand its base, propitiate hard-liners, and inject more political know-how into its deliberations.

In early December 1996, Zedillo fired Attorney General Lozano. Though a favorite of his U.S. counterpart Janet Reno and other American officials, many scorned Lozano for a "lack of results in most of the investigations and actions he had taken," in the words of an official in Los Pinos. He had neither found nor prosecuted the murderers of Colosio and Ruiz Massieu, while failing to stem the flood of drug trafficking. Known for personal honesty, the PAN lawyer had said that corruption claimed 80 percent of Mexico's judicial police and prosecutors during his tenure. As Lozano cracked down with dismissals and suspensions, he became the subject of murder threats and at least one attempt on his life. "It is difficult to say if Lozano resigned because of his failures or because he made life uncomfortable for the dinosaurs of the ruling party," observed Sergio Aguayo, a prominent academic critic of the country's judicial system. Needless to say, giving the boot to a prominent *panista* elated dyed-in-the-wool corporatists who regard National Action with all of the compassion of Cromwell ruling Ireland.

Within two weeks, PRI hard-liners had even more to cheer as the party's president stepped down. Even though Oñate had served in Congress and had intimate knowledge of grass-roots politics, he had disappointed modernizers by failing to quash the anti-reform, anti-technocratic excesses of the PRI's seventeenth National Assembly. Meanwhile, the old guard considered the

University of Wisconsin graduate as too close to Salinas, Zedillo, and other foreign-educated mandarins. They also decried his lack of combativeness with respect to the PRI's political foes whom he preferred to conciliate rather than excoriate. In addition, veterans blamed him for a flurry of resignations from the party—ex-governors Luis H. Ducoing (Guanajuato), Dante Delgado Ranuro (Veracruz), Francisco Luna Kan (Yucatán), and Elías Zamora Verduzco (Colima). In addition, Senator Layda Sansores and Luis Eugenio Todd also quit the party in the same period. Sansores, daughter of a former PRI president, bolted after failing to win the PRI's backing for governor of Campeche—where she became the unsuccessful PRD standard-bearer. Todd left to seek the PT's nomination for the Nuevo León governorship. Alberto Juárez Blancas, 70, leader of the CROC, the second-largest labor federation, lent his voice to the chorus of those threatening to abandon the revolutionary party. He expressed dismay over the dearth of leadership, the poor choice of candidates, and the PRI's resistance to change an organization torn between old power brokers and university-educated elites. Finally, despite their earlier modus vivendi, the PRI leader increasingly found himself at odds with Chuayffet—over who would direct the electoral reform as well as candidate selection—with the government secretary getting the upper hand as a virtual prime minister responsible for politics while Zedillo and Ortiz Martínez homed in on economic policy. Constant political battles inside and outside the party left the 47-year-old chain-smoking, overweight Oñate *"desgastado"* or "worn out."

Zedillo replaced Oñate with the feisty Roque, 53, who endeared himself to the chief executive by lining up party legislators behind controversial bills to boost taxes, to revitalize the social security system, to partially privatize petrochemicals despite PRI misgivings, and to enact the attenuated electoral reform. Roque's first assignment entailed collaborating with Zedillo and Chuayffet to recruit attractive, qualified legislative candidates who could unite the fractious PRI, while at the same time winning contests without recourse to the skulduggery long associated with the party. He subsequently assumed the role of attack dog in del Mazo's star-crossed race for Mexico City mayor.

Nevertheless, as part of a balancing act, progressive trade unionist Gordillo—a former ally of Hernández Juárez and harsh critic of Don Fidel—assumed the interim leadership of the PRI's popular sector until her election to the CNOP post in March 1997. Upon being sworn in, the fiery Chiapan answered backbiters who questioned her PRI bona fides. She denied ever disavowing her party militancy, but stressed her commitment to democracy and social justice, tolerance, and constructive self-criticism within the party.

Despite Gordillo's selection, graybeards filled the void left by Roque's elevation to party chief: Juan José Osorio Palacios—a genial 76-year-old violinist, secretary-general of the Music Workers' Union, and Don Fidel disciple—took over the PRI leadership in the Chamber. Augusto Gómez Villanueva, 66—a veteran mover and shaker in the peasant sector who had served five terms as a federal lawmaker—ascended to the number-two post vacated by Osorio. Within two years, Zedillo had moved 180 degrees—from a "healthy distance" from the party to a healthy (some claimed "unhealthy")—closeness to the PRI's corporatist elements. What accounted for the change in direction? The president finally realized the futility of trying to govern alone. While never a fan of the PRI, Zedillo came to power without a political base, failed to forge one through artful cabinet appointments, disdained his metaconstitutional faculties, allowed Pronasol to die on the vine, and encountered opposition parties thirsting for power not *concertación*. His only hope for retaining a legislative majority that would enable him to pursue his reformist agenda lay in aligning himself with the PRI, including its most reactionary elements who barely disguised their contempt for the technocratic chief executive.

A Reconsideration

Even with the reelection ban, Mexican presidents of previous years could look forward to four or more years of relative freedom to launch programs—if not bring them to fruition—before ambitious PRI insiders and their *camarillas* began jockeying for the selection of the next *número uno*. Although gubernatorial and local elections punctuated the presidential *sexenios* and congressional contests took place at midterm, the government-party hegemony ensured political support for the administration's objectives. As Mexico became increasingly integrated with the global economy, however, economic conditions—often influenced by external events—came to pose a greater constraint than domestic circumstances on executive decision making. The weakening of the PRI, the appearance of strong adversaries, the presence of vocal civic organizations aligned with kindred spirits in the United States and Canada, and the activities of a free press further narrowed the window of opportunity in which Salinas's successor could act. Indeed, Zedillo sought to begin advancing his agenda on Inauguration Day, no longer sure he would retain a pliable Congress after the midterm elections.

Ironically, Zedillo—a man who needed as long as possible to fix his political course—enjoyed less than a three-week honeymoon before the peso crisis disoriented him and his administration. As he abandoned his pre-election commitments to keep aloof from his own party, the least political man to hold the presidency since Madero came to appreciate three vital facts: First, several developments—many intensified by Salinas—had debilitated the traditional PRI. Second, rather than modernizing the governing party and broadening its base, Salinas had helped to erode the old corporatist amalgam without replacing it with a more modern, responsive organization. Third, the evolution of Mexican society as a whole and that of the revolutionary party in particular made it imperative to involve other parties in crafting—and thus legitimizing—policies crucial to Zedillo.

Convening the leaders of the four parties in Los Pinos in January 1995 proved a stroke of genius—a sign of respect for political opponents not witnessed since Calles summoned friends and foes to Querétaro after the assassination of Obregón. Though temper tantrums and walkouts enlivened the eighteen months of talks, the heads of the PRI, PAN, PRD, and PT demonstrated commendable skill and patriotism in negotiating, bargaining, compromising, transcending parochial interests, and—most crucially in a democracy—truly tolerating each other.

Spanish and English sages agree that "the best is the enemy of the good." This aphorism summarizes the shortcomings of the four-party talks. The principals and their aides-de-camp collectively devoted thousands of hours to attempts at perfecting an electoral system that—while far from ideal—had improved dramatically in recent years. Unlike 1988, few doubted that the PRI had prevailed in the 1994 presidential and congressional elections, which featured non-counterfeitable voter cards, citizen-dominated electoral bodies, a revised and audited voter registry, transparent ballot boxes, party observers at voting places, "international visitors," unprecedented media coverage, a 77 percent turnout, and an absence of post-election or second-round demonstrations. Within a year, Zedillo had also recognized PAN victories in three violence-free gubernatorial races. Admittedly, irregularities tarnished some contests, and PRI candidates enjoyed disproportional access to media and money. Yet realistically, could one expect Mexico's political leaders to hold themselves to a higher standard of financial circumspection than Bill Clinton's White House and House Speaker Newt Gingrich's GOPAC, both awash in early 1997 with charges of gross fundraising improprieties?

In many respects, the electoral reform was a matter of decidedly secondary importance. The negotiators concentrated on issues of concern to several thousand politicians, political scientists, pundits, and diplomats. Rather than asking them to undertake what for a majority of Mexicans were esoteric changes to a tolerable electoral system, Zedillo should have trained the negotiators' impressive bargaining skills on forging consensus on issues important to the other 94 million-plus Mexicans: namely, job creation, social initiatives, privatization and investment policy, public safety, industrial strategy, the labor law, and narcotrafficking, as well as acceptable modifications of the power relationship among major political actors and institutions.

Nothing guaranteed that the parties could have reached an accord on these undoubtedly complex questions. Yet Mexico faces such a daunting array of imperative issues that little would have been lost by concentrating on socioeconomic priorities. Moreover, the president, one or more parties, and other concerned organizations could have mobilized popular support for initiatives relevant to the lives of average citizens. As events turned out, the opposition chastised the PRI for diluting the electoral changes—while both sides abdicated their more fundamental responsibility to advance concrete policies to spur sustained, better-distributed economic growth and advance the well-being of the populace. The very exercise of devoting nearly two years to electoral reform not only preempted a collective examination of the nation's major problems, but also diverted the parties from developing sound individual programs to offer the people in 1997. Evidence of this shortcoming materialized in the general, cliché-infested platforms disseminated by candidates in the capital's mid-1997 mayoral contest.

Under closer scrutiny, comparisons with Spain prove simplistic as much as they beguile. Proponents of this parallelism overlook several key differences between Franco's regime and PRI rule. To begin with, by quelling organized labor activity and creating an extremely pro-business investment climate, the quasi-fascist generalissimo prepared his own succession in the highly favorable economic climate of a post-World War II boom distinguished by a 7.4 percent average growth between 1962 and 1966. Even as corruption flourished and competitive politics remained off-limits, city dwellers and villagers observed the proliferation of TV antennas; highway traffic jams featuring ubiquitous SEAT automobiles; and the replacement of iceboxes and wood-burning stoves with electric refrigerators and ranges. In the process, a growing middle class accrued an ever bigger stake in Spain's corporatist system. At the same time, Spanish workers and smallholders achieved a slow rise in their real incomes, in that case shrinking a huge chasm between rich and poor that continues to grow in Mexico. Laborers and campesinos unable to prosper in the hinterland found urban employment in Spain or became "guest workers" in France, Germany, and other affluent European nations. The absence of a large, culturally distinct indigenous population also eased the Spaniards' promotion of social mobility. And when Spain finally embraced widespread market restructuring as a condition of admission into the European Community, large infusions of EC aid and preferential access to other Western European economies became available to ease the transition.

Even if one accepts only political aspects of the PRI/Franco and Zedillo/Suárez analogies, a fundamental difference lies in the character of the two countries' heads of state. In Spain, the head of state is not the head of government and so the continuity of the state does not depend on the incumbent of a single office. Franco had the foresight to groom Juan Carlos—grandson of Alfonso XIII, Spain's last king—to become crown prince six years before the dictator's death. The country's political culture and society had changed radically while Franco lived. Once the old man passed from the scene, the young monarch stepped to the fore—his legitimacy and support enhanced by a felicitous marriage; prudent governmental appointments; a dignified bearing derived from military training; and the courage to face down Civil Guard irredentists who attempted to seize the government in February 1981. After quashing the coup, the King spoke on television to assure his countrymen that stability and democracy would prevail, further boosting his prestige. Above all, the decline of Spanish corporatism resulted from the death of one man. In contrast, the PRI is a complex party that will continue to exist even in the face of diminishing public support and stinging electoral defeats.

As opposed to post-Franco Spain, Zedillo takes perverse pride in moves to debilitate the authority of Mexico's presidential office. Despite a sad finale, Carlos Salinas realized the need to foster grass-roots support through Solidarity and to pursue sustained economic growth before creating channels and allowing grievants to articulate pent-up demands—especially when the government lacked sufficient resources to address these concerns. Salinas understood that while plunging headlong toward an open polity would win plaudits in many circles—among Washington lawmakers and editorial writers, for example—these moves might also unleash serious, shearing forces. Thus, Salinas chose to defer broad change until market-oriented restructuring had expanded Mexico's economic pie and enhanced the legitimacy of his regime. As events turned out, Salinas parceled out major slices of that pie to family members and cronies, which—along with the 1994 Christmas peso crisis—attracted public brickbats rather than bouquets to his successor's government.

With a vibrant economy and a respected political system, Zedillo might have moved gradually to strengthen Congress, devolve authority to the states and municipalities, and marginalize the dinosaurs. Instead, he unilaterally disarmed—or, at least, debilitated—the presidency and discarded Pronasol without reaching out to the masses with a new social program. At the same time, he and other reformers opened new avenues through which laid-off workers, crime victims, debtors, shabbily paid teachers, and chronic rabble-rousers could join broader segments of society in punishing the government, as they did, for example, in overwhelmingly electing Cuauhtémoc Cárdenas mayor of Mexico City in mid-1997.

Consequently, Zedillo's Mexico resembles a markedly less chaotic and dreary version of Gorbachev's Soviet Union more than the orderly Spain of Juan Carlos. Upon taking office in 1985, the party-state leader forged ahead with two simultaneous reforms—"*perestroika*" to liberalize a closed, inefficient, profoundly bureaucratized economy, and "*glasnost*" to open an authoritarian, repressive political system. Though no Soviet leader could have avoided these shifts, engaging both at the same time unleashed massive dissent, engendered a coup attempt, chilled production, scared off many outside investors, and made Western nations wary of supplying foreign aid.

Conclusion

Can Zedillo avoid a fate similar to Gorbachev's? If the analysis presented thus far is essentially correct, no one should underestimate the daunting scope and imposing historical depth of the challenges confronting Mexico's leadership today. Nor is it particularly useful to persist in armchair academic criticism of Zedillo's policy choices thus far, however questionable. Whether focusing on electoral reform or recoiling from it once its full implications became clear, Zedillo has labored under the inherent limitations of the very structure of political power that brought him to office and that he has moved aggressively to transform. Given the urgent circumstances attendant on his election to the presidency, it is doubtful that any member of the PRI would have managed the economic crisis of the last three years with greater aplomb. More importantly, any effective and hopeful approach to Mexico's future must be based on a reconciliation with, not an escape from, the country's past.

If they are to avoid the missteps of unsuccessful reformers elsewhere who aroused expectations without mustering the resources to satisfy them, Zedillo and his allies must take several steps.

First, they should get the PRI's house in order. Although multiple factions jostle for influence under the revolutionary party's tricolored banner, which flew at half-staff after the July 6, 1997 electoral debacle, two mutually antagonistic groups stand out. There are modernizers identified with an odd couple of winners in the mid-summer balloting: Deputy Arturo Núñez Jiménez, a seasoned *político*, and Senator Esteban Moctezuma. They share the president's belief that the PRI reverses argue strongly for democratizing the party's internal life, assuming a more critical attitude toward the government, accelerating economic reforms, and courting noncorporatist groups such as women, environmentalists, and young people, particularly because the latter awarded 82 percent of their votes to the opposition in Mexico City.

These progressives must contend with unrepentant dinosaurs epitomized by Governors Bartlett (Puebla), Madrazo (Tabasco), Cervera (Yucatán), and Manlio Fabio Beltrones (Sonora), who—thanks to relatively successful PRI electoral performances in their states—advocate business-as-usual modified only by incremental change. Like Bourbon kings who allegedly neither learned nor forgot anything, these sachems see no need to reshape their barnacled party's procedures, structure, program, and constituencies. Rather, they contend that the PRI's resurgence lies in nominating better candidates, waging more effective campaigns, giving no quarter to political foes, bringing pressure to bear on the media for positive coverage, and employing the patronage and assets at their disposal to reward loyalists and mobilize voters. Sympathetic to the governors' posture, the CTM's geriatric veterans threw caution to the wind and leapt into the intra-party fracas, seemingly oblivious to the thorny challenges within their own camp.

Experienced political insiders like Chuayffet, Millán, Gordillo, and Agriculture Secretary Francisco Labastida will play salient—perhaps crucial—roles in charting the course of the floundering revolutionary party. Although exhibiting links to both camps, these leaders realize the strategic importance of emphasizing change over the status quo, reform over retrenchment, and the "magic of the market place" over the "good old days" of boodle-generating statism.

Mexico City humorists may have hit the nail on the head by suggesting that, should Bartlett's forces gain the whip hand, their first task would be to relocate the PRI headquarters from its compound on Avenida Insurgentes Norte to Calle Rosas Moreno 151, site of the Gayosso funeral home that cared for Don Fidel's remains.

Second, now that IFE has proven its mettle in implementing a widely praised electoral mechanism, Zedillo must redirect the gaze of his fellow politicians from process to policy. That is, he must craft accords on major social and economic objectives—a goal complicated by preliminary results of the July voting showing that together the PRD (125 seats) and the PAN (122 seats) can outvote the PRI (239 seats) in the Chamber of Deputies. A commanding PRI presence in the Senate militates against a roll back of recent reforms; however, Los Pinos will rely heavily on such experienced consensus-builders as Nuñez and former Querétaro governor Mariano Palacios Alcocer, named PRI president in mid-September 1997, to reach out to the opposition in the lower house—with the forging of ad hoc alliances on specific issues more likely than the construction of a firm coalition.

In his search for votes, Zedillo will undoubtedly make overtures to the Right. Yet, despite having snatched two more statehouses from the PRI (Querétaro and Nuevo León), the PAN expressed dismay over its anemic performance in Mexico City where its nominee, Carlos Castillo Peraza (15.26 percent), ran third behind Cárdenas (47.11 percent) and Del Mazo (25.08 percent). Many analysts attributed this outcome to the party's having "cohabited" with Salinas, who recognized three PAN governors in return for *panista* congressional backing on key initiatives.

Moreover, post-election tensions buffeted the PAN as the flamboyant, populist Vicente Fox announced his presidential bid, much to the chagrin of party traditionalists who had thrown their weight behind Castillo Peraza's unfortunate mayoral candidacy.

While devising ways to cultivate the shell-shocked PAN, Zedillo wasn't expected to dismiss the possibility of tactical accords with the PRD in general and Cárdenas in particular. Their personal, generational, and ideological differences aside, the two men enjoy a productive rapport through their membership in the informal community of graduates and friends of the National Polytechnic Institute. As mentioned earlier, President Cárdenas founded the IPN to expand educational opportunities for gifted, disadvantaged youngsters. A poor kid from Mexicali, Zedillo won a scholarship to IPN, where he excelled. IPN provided the academic trampoline that propelled young Ernesto to a Yale doctorate before his meteoric rise in Mexico's financial bureaucracy—and his ultimate ascent to Los Pinos.

Although not an alumnus of the vaunted *"Politécnico,"* Cárdenas—as son of the school's founding father—belongs to the proud IPN family, described as a "tightly-knit clan" by a well-known *priísta* conversant with the country's Byzantine power networks. By no means beer-drinking buddies, Zedillo and Cárdenas have acquired mutual friends through the IPN connection. Such personal ties—in stark contrast to the animus between Cárdenas and Salinas—could spur understandings rather than the conflict that many observers predicted between Mexico's two most powerful politicians.

The stones of mutual interest pave the possible path to cooperation. Cárdenas evinces a messianic drive to follow his late father into Los Pinos presidential residence, where he cavorted as a child. His prospects of becoming *número uno* will evaporate if he falls on his face running Mexico City, which—along with contiguous Mexico state—constitutes 20 percent of the nation's population. His performance will depend—in part, at least—on support from the federal government that controls the city's security force, as well as 38 percent of its budget. Thus, Zedillo and Finance Secretary Ortiz Martínez, another presidential aspirant, could wield the budget axe to undercut Cárdenas's pledge to foster an "attractive and viable" capital.

Zedillo could also encourage harassment of the PRD mayor by PRI-linked unions, garbage collectors, and street vendors, as well as by PRI governors adept at dispatching demonstrators to the capital to publicize parochial issues. An upswing in work stoppages and demonstrations would sharpen the headaches of crime, unemployment, traffic snarls, and pollution that already afflict the city's 8.5 million residents. Hence, self-interest as much as statesmanship argues for Cárdenas to proffer Zedillo not a fist but a handshake—in the form of legislative backing for selective administration bills. Should such constructive behavior heighten Cárdenas's chances to become president, Zedillo—never a fervent *priísta*—could expect accolades from historians as the first chief executive in modern history to hand over the presidential sash to an opposition party member.

Third, Zedillo, whose public standing improved thanks to the cleanliness of the mid–1997 elections, must design a social program to minister to the needs of the 50 percent of his countrymen who endure hardscrabble poverty in fetid shantytowns or forlorn villages. At the very least, he should revive Solidarity, although under a new rubric because Salinas launched the anti-poverty venture and the ex-president's very name represents a "political swastika," in the words of Oscar Aguilar Asencio, political science professor at Mexico City's IberoAmericana University. As Salinas comprehended, social stability requires that the masses obtain a stake in—or, at least, don't feel ignored—as irreversible changes sweep through the economy.

Having made this point, it should be noted that Mexico's policymakers, even while facing greater social effervescence, still enjoy important safeguards against an upheaval: (1) a loyal, institutional military that obeys civilian leaders rather than deliberating over their orders; (2) the inclination of PRI dinosaurs to contend for power through orthodox means without themselves endeavoring to activate the barracks or engage in massive vote-rigging; (3) the absence of an Alberto Fujimori-style "man on horseback" seeking to exploit the problems flailing rank-and-file Mexicans, although pundits labelled as an abortive *Fujimorazo* Chuayffet's clumsy attempt to shatter a 259-deputy "Opposition Bloc" astutely forged by Muñoz Ledo, Creel, and Medina in mid-August; and (4) the willingness—albeit grudging at times—of the United States to extend a helping hand should destabilizing economic problems beset its southern neighbor.

Fourth, the president, along with major political parties, must address the first responsibility of government: the maintenance of public order. Rather than risk greater corruption of a military already penetrated by the drug mafia, Zedillo would do better to seek Canadian Mounties or British bobbies to supervise root-and-branch changes in police departments. While Indonesia's contracting of Swiss-based Société Génerale de Surveillance to operate the country's blatantly corrupt customs service bears watching, Hong Kong's no-holds-barred battle against police malfeasance in the 1970s furnishes a successful example that Mexico's fellow OECD members might commend to Zedillo if his spring 1997 initiatives to clean up the Federal Judicial Police come a cropper. Such loud public outrage followed revelations of illicit activities by the Royal Hong Kong Police that local decision makers felt emboldened to create the Independent Commission against Corruption (ICAC), despite the claims of Cassandras that culturally ingrained corruption would prove impervious to attack. Though not without problems, the ICAC achieved notable results thanks to its (1) selection of a distinguished head; (2) successful prosecution of several "big fish;" (3) administrative independence; (4) substantial budget; (5) recruitment of British and other Commonwealth professionals to supervise young, highly qualified Chinese recruits, who earned preferential salaries during their two-and-a-half-year, renewable contracts; (6) opening of new channels to the public for lodging complaints about police misconduct; and (7) shifting the burden of proof so that police officers whose wealth exceeded earnings had to prove that they had not pocketed payoffs.[8]

Fifth, while Mexicans will decide how best to wage their internal war against drugs, Zedillo should alert Washington to the dangers of enlarging the role of Latin American militaries in the anti-narcotics fight. In February 1997, for example, authorities arrested the head of Mexico's anti-drug law enforcement agency, General Jesús Gutiérrez Rebollo, on charges that he had accepted bribes from dealers. This program has proven ineffective, as 80 percent of the cocaine and huge quantities of heroin and marijuana pour into the United States through Mexico, where the Juárez Cartel has eclipsed its Colombian counterparts in power and resources. As Mexican officials continually remind their American peers, "drug trafficking would decline dramatically were it not for the insatiable demand in the United States." To his credit, President Clinton recognized this fact during his May 1997 visit to Mexico.

In light of a 105 percent upswing in the use of controlled substances by America's youth in the 1992-1995 period, reported in August 1996 by the U.S. Public Health Service, Washington should focus its attention and resources on programs to reduce consumption in American cities, towns, and rural areas rather than pressuring Mexico and other nations to pursue policies likely to increase corruption in the armed forces, a corporatist institution that Zedillo has courted since taking office.

Sixth, as discussed in Chapter 5, Zedillo should cast his lot instead with moderate trade unionists—those with a foot in both the technocratic and dinosaur camps—to influence developments in Mexico City and other urban centers. Although several leaders boast important skills, PRI Secretary-General Millán has the best chance to revamp and modernize the CTM and the Labor Congress, but he may have to settle for encouraging gradual change under the watchful eye of Rodríguez Alcaine   at least for several years. Cárdenas's victory in the D.F. could deliver the coup de grâce to CTM boss-manipulated "letter-head" unions—with positive consequences for the new labor culture nationwide.

Finally, Mexico must continue its support for NAFTA, while convincing Washington of the imperative for Mexico to postpone the elimination of its tariffs on corn and other grains. Most *ejidos*, even if reformed or modernized under the 1992 constitutional amendment, will find themselves unable to compete with Cargill, Archer Daniels Midland, and other world-class grain companies that will achieve full entrée to the Mexican market early in the next century. By that time the campesino population, most of whom have little or no formal education, will double to 30 or 40 million people. The Mexican government must launch a Herculean effort to build infrastructure and design a comprehensive, rural-focused development strategy that emphasizes education, irrigation, and health care for elements of the population most vulnerable to the neoliberal changes besetting Mexico. Failure to devote resources to the PRI's most loyal corporatist sector will find its members pouring into already saturated Mexican cities, crossing illegally into the United States, or casting their lot with EZLN- or ERP-style rebel movements.

The opposition's impressive showing in the mid-1997 elections for legislators, governors, and mayor of Mexico City administered the strongest blow yet to Mexico's PRI-government system. That President Zedillo insisted on a fair count in most contests enabled both the PAN and the PRD to register important gains and to capture nearly half of the Chamber of Deputies, while raising to six the number of governorships in opposition hands.

In addition to weakening corporatism, however, the outcome betokened the increasing complexity and regionalism of the country's polity. Pluralism reigns in the U.S.-focused north, where the PAN—as is the increasing case nationwide—controls most large- and medium-sized cities and can hold its own with the PRI in virtually any other election in any state. There, Monterrey's *El Norte* and Tijuana's *Zeta* newspapers set high standards for objective news reporting; entrepreneurs cut thousands of deals a day with their American counterparts with whom they see their future intertwined within the context of NAFTA; and the Roman Catholic Church regularly advocates civic responsibility and condemns political venality. For proof of competitive two-party politics, one only has to observe that National Action boasts three governorships, a majority of city halls, and a substantial number of state and federal legislative seats in the region. Yet, even as the PRI and the PAN engage each other in ever more transparent and democratic elections, new power contenders have sprung to life near the border in the form of the Tijuana, Juárez, and Gulf drug cartels. With tens of billions of dollars at their disposal, the leaders of these hierarchical, authoritarian, corrupt organizations will undoubtedly seek to influence policies, particularly at state and local levels. To date, the narco-criminals' success in suborning poorly paid, unprofessional local judges and prosecutors has diminished the need to buy elected officials as has taken place in Colombia.

In the center of the country, pivoting on metropolitan Mexico City, pluralism coexists with corporatism, although the latter's institutions are reeling as evidenced by CTM candidates having lost most races for direct-election congressional seats on July 6. Three parties vigorously contend for elective posts; *Reforma* and other major newspapers offer readers objective, comprehensive coverage of political events; the cardinals of Mexico City and Guadalajara have enhanced their roles as opinion leaders; and civil society continues to flourish thanks to an ever thicker network of independent unions, professional associations, community groups, and NGOs. At the same time, the PRI retains the preeminent political organizations in Mexico City, Guadalajara, and Puebla, even though opposition parties have captured the mayor's offices in these cities; most bureaucrats owe their jobs to the ruling party; and, while notably weaker than they were twenty-five years ago, corporatist entities such as the CTM, CNC, and CNOP still report millions of adherents. The disputed validity of such numbers makes little difference because sectoral chiefs can no longer deliver their members' votes.

In contrast, the south remains a bastion of corporatism, even though the PRD boasts enclaves in Campeche, Tabasco, Oaxaca, and Guerrero, and the PAN presents a serious challenge to the PRI in Yucatán. In this largely rural, impoverished part of the nation, the PRI captures the lion's share of elections outside of major cities, often with the connivance of local party *caciques;* union bosses continue to serve as patrons for the workers in their bailiwicks; and the government systematically dispenses largesse with an eye to outbidding guerrilla movements for the hearts and stomachs of the downtrodden. In the years ahead, Mexico City will have to increase its ante as the influx of cheap grain from the United States uproots hundreds of thousands—perhaps millions—of subsistence farmers.

For years, it was said: *"México—No Hay Dos"*—literally translated, "There's only one Mexico." In fact, the changes accentuated by industrialization, urbanization, and increasing integration with the global economy give lie to this aphorism. On the eve of the twenty-first century, there are at least three—and arguably more—Mexicos: each following a different path of development as pluralism inexorably eclipses corporatism.

Notes

1. Although politicians from most parties extolled the Spanish model, Zedillo himself insisted that the evolution of Mexico, already "democratic," was *sui generis.* Analysts examining this analogy, often with a skeptical eye, include: Gustavo Esteva, "La transición sin pacto," *Reforma,* March 3, 1996, p. 9-A; Luis Rubio, "El modelo español de transición," *Reforma,* April 7, 1996; and Carlos Castillo Peraza, "El ejemplo de felipe," *Reforma,* July 25, 1996, p. 8-A.

2. See, Stanley Payne (ed.), *Politics and the Military in Modern Spain* (London: Oxford University Press, 1976); and David Gilmour, *The Transformation of Spain: From Franco to the Constitutional Monarch* (London: Quartet Books, 1985), pp. 133–210.

3. Zedillo, "'Queremos una patria en paz,'" *Reforma,* December 2, 1994, p. 71.

4. Quoted in Lowry McAllen, "Nation Awaits Passage of Reforms," *The News* (Mexico City), July 29, 1996, p. 3.

5. Magdelena Robles, "Retroceden priístas 50% in el Edomex," *Reforma,* November 11, 1996.

6. Rafael Jiménez, "Malestar económico influye en votantes," *Reforma,* November 14, 1996.

7. "Mexico's PRI Ditches All-Party Accord and Imposes Its Own Electoral 'Reform'," *Latin American Weekly Report,* November 28, 1996, p. 541.

8. Robert Klitgaard, *Controlling Corruption* (Berkeley: University of California Press, 1988), pp. 98–121.

Glossary

The following is a list of Mexican and American translations of abbreviations found in the text.

Companía Nacional de Subsistencias Populares (CONASUPO)—National Food Distribution Company

Confederación de Trabajadores de México (CTM)—Mexican Workers' Confederation

Confederación Nacional Campesina (CNC)—National Peasant Confederation

Confederación Nacional de Camaras Comerciales (CONCANACO)—National Confederation of Chambers of Commerce

Confederación Nacional de Camaras Industriales (CONCAMIN)—National Confederation of Industrial Chambers

Confederación Nacional de Organizaciones Populares (CNOP)—National Confederation of Popular Organizations

Confederación Regional Obrera Mexicana (CROM)—Mexican Regional Confederation of Workers

Confederación Revolucionaria de Obreros y Campesinos (CROC)—Revolutionary Confederation of Workers and Peasants

Corriente Democrática (CD)—Democratic Current

Ejército Revolucionario Popular (ERP)—People's Revolutionary Army

Ejército Zapatista de Liberación Nacional (EZLN)—Zapatista National Liberation Army

Federación de Sindicatos de Empresas de Bienes y Servicios (FESEBES)—Federation of Goods and Services Unions

Federación de Sindicatos de Trabajadores al Servicio del Estado (FSTSE)—Federation of State Workers' Unions

Fondo Nacional para el Consumo of de los Trabajadores (FONACOT)—National Fund for Workers' Needs

Frente Democrático para la Reconstrucción Nacional (FDN)—Democratic Front for National Reconstruction

Frente Nacional Ciudadano (FNC)—National Citizens Front

Instituto de Seguridad y Servicios Sociales de los Trabajadores del Estado (ISSSTE)—Institute for Social Security and Social Services for State Employees

Instituto del Fondo Nacional para la Vivienda de los Trabajadores (INFONAVIT)—National Fund for Workers' Housing

Instituto Mexicano de Seguro Social (IMSS)—Mexican Social Security Institute

Instituto Politécnico Nacional (IPN)—National Polytechnic Institute

Ley Federal de Organizaciones Políticos y Procesos Electorales (LOPPE)—Federal Law of Political Organizations and Political Processes

Movimiento de Acción Popular (MAP)—Popular Action Movement

Movimiento Electoral Democrático (MED)—Democratic Electoral Movement

Movimiento Popular Territorial (MPT)—Popular Territorial Movement

Movimiento Sindical (MS)—Union Movement

Pacto Obrero-Campesino (POC)—Worker-Peasant Pact

Partido Acción Nacional (PAN)—National Action Party

Partido Auténtico de la Revolución Mexicana (PARM)—Authentic Party of the Mexican Revolution

Partido de la Revolución Democrática (PRD)—Democratic Revolutionary Party

Partido del Frente Cardenista para la Reconstrucción Nacional (PFCRN)—Party of the Cardenist Front for National Reconstruction

Partido Mexicano de los Trabajadores (PMT)—Mexican Workers' Party

Partido Nacional Revolucionario (PNR)—
Revolutionary Nationalist Party
Partido Revolucionario Institucional (PRI)—
Institutional Revolutionary Party
Partido Revolucionario Mexicana (PRM)—Party
of the Mexican Revolution
Partido Socialista Unificado de México
(PSUM)—United Socialist Party of
Mexico
Programa Nacional de Solidaridad (Pronasol)—
National Solidarity Program

Secretaría de Desarrollo Urbano y Ecología
(SEDUE)—Urban Development Ministry
Secretaría de Relaciones Exteriores (SRE)—
Foreign Relations Ministry
*Sindicato de los Trabajadores Petroleros de la
República Mexicana* (STPRM)—Oil Work-
ers' Union

*Sindicato Nacional de Trabajadores de la Edu-
cación* (SNTE)—National Union of Edu-
cational Workers
*Sindicato Unico de Trabajadores de la Industria
Nuclear* (SUTIN)—Nuclear Workers
Union
*Sindicato Unico de Trabajadores Electricistas de la
República Mexicana* (SUTERM)—Electri-
cal Workers' Union

Teléfonos de México (Telmex)—state-owned
telephone company
Tribunal Federal de Electoral (TFE)—Federal
Electoral Tribunal

Universidad Nacional Autónoma de México
(UNAM)—National Autonomous University of Mexico

Selected Bibliography

Books and Monographs

Aguilar Camín, Héctor, *Despues del milagro*. Mexico City: Cal y Arena, 1988.

Aquinas, St. Thomas. *On Kingship: To the King of Cyprus*. Toronto: The Pontifical Institute of Mediaeval Studies, 1949.

Beals, Carleton. *Porfirio Díaz: Dictator of Mexico*. Westport, CT: Greenwood Press, 1971.

Beer, Samuel. *To Make a Nation: The Rediscovery of American Federalism*. Cambridge: Harvard University Press, 1993.

Brandenburg, Frank. *The Making of Modern Mexico*. Englewood Cliffs, NJ: Prentice-Hall Inc., 1967.

Burns, N. Bradford. *A History of Brazil*. 2nd ed.; New York: Columbia University Press, 1993.

Camp, Roderic A. *Entrepreneurs and Politics in Twentieth Century Mexico*. New York: Oxford University Press, 1989.

———. *Mexican Political Biographies, 1935–1993*. 3rd ed.; Austin: University of Texas Press, 1995.

Centeno, Miguel Angel. *Democracy within Reason: Technocratic Revolution in Mexico*. University Park, PA: Pennsylvania State University Press, 1994.

Cline, Howard F. *Mexico: Revolution to Evolution 1940–1960*. Westport, CT: Greenwood Press, 1981.

Connor, Carolyn. *Industry and Underdevelopment: the Industrialization of Mexico, 1890–1940*/Stephen H. Haber. Stanford: Stanford University Press, 1989.

Dye, Thomas R. and Harmon Zeigler. *The Irony of Democracy*. Belmont, CA: Wadsworth Publishing Co., 1996.

Flynn, Peter. *Brazil: A Political Analysis*. London: Anchor Press, 1978.

Gilmour, David. *The Transformation of Spain: From Franco to the Constitutional Monarch*. London: Quartet Books, 1985.

Grayson, George W. *The North American Free Trade Agreement: Regional Community in the New World Order*. Lanham, MD: University Press of America, 1995.

———. *A Guide to the 1994 Mexican Presidential Election*. Washington, DC: Center for Strategic & International Studies, 1994.

———. *The Church in Contemporary Mexico*. Washington, DC: Center for Strategic & International Studies, 1992.

———. *The Politics of Mexican Oil*. Pittsburgh: University of Pittsburgh Press, 1980.

Gruening, Ernest. *Mexico and Its Heritage*. New York: D. Appleton-Century Co., 1934.

Haber, Stephen. *Industry and Underdevelopment: the Industrialization of Mexico, 1890–1940*, Stanford, CA: Stanford University Press, 1989.

Hansen, Roger D. *The Politics of Mexican Development*. Baltimore: Johns Hopkins, 1980.

Heller, Judith A. *Mexico in Crisis*. 2nd ed.; New York: Holmes & Meier, 1983.

Katzenberger, Elaine (ed.), *First World, Ha Ha Ha! The Zapatista Challenge*. San Francisco: City Lights, 1995.

Klitgaard, Robert. *Controlling Corruption*. Berkeley: University of California Press, 1988.

Levy, Daniel and Gabriel Székely. *Mexico Paradoxes of Stability and Change*. Boulder, CO: Westview Press, 1983.

Lieuwen, Edwin. *Arms and Politics in Latin America*. Rev [i.e. 2d] ed.; New York: Published for the Council on Foreign Relations by Praeger, 1961.

Lovejoy, Arthur. *The Great Chain of Being*. Cambridge: Harvard University Press, 1964.

Lowi, Theodore J. *The End of Liberalism: the Second Republic of the United States*. 2nd ed.; New York: Norton & Co., 1969.

Mabry, Donald. *Mexico's Acción Nacional: A Catholic Alternative to Revolution*. Syracuse, NY: Syracuse University Press, 1973.

Marcos, Subcomandante. *Shadows of Tender Mercy: The Letters and Communiqués of Subcomandante Marcos and the Zapatista Army of National Liberation*. New York: Monthly Review Press, 1995.

Meyer, Michael C. and William L. Sherman. *The Course of Mexican History*. New York: Oxford University Press, 1983.

———. *The Course of Mexican History*. 3rd ed.; New York: Oxford University Press, 1987.

Middlebrook, Kevin J. *The Paradox of Revolution: Labor, The State, and Authoritarianism in Mexico*. Baltimore: Johns Hopkins, 1995.

Morris, Stephen D. *Political Reformism in Mexico: An Overview of Contemporary Mexican Politics*. Boulder, CO: Lynne Ridenner, 1995.

Newell, Roberto G. and Luis Rubio F., *Mexico's Dilemma: The Political Origins of Economic Crisis*. Boulder, CO: Westview Press, 1984.

Padgett, L. Vincent. *The Mexican Political System*. 2nd ed.; Boston: Houghton Mifflin Co., 1976.

Partido Revolucionario Institucional. *Ernesto Zedillo: Architect of a Modern Mexico: Profile and Policies of a Candidate for President*. Mexico City: PRI, 1994.

Payne, Stanley (ed.). *Politics and the Military in Modern Spain*. London: Oxford University Press, 1976.

Philip, George D. E. *The Presidency in Mexican Politics*. New York: St. Martin's Press, 1992.

Riding, Alan. *Distant Neighbors: A Portrait of the Mexicans*. New York: Alfred A. Knopf, 1985.

Roberts, J. M. *The History of the World*. New York: Oxford University Press, 1993.

Romero Deschamps, Carlos. *Discurso: lvii aniversario de la expropiación petrolera 18 de marzo de 1995*. Mexico City: STPRM, 1996.

Russell, Philip L. *Mexico under Salinas*. Austin, TX: Mexico Resource Center, 1994.

Salinas de Gortari, Carlos *Producción y participación: política en el campo*. Mexico City: Fondo de Cultura Económica, 1987.

Sanders, Sol. *Mexico: Chaos on Our Doorstep*. Lanham, MD: Madison Books, 1986.

Scott, Robert E. *Mexican Government in Transition*. Urbana: University of Illinois Press, 1964.

Skidmore, Thomas E. and Peter H. Smith. *Modern Latin America*. 3rd ed.; New York: Oxford University Press, 1992.

Smith, Peter H. *Mexico: The Quest for a U.S. Policy*. New York: Foreign Policy Association, n.d.

Stevens, Evelyn. *Protest and Response in Mexico*. Boston: MIT, 1974.

Story, Dale. *The Mexican Ruling Party: Stability and Authority*. New York: Praeger, 1986.

Tannebaum, Frank. *Mexico: The Struggle for Peace and Bread*. New York: Knopf, 1950.

———. *Ten Keys to Latin America*. New York: Alfred A. Knopf, 1965.

Thomas, Hugh. *The Mexican Labyrinth*. New York: Twentieth Century Fund, 1990.

Trimberger, Ellen Kay. *Revolution from Above: Military Bureaucrats and Development in Japan, Turkey, Egypt and Peru*. New Brunswick, NJ: Transaction Publishers, 1978.

Vernon, Raymond. *The Dilemma of Mexico's Development: the Roles of the Private and Public Sectors*. Cambridge: Harvard University Press, 1963.

Zárate, Alfonso. *Los usos del poder*. Mexico City: Raya en el Agua, 1995.

Articles and Chapters in Books

Bailey, John J. "The Bureaucracy," in George W. Grayson (ed.) *Prospects for Democracy in Mexico*. Washington, DC: Center for the Study of Foreign Affairs, 1988, pp. 18–19.

Black, Antony. "St. Thomas Aquinas: The State and Morality," in Brian Redhead (ed.), *Political Thought from Plato to NATO*. London: Ariel Books, 1988, pp. 66–67.

Camp, Roderic. "Camarillas in Mexican Politics: The Case of the Salinas Cabinet," *Mexican Studies*, Vol. 6, No. 1 (Winter 1990): pp. 85–108.

Cox, N. "Recent Changes in the Mexican Political System," in George Philip (ed.) *Politics in Mexico*. London: Croom Helm, 1985: pp. 15–53.

"Democracia o anarquía: escenarios para el futuro político de méxico," *La carpeta púrpura*, IX (April 30, 1996).

Dore, Elizabeth Wilkes. "Audiencia," in Helen Delpar (ed.) *Encyclopedia of Latin America*. New York: McGraw-Hill, 1974, pp. 48–49.

Goodsell, James N. "Mexico: Why the Students Rioted," *Current History*, Vol. 56, No. 329 (January 1969): pp. 31–35.

Grayson, George W. "Mexico: Embattled Neighbor," *Great Decisions*. New York: Foreign Policy Association, 1996.

Klarén, Peter F. "Lost Promise: Explaining Latin American Underdevelopments," in Roderic Ai Camp, *Democracy in Latin America: Patterns and Cycles*. Wilmington, DE: Scholarly Resources, 1996: pp. 91–120.

Morse, Richard M. "Recent Research on Latin American Urbanization: A Selective Survey with Commentary," *Latin American Research Review*, 1 (Fall 1965): pp. 35–74.

Needler, Martin C. "Pendulum Effect," *Politics and Society in Mexico*. Albuquerque, NM: University of New Mexico Press, 1971: pp. 46–49.

Riding, Alan. "The Mixed Blessing of Mexico's Oil," *New York Times Magazine*. January 11, 1981: p. 25.

Rubio, Luis. "The Changing Role of the Private Sector" in Susan Kaufman Purcell (ed.), *Mexico in Transition: Implications for U.S. Policy*. New York: Council on Foreign Relations, 1988.

Schmitter, Philippe C. "Still the Century of Corporatism?" in Frederick B. Pike and Thomas Stritch (eds.), *The New Corporatism: Socio-Political Structures in the Iberian World*. Notre Dame: University of Notre Dame Press, 1974: pp. 85–131.

Stevens, Evelyn P. "Mexico's PRI: The Institutionalization of Corporatism"in James Malloy (ed.), *Authoritarianism and Corporatism in Latin America*. Pittsburgh: University of Pittsburgh Press, 1977.

Weintraub, Sidney and M. Delal Baer, "The Interplay between Economic and Political Opening: The Sequence in Mexico," *The Washington Quarterly*, 15, No. 2 (Spring 1992): pp. 187–201.

Wiarda, Howard J. "Toward a Framework for the Study of Political Change in the Iberic-Latin Tradition: The Corporative Model," *World Politics*, 25 (January 1973): pp. 206–235.

———. "Dismantling Corporatism: The Problem of Latin America," in *World Affairs*, 156 (Spring 1994): pp. 199–203.

Magazines and Newspapers

Daily Report (Latin America). 1979–1997.

Economist. 1986–1997.

El Finaciero. 1989–1997.

El Norte. 1992.

El Universal. 1992.

Excélsior. 1977–1997

Financial Times. 1987–1996.

International Commerce. 1996.

Journal of Commerce. 1988–1997.

La Jornada. 1992–1997.

Latin America. 1970.

Latin American Newsletters. 1991–1997.

Latin American Regional Reports: Mexico and Central America. 1991.

Latin American Weekly Report. 1982–1997.

Los Angeles Times. 1989.

Mexican Business. 1996–1997.

Mexico City Times. 1995–1997.

Multinational Monitor. 1993.

New York Times. 1974–1997.

Newsweek. 1989–1997.

Proceso. 1978–1997.

Reforma. 1995–1997.

The Nation. 1993.

The News (Mexico City). 1986–1997.

Unesco Courier. 1995.

Unomásuno. 1986.

U.S. News & World Report. 1990–1997.

Wall Street Journal. 1984–1997.

Washington Post. 1982–1997.

Interviews

Aguirre Velázquez, Ramón. Former Mayor of Mexico City. Mexico City, June 17, 1996.

Bailey, John J. Professor of Government. Georgetown University. Telephone Interview, May 19, 1996.

Millán Lizárraga, Juan S. PRI Secretary-General. Mexico City, August 1, 1996.

Silva Herzog Flores, Jesús. Ambassador. Washington, DC, June 28, 1996, and December 13, 1996.

Vázquez Gutiérrez, Hebraicaz. President, the National Petroleum Movement. Mexico City, May 31, 1978.

Index